The death of an emperor

Also by Thomas Crump

The Law for Everyman (Collins, 1963)
Man and his Kind (Darton, Longman & Todd, 1974)
The Phenomenon of Money (Routledge & Kegan Paul, 1981)
The Anthropology of Numbers (CUP, 1990)

THE DEATH OF
AN EMPEROR

Japan at the crossroads

THOMAS CRUMP

Oxford   New York
OXFORD UNIVERSITY PRESS
1991

Oxford University Press, Walton Street, Oxford OX2 6DP

Oxford New York Toronto
Delhi Bombay Calcutta Madras Karachi
Petaling Jaya Singapore Hong Kong Tokyo
Nairobi Dar es Salaam Cape Town
Melbourne Auckland

and associated companies in
Berlin Ibadan

Oxford is a trade mark of Oxford University Press

First published 1989 by Constable and Company Limited
First issued as an Oxford University Press paperback
with a new Afterword 1991

British Library Cataloguing in Publication Data
Data available
ISBN 0-19-285242-6

Library of Congress Cataloging in Publication Data
Crump, Thomas.
The death of an emperor : Japan at the crossroads / Thomas Crump.
p. cm.
Reprint. Originally published: London : Constable, 1989.
Includes bibliographical references (p.) and index.
1. Hirohito, Emperor of Japan, 1901– . 2. Japan—Emperors—Biography.
3. Japan—Politics and government—1926–1989
I. Title.
DS889.8.C78 1989b 952.03'3'092—dc20 [B] 90-25696
ISBN 0-19-285242-6

Printed in Great Britain by
The Guernsey Press Co. Ltd.
Guernsey, Channel Islands

Contents

[v]

Illustrations

Acknowledgements

THIS research upon which this book is based would not have been possible without the help and support of the Faculty of Political, Social and Cultural Sciences of the University of Amsterdam, the National Museum of Ethnography in Osaka and the Japan Foundation, and in London, the Mercers' Company and the School of Oriental and African Studies. In particular I would like to thank both the staff and students of the Anthropological Sociological Centre of the University of Amsterdam for allowing me to attend the funeral of the Showa Emperor in February 1989, and the installation of his successor, the Emperor Akihito, in November 1990.

In Japan itself I am indebted to many for both advice and hospitality. I would particularly like to thank Prof. Masaru Akasaka of the University of Toyama, Prof. Takeshi Hatta of the Osaka Education University, Prof. Takao Hayashi of the Doshisha University, Kyoto, Prof. Takakuni Hirano and Prof. Hitoshi Ueda of the University of Niigata, Dr Etsuko Kuroda and Dr Hirochika Nakamaki of the National Museum of Ethnology, Osaka, Prof. Yoshinobu Kotani and Prof. Hirofumi Saito of the University of Nagoya, Mr Osamu Odawara of Fukuoka, Mrs Marion Pennink, First Secretary in charge of Press and Cultural Affairs at the Royal Netherlands Embassy, Tokyo, Prof. Paul D. Scott of the Kansai University of Foreign Studies, Hirakata, Prof. Halldor Stefansson of the Osaka Gakuin Junior College, Mr Masamichi Sugihara of the Japan Foundation, Kyoto, Prof. Yoshio Yano of the Kyoto Education University, Prof. Yasukichi Yasuba of the University of Osaka, Prof. Toshinao Yoneyama of the University of Kyoto and Prof. Teigo Yoshida of the University of the Sacred Heart, Tokyo.

Outside Japan I have received most welcome help and advice from Prof. Adrian Mayer, Prof. Brian Moeran and Mr John Breen of the School of Oriental and African Studies of London University, Dr Carmen Blacker of the University of Cambridge, Dr Roger Goodman of the University of Essex and Dr Ian Reader of the Centre for Japanese Studies of the University of Stirling.

T. C.

Preface

To the Japanese people, their emperor or *tennō* is a conundrum as he would be also to the world outside Japan, if he were better understood there. In writing this book and choosing its title, I have set out to explain to the outside world something of the significance of the emperor to the Japanese people, and of his death.

The death of the man known in the Western world as the Emperor Hirohito of Japan is significant, within Japan, for the opportunity it provides for almost unrestricted public debate and private discussion about the nature of both the man and his office. In Japan there is a whole science, known as *tennōsei*, relating to this question, but in any normal time its exercise is subdued, even quiescent. The subject, quite simply, is taboo, and even foreigners, or *gaijin* (to whom much is permitted in Japan), are steered away from it.

At the heart of the conundrum is the status of the emperor as a *theocratic* ruler. First and foremost the emperor is – for want of a better word – a *priest* in the traditional Japanese religion of Shinto. In Shinto this priestly office is unique in that the holder for the time being has acquired it by a rule of succession which has operated, without any interruption, from the beginning of time. The unbroken line of succession (however uncertain its historical basis) is as important to the Japanese belief in their emperor as the apostolic succession is to Roman Catholics. The emperor for the time being is what he is simply because he succeeded to his office, first by a rule of descent, and second by his performing the traditional accession rituals. By the standards of any European royal house (of which none is as old as that of the *tennō*), the rules of descent are extremely flexible. It is sufficient that the emperor be descended, by blood, from one of his predecessors, so that all the emperors are so descended from the first emperor, Jimmu. (The Showa Emperor, born in 1901, was the first legitimate child of an emperor to succeed to the Chrysanthemum Throne since Go-Momo-zono, born in 1758.)

It is because the accession rituals are essential for making the new emperor, and establishing his status according to Shinto tradition, that I describe them in some detail in Chapter 6. If, because of the strangeness of the rites described, this is the most difficult chapter of the book, it is also the most important. My subtitle 'Japan at the Crossroads' is deliberately chosen in the light of the decision that the new emperor of Japan, Akihito, must make about the performance of the most ancient and important ritual known as the *daijōsai*. The effect of this ritual is to establish the new *tennō*'s status as *arahitogami*, a word which sums up the whole traditional Shinto theology relating to the *tennō*. That is, the emperor is not just a priest, but he is that unique sort of priest connoted by this word, *arahitogami*.

The word is a compound of *ara*, meaning 'present', 'actual' or 'real', *hito*, meaning simply 'man', and *kami*, generally but misleadingly translated by 'god'. The whole word, *arahitogami*, is generally translated as 'divine present emperor', which is reasonable enough, for none but the emperor, or *tennō*, can combine the three components in one person. (There is a category of *kami*, known as *ikigami*, or 'living gods', which may include other individuals besides the emperor, but none of them will share his status as *arahitogami*.) The principle is that there is always one, and only one *arahitogami*, just as there is but one Pope (although Japan also had a sort of Avignon period, and at much the same time in history. In Shinto, as much as in Catholicism, the inconveniences of history are not allowed to override dogma.). The *arahitogami*, or *tennō* for the time being, is somewhere between heaven (the *ten* of *tennō*) and earth, and his throne is above the clouds.

In terms of comparative religion (free from any bias in favour of Western Christianity) the *tennō*, according to Shinto, is simply a 'Pastor Aeternus', a title bestowed on the Pope by the Vatican Council of 1870. On this point, the essential difference between Shinto and Catholicism is twofold. First, the function of the *tennō* is almost purely ritual (although a pastoral commitment can be read into the Imperial Rescript of Education of 1890, which I consider in detail in Chapter 4). Second, Shinto never had any interest in proselytes: even in Japan's overseas empire, no one ever confronted a Shinto missionary. Shinto is best seen as the religious dimension of being Japanese (which is how the Japanese themselves see it).

The problem with the Showa Tenno (as the Emperor Hirohito must be known after his death on 7 January 1989) is that he was forced to assume a political role, which in principle has nothing to do with being the *tennō*, at the same time, being constrained by the circumstance of the allied occupation of Japan from 1945 to 1952 (which I describe in Chapter 9) to renounce his status as *arahitogami*, which traditionally is what being *tennō* is all about. So long as the Showa Emperor remained alive, the question of the status of the *tennō* could be left pending. This is another reason for the title of my book, *The Death of an Emperor*, because it is the death of the old emperor which makes it imperative to find an answer to the question of the status of the new emperor, his son Akihito.

The Showa Emperor, if he had taken a simple view of what he had achieved in a reign of more than sixty years, might have been content with the transition from *arahitogami* to constitutional monarch. If this was all there was to it, I could have written a much shorter book, but, to quote Oscar Wilde, 'truth is never pure, and rarely simple'. Considering that the Showa Emperor's reign saw his own country left in ruins after a war which engulfed nearly the whole world at the cost of millions of casualties, if this was necessary to achieve the transformation of his own status which he found so important, then, certainly, we have a case of overkill without any historical precedent.

From whatever perspective I have been able to look at the record, I have always come back to accepting General MacArthur's judgement, given after he had met the Showa Emperor for the first time in September 1945, that this was 'the first gentleman of Japan'. Why then are the authors of the first two books to appear in the West after the death of the Showa Emperor, Edward Behr's *Hirohito* and (in German) Peter Crome's *Der Tenno*, so intent on a verdict of guilty? Both these authors are professional journalists, and the journalist, more than any other writer, is sensitive to the instant demands of his readers: he must know his public, and identify with it. From this perspective, the essence of the Showa Emperor's crime is not only that he survived, but that he survived so long. Who else, in 1989, could still be held responsible for the rape of Nanking, the Bataan death march or the Burma railway? Significantly, another journalist, the

Frenchman Robert Guillain, in his *La Guerre au Japon*, never even suggests that the Showa Emperor should answer for Japanese war crimes: Guillain, who spent the whole war in Tokyo, saw at close hand the forces which led Japan to the catastrophe of the Pacific War.

Living in Holland, I cannot possibly be insensitive to the feelings of the thousands who can still remember the horrors of the Pacific War, and the indignities suffered in the name of the Emperor of Japan. Much was lost in the Pacific War which, even after the defeat in Japan, was never retrieved. All I can ask of those who still suffer, and often acutely, from this loss is that what they in the end must judge is not a man called Hirohito, but a projection on an institution of which he, by the accident of history, was the nominal incumbent. This is summed up in the Japanese phrase, *yūmei mujitsu*, literally 'having a name, but no substance'. The tragedy of Japan, in the years up to 1945, is that its leaders, in purporting to carry out the will of the emperor, did but 'hide themselves behind the throne and fire at their . . . enemies from this secure ambush': these words, from the year 1913, were spoken in the Japanese parliament by an opposition member of the Diet, Yukio Ozaki. (I give the full context in Chapter 5.) The emperor was the pretext for, and not the originating cause of, all that was done in his name.

Finally, I remain alone responsible for the contents of this book: in writing about Japan, one has a wealth of sources, and almost unlimited opportunity for misreading them. My most important written sources are given at the end of the book under the heading Further Reading. Still more important to me are my many friends and colleagues in Japan, and elsewhere, who have found the time to discuss many of the points arising in this book. Particularly in the month of February 1989, when I was in Japan for the Showa Emperor's funeral, I was helped by many different people, from Hokkaido in the far north to Kyushu in the south. This is detailed under the heading Acknowledgements, but I would like to make clear that the help I acknowledge was absolutely indispensable. I could not have written this book without it. Only the faults remain my own.

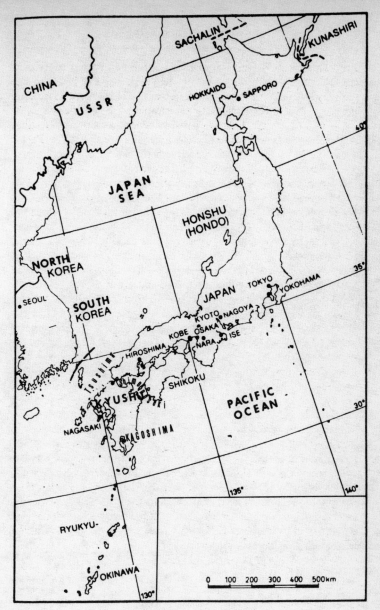

Map of Japan in 1989

A year of reckoning

BY any reckoning, the Chrysanthemum Throne, to which the present emperor of Japan, Akihito, succeeded on 7 January 1989, is one of the world's oldest public institutions. The nature of the institution is little understood, even by many Japanese, if only because its historical development since its ancient origins is so strange to the modern world. This explains why, in the months before the death of the old emperor, whom the world outside Japan knew as Hirohito, the attention of the media was focused upon the man, and not the institution he represented.

Such interest reached its climax in the period between the emperor's death, on 7 January, and his funeral, some seven weeks later, on 24 February. In Japan, every supermarket, news-stand and bookshop had its display of books and magazines, illustrated with photographs retrieved from archives going back to the beginning of the century, and recounting every possible event, not only in the life of the emperor himself, but in the history of the nation which recognized him as its sovereign.

The story to be told was phenomenal. The emperor himself, when he died at the age of eighty-seven, was older than any of his predecessors, and had reigned far longer. More than that, in the sixty-three years of his reign, the defeat of Japan in 1945, following the cataclysmic destruction caused by the only atomic weapons ever used in warfare and the reconstruction which then followed, brought about changes more profound than had occurred in any previous time. In a country in which the Pacific War had reduced the cities to dust and ashes, and brought the population to a point where even survival was uncertain, the emperor, then a comparatively young man, remained in the capital city, and after his country's defeat was allowed to remain on the throne. He was to be there for another forty-three years, but even at his death controversy still surrounded him – surprising for a man who, both by his own nature and by that of his office, was essentially a very private person.

For the Japanese he hardly even had a name. He was just simply the *tennō*, a Japanese word misleadingly translated as 'emperor', as if the *tennō* was to be equated with Julius Caesar, Peter the Great, Napoleon or, in our own century, Haile Selassie. Such an equation could hardly be right for any of the more than one hundred *tennō*'s recorded in Japanese history, although some Japanese wish that it were so. There is no indication that Hirohito ever was, or wished to be, such an emperor. In the nineteenth century, when Japan first became open to the West, the reports of the visitors to the court referred to the emperor by an alternative title, *mikado* (which is like referring to the Holy See instead of the Pope), but, correctly according to Japanese practice, did not mention his name. This was adopted by Gilbert and Sullivan as the title of one of the best known of the Savoy operas, in which only the costumes and décor could possibly be recognizable to the Japanese themselves: the plot is pure fantasy. The title of *Mikado* was revived, in 1986, by the Tokyo journalist, Naoki Inose, whose book *Mikado no Shōzō (Images of the Emperor)* looks at all the different ways in which people, particularly outside Japan, have projected their own images on to the person and office of the Japanese emperor. Such projections will be a constant theme of this book.

Over the two thousand-odd years of Japanese history, the *tennō* was more a pope than a king. The office he held conferred upon him certain powers, which were religious more than political. There was no need to refer to him by name: there was always one, and only one, *tennō* at any given time. There was generally a recognized successor, known as the *kōtaishi* or *tōgū*, words generally, if somewhat misleadingly, translated as 'crown prince'. Even when there was no designated successor, the problem of succession was always solved, so that the provision of the first article of the modern constitution (promulgated by the Emperor Meiji in 1889) that 'The empire of Japan shall be reigned over and governed by a line of emperors unbroken for ages eternal' stated a proposition which had been true throughout Japanese history. The Imperial Rescript on Education, which followed a year later, put the matter in even more cosmic terms: 'Our Imperial Throne is coeval with heaven and earth'.

After the defeat of Japan in the Pacific War, such pretensions were not acceptable to the occupying forces, known simply as SCAP (Supreme Command for the Allied Powers); in 1947 a new constitution replaced that of 1889, and the whole of the Imperial Rescript on Education was repealed – much against the wishes of the Japanese bureaucracy, which had survived the war almost intact.

The emperor, at the same time, helped matters in the same direction by renouncing, on New Year's Day, 1946, all claims to divine status, so that he was no longer the *arahitogami*, that is to say, the 'divine present emperor'. Just what this involved is a point to be returned to later, in Chapter 9, but for the present it is to be noted that the emperor still remained the *tennō*, whose name needed never to be mentioned, although that of the era defined by his reign, Showa, was an essential part of the Japanese calendar.

He acceded automatically to the throne, as *tennō*, when his father died on Christmas Day, 1926, although the rites of succession were protracted over a period of nearly two years – as they may well be in the case of his son, the present, new *tennō*, Akihito. The accession, as already noted, was automatic since he was already the Crown Prince, having been installed at the age of fifteen and a half as the *kōtaishi*, on 3 November 1916. Hirohito's father, today known as the Taisho Tenno, had succeeded his father, Meiji, as emperor in 1912. Once Hirohito was the *kōtaishi*, his name need not be, and indeed was not, spoken even within the imperial court and his own family. Only before then could Hirohito, born in 1901 as the first son of the then *kōtaishi*, be called by the name given to him – and he had no other – in a Shinto ceremony which took place when he was a month old. Even then, it was probably only his father and his grandfather who could use this name. The young prince, having his own household almost from birth, saw them but occasionally, and they may still have preferred a number of familiar alternatives, such as parents are often inclined to adopt for their children.

If this all seems very involved, it causes no particular difficulty to the Japanese. Their idea of a name is that it provides a label, ideally not shared by anyone else in the whole country, which is used to refer to its bearer in the third person. It is written, if anything, more often than it is spoken, so that it is first and foremost what determines the public identity of any individual Japanese. This explains the constant exchange of visiting cards, or *meishi*, which is part and parcel of daily life. In a country where all relationships are governed by principles of seniority, a given name can only be used in conversation by a senior speaking to a junior, and that within the confines of the family. President Reagan, when he addressed the Japanese Prime Minister, Nakasone, as Yasuhito, would have been, if Japanese, guilty of an almost unthinkable solecism, although as a foreigner, or *gaijin*, he could hardly have been expected to know better. None the less Nakasone's successor, Takeshita, Prime Minister at the time of the Showa Emperor's death, made clear that he would not encourage such familiarity, even with the President of the United States. (Tashiki Kaifu, now Prime Minister after scandal had forced the resignation of both Takeshita and Takeshita's successor Sosuke Uno, will almost certainly take the same position.)

The principle, if extended to the emperor, rules out any possible use of an actual given name, for he is by definition senior to all his subjects, and the title *tennō*, or the more polite *tennō heika* – roughly equivalent to 'His Majesty the Emperor' – is sufficient for any reference in the third person. But all this changes on the death of a *tennō*. A dead *tennō* must have a name, as an imperial ancestor, or *kōsō*, simply to distinguish him from all his predecessors, so that once the old emperor died, he immediately became the Showa Tenno, and as such was referred to in every possible publication. A Japanese emperor, therefore, while he lives, is a person without a name where as once dead, he becomes a name without a person. This has the somewhat contrary result that any list of Japanese emperors, or indeed the mention of any one of them in a historical work, refers to them by names never used as such while they were alive: when the little prince Hirohito was born, grandson of the emperor now, but not then, known as Meiji, no one could possibly tell that he, after his death nearly ninety years later, would be known to history as Showa. This again is not too difficult for the Japanese to grasp, since almost everyone receives a new name after he dies, generally from the priests of the Buddhist temple where the mortuary rites are carried out. Under the present order this is not possible in the case of the emperor, since following the precedent established at the time of the Meiji Emperor's death in 1912 the funeral is strictly Shinto (other members of the imperial family have normal Buddhist funerals, followed by crem-

[4]

ation). The change in the emperor's name, at death, is simplified by a precedent established for the Meiji Emperor, by which the name of the era becomes the posthumous name. This still has to be communicated to the imperial ancestors, some three weeks after the death, in a private court ceremony called the *tsuigō hōkoku no gi*. In this way, the old emperor, who died on 7 January, was presented to his ancestors, as the Showa Tenno, on 31 January 1989. These points come up again in Chapter 12, where I describe the whole ritual process which followed the emperor's death.

In addition to acquiring a new name, a deceased emperor, after the first fifty-odd days of protracted funeral rites, comes to his final resting place in a funeral mound, known in the first instance as *sanryō*. The old emperor, Showa, came to rest in the *sanryō* specially built for him in Hachioji, a satellite town of Tokyo, in the evening of 24 February 1989, after a day almost entirely devoted to mortuary ritual, both public and private. There his body was committed, by a ceremony known as *ryōsho no gi*, to lie next to the *sanryō* built for his father, Taisho, in 1927. This was the sixteenth in a succession of rituals which had been performed in the forty-eight days following the death on 7 January, and there were almost as many still to be performed, the last only at the end of the year, 1989. On the actual death the body was transferred to a purpose-built structure within the Imperial Precinct, known as the *hinkyū*, and it was only on the day of the funeral that it was brought to the building, known as the *sōjōden*, in the Shinjuku Gyoen – a Tokyo park which was originally an imperial foundation – for the main rites to be performed. This is what television viewers could see, in many different parts of the world.

The protracted funeral ritual is an example of what anthropologists call a *rite de passage*, or more specifically, a *rite de transition*. In Shinto, a religion preoccupied with the need to avoid pollution, and particularly that associated with death, it is hardly surprising that both the *hinkyū* and the *sōjōden* are temporary structures. On the death of the emperor, they were built to order, out of wood, to a traditional design, executed by skilled craftsmen at very considerable cost. They no longer exist, and the visitor to the Shinjuku Gyoen, now once more open to the public, will find no trace of the *sōjōden* built, and dismantled, at the beginning of the year. It is significant that the first Chinese character in the written form of *hinkyū* has an alternative reading, *mogari*, which means an intermediate stage between this world and the next. The deceased emperor is in a state of *mogari* while he is in the process of becoming an imperial ancestor. In the oldest Shinto tradition of a period long before the move to Kyoto in the year 794, the transitory nature of human life, manifested in that of the emperor for the time being, was itself represented by the destruction of every imperial residence, as soon as death supervened, so that the period of *mogari* can be seen as no more than an extension of that of the life preceding it. It is the announcement of the new name, or *tsuigō*, to the ancestors, and the consignment of its bearer to the *sanryō*, which give a *tennō* his place in history.

The *rites de transition* lead, in the end, to the *sanryō* built for the most recently deceased emperor becoming a new point in the imperial topography. For obvious historical reasons, most such points are scattered in and around the old capital of Kyoto, where they are known as *goryō* or *misasagi* – the distinction is difficult to make since both terms are written with the same Chinese characters. The aggregate of such *goryō* provides a permanent physical refraction of the imperial line, at least from a date, some hundreds of years ago, when the bodies of deceased emperors came to be buried, rather than cremated according to normal Buddhist practice. These monuments are not conspicuous, although they are often to be found in a small local park. The emperors whom they commemorate have for the most part passed into oblivion. The most imposing of the Kyoto *goryō* is also the most recent, that built in the suburb of Momoyama for the Emperor Meiji on his death in 1912: in this case the approach is watched over by a *torii*, the sacred gateway to all Shinto holy places, and in the period of mourning for Meiji's grandson, Showa, occasional visitors did come to pay their respects.

If one looks at the line of imperial ancestors, defined as the class of all previous emperors, every one of them is descended, through the male line, from at least one of his predecessors. This is equally true of the occasional empresses who reigned over Japan, although such possibility is now excluded by the Salic law of succession, adopted from Prussia in the nineteenth century, which disbars women from succession. The rule of descent has always excluded any possibility of a succession of dynasties, such as is to be found in the history of China, a country from which the Japanese, in other ways, have borrowed many of their political and religious institutions. Japan has simply one line of imperial descent, and the logical need for a starting point is satisfied by the Emperor Jimmu, a mythical rather than a historical character, who is claimed to have started his reign in the year 660 BC.

From the very beginning the emperor's authority has been established by his receiving the three imperial regalia, or *sanshū no shinki*, consisting of the mirror, jewel and sword. Of these the mirror is the most significant for understanding not only the imperial institution, but also what is at the heart of the Japanese character. It was the mirror which the other gods, or *kami*, used to entice the sun-goddess out of a cave where she had hidden herself in a fit of pique with her brother, the god of thunder. By going into the cave, and closing it behind her, the sun-goddess had plunged the world into darkness: when she emerged, it was only to see her own reflection in the mirror. But it was too late to turn back: the *kami* had blocked the mouth of the cave by tying a rope across it. From this point on the sun-goddess was concerned to restore order to the land, which is now Japan, created, in an extremely complicated way, by her heavenly ancestors. For this purpose she sent her grandson Ninigi to rule from his palace at Mount Takachiho, which is above the cave. She then bestowed on him not only the mirror (which was from then on to be thought of as if it were the sun-goddess herself), but also the necklace or jewel (which she had received from her own father, Isanagi), and the sword which she had had specially made from the tail of a dragon. These in turn descended from Ninigi to his great-grandson, Jimmu, who on 11 February 660 BC established himself as the first emperor of Yamato, as Japan was originally known. This day, known since 1965 as *kenkoku kinenbi* or 'national foundation day', was declared a public holiday in the late nineteenth century, when the mythical descent of the Meiji Emperor, together with the whole chronology, became part of the doctrine of the official State Shinto.

The cave, known as Ama no Iwato, and the rope are still where they always have been, just outside the village of Takachiho, lost in the mountains of Kyushu, the most southerly of the four main Japanese islands. The mirror is kept in the *naigū*, or 'inner shrine' of the imperial temple of Ise, which is dedicated, needless to say, to Amaterasu Omikami, the sun-goddess, herself. The oddest thing about the *naigū* is that tradition requires it to be destroyed, and built anew, every twenty years, always on the same plan. This is done by alternating between two adjacent but otherwise identical sites, so that as every cycle nears its end, the new shrine is constructed on the vacant site, the destruction of the old beginning with the dedication of the new. The visitor to Ise sees a building whose design, as familiar to the Japanese as Big Ben is to the British, is of great antiquity, but which in actuality cannot be more than twenty years old.

This curious point, if somewhat laboured, is important for establishing the way in which the imperial succession is related to time. No emperor ever has the name of a predecessor: that is, the posthumous names by which the emperors are known to history are all different. In the earliest Japanese chronicle, known as the Kojiki and completed under the auspices of the imperial court in AD 712, the succession of emperors is simply given by their names. This information, together with the length of the reign given for each individual emperor, is what determines the year 660 BC as that in which the reign of the first emperor, Jimmu, began.

The Kojiki is not be trusted as a historical document, at least as it relates to the first twenty-eight emperors whose reigns it records. This means that the dates given for the emperors reigning in the first 1,200 years cannot be relied upon. This is obvious enough when one notes, for instance, that the sixth emperor, Koan, is stated as having reigned for ninety-nine years, and that others, also, reigned for unbelievably long periods.

Before the Kojiki, Japan had no written language of its own. The first writing known to the Japanese came from China or Korea, in the form of mirrors and swords, inscribed in Chinese characters, and imported some time before the fourth century AD. It was not until the beginning of the seventh century that the Japanese began to produce their own written texts, and even then they first did so in a version of Chinese known as *kanbun*. Then the Prince Shotoku (574–622), who was regent for his aunt, the Empress Suiko, composed, in the year 604, the Constitution of Seventeen Articles, which was a code of general ethical principles of Chinese origin. Even the Kojiki was mainly written in *kanbun*, but the poems and proper names occurring in it do represent the earliest example of written Japanese, in which the Chinese characters were used, where necessary, in a distinctive Japanese phonetic form now known as *man'yōgana*, after an anthology of poems, the *man'yōshū* which appeared in 759.

The Prince Shotoku is a key figure in Japanese imperial history. The fact that he himself never became the emperor allows his likeness to appear, now, on the 10,000 yen banknotes, for the likeness of a *tennō*, live or dead, may never be impressed upon a note, coin or stamp. By establishing, in 607, a monastery in Horyu-ji, close to the capital of his day, as a centre for Buddhist worship, Shotoku, more than anyone else, ensured the place of Buddhism in Japanese society, where it would greatly influence the further development of the traditional, indigenous Shinto, particularly in its relation to the imperial court. His monastery, located some thirty miles outside Osaka, still survives, in part, as the oldest wooden building in the world.

More important for the imperial chronology was the adoption by Prince Shotoku of the traditional Chinese calendar in the same year as he published the Constitution of Seventeen Articles. The basis of this calendar is a sixty-year cycle maintained by the so-called *kan-shi* system, consisting of the ten heavenly stems, *kan*, and the twelve earthly branches, *shi*. The former are based on the five elements of Chinese alchemy, wood, fire, earth, metal and water, alternating according to the principle of 'elder and younger brother', or in Japanese *e* and *to*; the latter are based on the twelve animals of the Chinese zodiac. The two cycles begin at the point defined by the *kan* character which is read as *kinoe* (the elder brother of wood), and the *shi* character which is read as *ne* (rat). If each cycle moves on one step every year, *kinoe* and *ne* will not coincide until sixty years later. (The mathematician will note that 60 is the lowest common multiple of 10 and 12.) The *kanshi* system, applied to years, will determine any date exactly, so long as other extraneous factors rule out all but one possibility. To give an example, someone who were now to say that he was born in the year *kanoto no hitsuji*, defined by the *kan* for 'the younger brother of fire' (*ka no to*) and the *shi* for 'sheep' (*hitsuji*), could only have been born in 1931, since if born in 1871, let alone 1811, and so on into the indefinite past, he would be impossibly old.

If the *kanshi* system is imposed upon another system, based upon successive periods, of no fixed length, but each with its own distinctive name, then the combined use is sufficient to give every year its own unique designation. In this way the combination of *kanoto no hitsuji* and Showa must also mean 1931, since this is the only year in the Showa era which coincided with that point in the Chinese calendar. This means, in any case, that the Japanese emperors, past and present, make an indispensable contribution to maintaining the calendar, so that the end of the Showa era, and the beginning of Heisei, do make

1989 a year of reckoning. It is easy for someone from the West to reduce all this to the level of fortune telling and horoscopes in the popular press, and at this level also one finds much of its appeal to the Japanese at the present time.

The importance of the system, as it incorporates the name of the era, or *nengō* in Japanese, is to be seen from the fact that it was made the only legal basis for calendar reckoning by an enactment passed as recently as 1979. For all official use, instead of the *kanshi* reckoning, the years are counted from the beginning of the era which coincides with that of the first year of the emperor's reign. It is this which explains how, at midnight on 7 January 1989, Showa 64 became Heisei 1. The only difficulty about this innovation is that it makes the naming of future dates somewhat problematical. To give one example, a new Buddhist temple is under construction in the Kyoto ward of Higashiyama, and so long as the old emperor lived a contractors' notice-board stated that it was due for completion in the spring of Showa 65, that is our year 1990. But there will be no Showa 65, and even though the year is now stated as Heisei 2, the problem has been shelved rather than solved. In the *kanshi* system, the name of the era need not even have been mentioned, since the *kan* and the *shi* for 1990 would not again coincide until the year 2050, which is hardly a realistic alternative.

The matter does not end here, for nothing is that simple in Japanese number mysticism. The Chinese empire, with its successive dynasties, applied the calendar based on the sixty-year cycle to a succession of era names, chosen according to astrological principles. Not long after the adoption of the Chinese calendar, the Japanese adopted the same system, so that the reign of the thirty-sixth emperor, Kotoku (645–54), was divided into two eras, Taika (645–50) and Hakuchi (650–55), establishing a precedent which was to be followed for more than 1,200 years, being abandoned only with the accession of the Emperor Maiji in 1868. It was then that the practice was established of having the emperor announce the name of his era on the day of his accession, with the provision that this should also be his own name after his death. With Hirohito, in 1926, the name first chosen was printed by a daily newspaper, the *Mainichi*, while the old emperor was still alive. This was so serious a lapse that the name of Showa, actually announced two days after the death, was only chosen at the last moment. The merits of this name were to be found in the meanings of the two

Chinese characters of its written form, 'light' and 'harmony', but then the meaning of every *nengō* was equally auspicious according to such criteria.

This is equally true of the name, Heisei, chosen for the era of the present emperor and announced on 8 January 1989. The factors determining this particular choice were much more complicated, and required the advice of a number of leading Japanese historians. The starting point was a list of seventy-two *kanji*, or Chinese characters, from which the two components of every one of the 240 *nengō* known to history had been chosen. None of these was of course available for the new era. What is more, any possible combination must be one which occurred in one of five or six sacred texts, or *shūkyō*, including the Kojiki and the Ekikyō, better known in the West by its Chinese name, I Ching. The learned advisers came up with three possibilities, but of these two began with the letter S when written in *rōmaji*, as the Japanese call the Roman alphabet. These had to be ruled out, since in many computer systems the data base already recorded years in the Showa era simply with the prefix S. This left only Heisei, which was acceptable according to any criteria, ancient or modern. (Of course the imperial ancestors will not learn this name until the ceremony of *tsuigō hōkoku no gi* takes place some four weeks after the death of the present emperor, in the first year of an era whose name cannot possibly now be known.)

The present official calendar may well have the worst of all possible worlds, and it is difficult to see why, in 1979, the Japanese government preferred it to the Western Gregorian calendar, which the Japanese themselves use, unofficially, all the time. There are political reasons for the government's policy, but these, though important for understanding it, are still somewhat abstruse. They will in any case be discussed further in Chapter 11. There is however one practical reason, at least, for abandoning the *kanshi* system of reckoning. This system is ambiguous for recording any period of time longer than sixty years, with the result that anyone entering into the sixty-first year of his life will repeat the year of his birth. This process is familiar to the Japanese under the name, *kanreki*, which means 'returning to the calendar'. In the life of the individual this calls for special ceremonies which represent, symbolically, the beginning of a second childhood, and few families allow the occasion to pass by unnoted. The ambiguity in this case hardly matters, because there is no difficulty in distinguishing events separated by a period of sixty years in the life of an individual.

If an emperor reigns for more than sixty years, quite different questions arise, but then this was never a real problem until the year 1985, when the Showa Emperor entered the sixty-first year of his reign. Since the Chinese calendar had been officially abandoned one might have expected the government to have ignored this event: instead they treated it as if it were a sort of *kanreki*, although there was, by the very nature of the case, no precedent for their doing so. But the celebrations were muted and idiosyncratic: ten million gold coins, each of a denomination of 100,000 yen (about $700) were minted, and there were special issues of silver coins of lesser denominations. There was also a special joint session of the Diet, over which the emperor presided. There was none of the torrent of publicity about his life and times which was released at the time of his death some four years later.

The public events, which focused on the person of the emperor, organized by the government in the autumn of 1940 to celebrate the fact that twenty-six centuries had elapsed since the nation was founded with the accession of the Emperor Jimmu in 660 BC, were of a quite different order. The government of that time, led by Prince Konoye but dominated by the armed services, wished to present the emperor as the head of a conquering army, and he played the role assigned to him in the masquerade. In the photo-reportage following his death nearly fifty years later, the picture of the young emperor, mounted on his white horse and wearing the uniform of the commander-in-chief of the armed forces, constantly recurred, providing one of the most familiar images of his long reign.

It is worthwhile to take a last look at this mythopoeic year, 660 BC, and to see why it counts for so much. True, to abandon it would require rewriting the Kojiki and other ancient chronicles – but how did these arrive at this date in the first place? Once more the answer is to be found in the Chinese calendar and the establishment of Buddhism in Japan. The point is that for esoteric reasons to be found in traditional Chinese number mysticism, Buddhism was to come to Japan twenty-one complete sixty-year cycles after the accession of the first emperor. The year, 604, in which the Chinese calendar was adopted was chosen to coincide with the first year of a new cycle, which event last occurred in 1984. The establishment of Buddhism was dated from four years earlier, which, in the Western calendar, happened to be the year 600: 21 x 60 = 1,260, and 1,260 years before AD is 660 BC. QED.

The fact that this predates the emergence of the Japanese imperial line by some 600 years is not to the point: the cold logic of arithmetic must win over the historical record. (In all these calculations the Japanese knew nothing of the Western calendar: the point is that the compilers of the Kojiki worked backwards from their own time to find out first the date when Buddhism was established and then, derivatively, the chronology of the first emperors.) The approach dominates Japanese popular historiography: the abstract principles governing the course of history, which can be said to be based on Japan's idea of its manifest destiny, cannot be faulted. The fact that the emperors, in particular, can hardly escape from their rule goes a long way towards explaining why they have always found it so difficult to establish any distinctive personality. The consequences of this for Emperor Hirohito are worked out in Chapter 11.

Before leaving the arithmetic of the calendar and its historical – or better, mythical – implications, it is important to note that there is nothing in the explanations given above that did not appear in countless articles in the popular press appearing in the last months of 1988 and the first months of 1989. The arithmetical demands (which are hardly more than are required for betting on horses or working out baseball averages) come naturally to the Japanese. It is, however, instructive that after the end of the Pacific War, Yuji Aida, a young Japanese soldier captured in Burma, published a book entitled *Prisoner of the British*, which included a short section headed 'British troops can't count'. This tells how the Japanese prisoners, made to work in British Army food depots, had no difficulty in breaking bulk in order to make up the exact consignments indented for out of the stores. The Japanese performed, correctly and almost instantaneously, arithmetical calculations which quite baffled the British private soldiers working with them. The details given by Aida show, in fact, that the calculations so easily made by his compatriots were precisely those which arise in working with the Chinese calendar, although no one seemed to realize this. The key point here is not so much the proficiency of the Japanese in mental arithmetic, but their almost inborn feeling for working with numbers, and accepting that life is governed by the way numbers combine with each other. In the history of Western thought this is precisely the approach of the school of Pythagoras: Japan, on the other hand, certainly borrowed it from China, in much the same period as it adopted the Chinese calendar.

The point has come to establish a chronology of Japan, which can be related to changes in the position of the imperial court. In the life span of any Japanese, certain years are known as *yakudoshi*: these are fateful years in which special precautions must be taken to guard against misfortune. The history of Japan can also be related to a small number of key years, although it would be wrong to refer to those as *yakudoshi*: this is particularly true when it comes to the reign of the Showa Emperor. Many of these years have already been mentioned, but it is useful to present them once again, as the major landmarks in Japanese history.

The first year, 660 BC, is that of the founding of the imperial line with the Emperor Jimmu. There is no adequate historical basis for this year, and it is best to accept that the imperial line emerged, from uncertain origins, some time around the beginning of the Christian era.

The year AD 604, in contrast, is an important historical landmark. The year of the adoption of the Chinese calendar, it occurs in the middle of the regency of the Prince Shotoku, who more than any other person was responsible for establishing Buddhism in Japan.

In the year 794 Kyoto became the imperial capital, following the abandonment, in 784, of Nara, thirty miles to the south, where the Buddhist monasteries had denied any freedom of action to the court.

In 1600, the commander-in-chief, or Shogun, Tokugawa Ieyasu, established an effective government for the whole country, based upon his castle in Edo, which is now the Imperial Precinct in the city known to the world of today as Tokyo. The Edo or Tokugawa period is critical for understanding the imperial institution, since almost from the very beginning the emperors were confined behind the walls of the *gosho*, as the imperial compound in Kyoto was known: denied all political power, and forced to exercise their administrative prerogatives at the behest of the Shogun, the emperors were left to perform the magico-religious court ritual, established by ancient tradition, and find, for the rest, what pleasure and entertainment could be enjoyed in a confinement from which abdication or death provided the only possible release. All this is looked at in much greater detail in Chapter 3.

This state of affairs lasted until 1868, the year of the so-called 'Meiji restoration'; in this year, on 9 January, the last of the Tokugawa Shoguns gave up his office, and the family which had ruled Japan for 268 years disappeared, almost without trace, from the political scene. The government which then came to power derived its legitimacy from the principle of *sonnō-jōi*, which had been developing over the fifteen years following the arrival of Commodore Perry in the Bay of Edo in July 1853.

The Meiji restoration is considered in detail in Chapter 4, so now no more is needed than a short explanation of the meaning of *sonnō* and *jōi*. *Sonnō* need mean no more than the traditional Japanese reverence for the emperor, but in the years leading up to the Meiji restoration, it came to mean also a statement of policy which would lead to the setting-up of a government presided over by the emperor, to replace the *bakufu*, as that of the Tokugawa Shoguns was known. *Jōi* was the policy that this new government was to follow: its aim was to frustrate the policy of *kaikoku*, which meant opening the country to foreigners. Following the uninvited visit of Commodore Perry this was the most critical issue in Japanese politics in more than 250 years.

The status of the new emperor, who at the beginning of 1868 was but fifteen years old, was confirmed by moving the capital from Kyoto (where it had been for more than a thousand years) to Edo, which the *bakufu* had long established as the seat of effective government in Japan. By changing the name to Tō-kyōto (which is still used officially and means 'Eastern Capital') the message conveyed was that the new emperor combined the ritual and religious functions of his predecessors with the political functions of the Tokugawa Shoguns.

In any case the result of this reform was the opposite of that intended by those who had brought it about. *Kaikoku* triumphed over *jōi*. Under the Emperor Meiji Japan became a modern country, which within forty years would defeat a major European power, Russia, in a war fought with modern weapons. When in 1868 Meiji travelled to his new capital, he was carried the whole way from Kyoto – a distance of more than 300 miles – in a palanquin, and the advance news of his arrival was carried by a succession of runners. When he died in 1912, his body was carried back to Kyoto by train, and the news was transmitted by electric telegraph.

In the 121 years (almost to the day) which elapsed between the Meiji restoration and the death of Meiji's Showa grandson on 7 January 1989, the year 1945 was the most cataclysmic in all Japanese history.

If one focuses on this year from the perspective of the life of the Showa Emperor, it is seen to occur almost exactly at the half-way point. Showa was born as the Prince Hirohito in 1901: Hiroshima was destroyed by the first atomic bomb when the emperor was forty-four years old, and he was to die not long before his eighty-eighth birthday.

The period of 121 years is but a year longer than two complete cycles of the Chinese calendar. The character of the whole period can be summed up in the two names of Meiji and Showa, for the Emperor Taisho, Meiji's son and Showa's father, counted for little, and for the last five years of his short reign (1912–26) his son acted as regent.

The questions asked in this book focus upon Showa. Who was he? What did he represent? What did he really achieve? Such questions cannot be answered adequately unless they are asked also of Showa's grandfather, Meiji. Meiji was a remote but none the less dominant influence upon the life of his young grandson, Hirohito, and the death of the grandfather was to confront the eleven-year-old grandson with fundamental questions about his role and identity, not only in Japan, but eventually also in the whole world. The confrontation was one which the Emperor Showa could never escape at any time, neither in the sixty-three years of his reign, nor in the years preceding it. It caused him at times immense anguish, and left him alone with decisions for which the undoubted wisdom of his grandfather was little help. He was an actor on a world stage, in a drama of which he was not the author, playing a role open to many different interpretations, many of which did him no justice at all. The script was continually being rewritten about his head, on a basis claimed to be historical, but grounded in myths, which themselves were continually being recast, not in the interests of the emperor himself (to which few outside his own family ever paid much heed), but in the interests of those who wished to use him for their own ends. The story to be told is of an essentially unpretentious man longing to be himself, to be free of a confinement which at times must have seemed as drastic as that to which the Shoguns had subjected his ancestors, imprisoned within the walls of their Kyoto precinct.

2

Gods, ancestors and rice

THE first part of the word *tennō*, which the Japanese use to refer to their emperor, means, in different connotations, heaven, providence, destiny, and none of these connotations escapes them when they think about the status of the *tennō*. But if the Japanese themselves understand the position, at least in its present-day form, more or less correctly, they tend to explain it to outsiders in a way which leads only to mystification.

The problem is essentially religious. At its heart is the fact that three quite different religious traditions, Shinto, Buddhism and Confucianism, have governed daily life in Japan for well over a thousand years, and the emperor of the day has been involved in every one of them. Following the Meiji restoration, in 1868, a form of Shinto, known as State Shinto, was promoted as a matter of government policy, with such success that when the Showa Emperor died at the beginning of 1989 most of his subjects accepted that this was the only religion he adhered to. The implications of his disclaimer of divine status in the course of the New Year Celebrations in 1946, as much as of the provisions in the 1947 constitution providing for a purely secular state, were generally disregarded. The present government of Japan would be happy to see these matters forgotten.

Among ordinary Japanese there is little question of Buddhism having been supplanted by Shinto, although a number of recent surveys do suggest that Shinto, relatively speaking, is gaining some ground. And in the background the ethical precepts of Confucianism are far from being abandoned. In fact, since their earliest contacts with Buddhism some time before the seventh century, the Japanese have consistently mixed different religious traditions. This allows for the coexistence of heterogeneous religions in one family, or even one person.

If syncretism was never a problem for the Japanese, it is still necessary, if the religious position is to be understood, to separate the different strands comprised in the whole – particularly in its changing relationship to the court.

An historical approach allows the analysis to proceed on the basis of four periods. The first is that of pure Shinto, as it was in the period before contact with China and Korea introduced Buddhism and Confucianism into Japan. This period goes back to the beginning of time, as the Japanese understand it, which means the reign of the Emperor Jimmu from 660 BC. On this basis the first period comprises nearly half of Japanese history to the present time. Modern historical scholarship allows it a much shorter duration of hardly more than 600 years, but the exact length of time is much less important than the actual content of this primordial Shinto. This itself is problematical in so far as the historical process which made any record possible, that is, the adoption and adaptation of written Chinese, also put an end to this ideal state.

This enables the Japanese, even today, to allow the play of fantasy to define the origins and early history of Shinto, together with that of the first twenty-odd emperors. The surviving forms of Shinto, which are well recorded throughout the historical period, provide, of course, some guidance, varying according to circumstance. Reconstruction by means of a process comparable to that used by Old Testament scholars concerned with the earliest history of Judaism is an uncertain matter, since Shinto, in pronounced contrast to Judaism, developed on its own, in complete isolation from any foreign influences. None the less, the rite of *daijōsai* for the installation of a new *tennō* (which I describe in detail in Chapter 6) can be traced back to a very early time. Other rites, clearly influenced by Buddhism, must be much more recent, but however uncertain the actual origins of the Japanese, even the most rigorous historian must accept that there was an important and protracted period of time during which they established, unaided by any outsider, their own religion and polity. What is more, there was always an emperor, who in some quite essential way was involved in the development of Shinto. These are the factors which today still give many Japanese the sense that they are radically different from any other people.

This still does not answer the question, what is Shinto? The word itself, which is of Chinese origin, means 'the way of the gods', and the gods, or *kami*, are innumerable, are present everywhere and take almost any possible form. Shinto is, and always has been, a pervasive element in Japanese daily life. It emphasizes life rather than death (which is seen as essentially polluting), and conceives of nature as capricious, but essentially beneficent. In Shinto the numerous festivals reflect more a love of theatre than any concern for morality: the behaviour required of its adherents is focused on the correct performance of ritual, rather than respect for any sort of ethical code, or concern for any form of judgement. The reward for the right ritual at the right time is to be found in the favourable response of the *kami* to whom it is addressed.

The foremost demand made of any *kami* is that the caprice of nature be kept within bounds, which must mean, in a modern urban society such as that of modern Japan, that the *kami* have less work to do. None the less, at almost any shrine, hundreds of wooden tablets, known as *ema*, will bear messages, addressed to the *kami*, in which young married women will petition for help in conceiving a child, or for intervention in the course of a child's illness. In the original tradition such petitions played a relatively unimportant role, for Shinto is a religion concerned with the fruitfulness of the land, which in Japan is measured, above all else, by the abundance of the rice harvest. Within Shinto there is a special and complicated cult of the fox-god, Inari, who symbolizes the spirit of rice. Where there is a household shrine, two cups of rice will be offered every morning.

It is in the cultivation of rice that the local *kami* really come into their own. Until the present century, this was the traditional economy of almost the whole Japanese population. The required level of productivity could only be achieved by means of irrigated terraces, laboriously constructed and maintained by the local population. These are still to be seen in every part of Japan, even near the centre of the largest cities. In the countryside the increasing scale of commercial agriculture has led to the abandonment of many small and inaccessible terraces, but small-holdings, often worked by housewives, are still very common. The cultivation of rice was the main activity of the *ie*, or Japanese household, for which the imperial household provides an ideal prototype.

From the very beginning the imperial line has been associated with the cultivation of rice (although this may be more a matter of myth than of history). The sun-goddess originally hid herself in the cave at Takachiho because her tiresome brother, Susonowo no mikoto, the god of thunder, had broken down the divisions between her plots of rice, and defecated on her new palace just as she was about to celebrate the first fruits ceremony. This is enough to cause anyone to go into a sulk, particularly in a land such as Japan which is so obsessive about both boundaries and pollution.

If the court, as such, has not grown rice in historical times, the emperor still attends ceremonies for the transplanting of rice – an essential stage in the process of cultivation – at the inner shrine at Ise, which is dedicated to his divine ancestress, the sun-goddess. Furthermore, the *daijōsai* is essentially a celebration of the first fruits of the rice harvest, which on this occasion are symbolically consumed by the new emperor.

The successful cultivation of rice depends upon two factors, both of which play a major role in Shinto. The first factor is the timing of every stage in the cultivation process. This is essential for the operation of the system of wet-rice cultivation traditionally followed in Japan, although it is known also throughout East and South East Asia. The agricultural basis of this system is that a very high yield can be obtained from a very small area, without in any way exhausting the soil, provided that the rice plants (which look not unlike any other grain) can grow in a bed of water, maintained at a level just below that of the kernel. This requires an absolutely flat field, to which water can be supplied at every stage in the growing season. Until well into the present century the only way of achieving this result was to build hillside terraces in an area where rain could be relied upon whenever required. It was an advantage if the soil was volcanic, because the flow of water for irrigation would then bring with it a rich supply of minerals.

Japan, where nearly 90 per cent of the total area is mountainous, with a long history of volcanic activity, is a country ideally suited for wet-rice cultivation. Not only the socio-economic, but also the religious implications are far-reaching. As for the former, this sort of agriculture is tied, absolutely, to one place, for everyone involved in it. There is no question of any sort of shifting cultivation or crop rotation (although the Japanese family always tried to supplement its diet with roots, fruit and vegetables, and fish if it was settled near the coast.) At the same time, the basic unit or *ta* (represented by the Chinese character 田 which frequently occurs in names such as that of the new Tokyo airport, Narita, or of the Prime Minister involved in the Lockheed scandal of the 1970s, Tanaka) is almost always small, simply by force of circumstance. In actual cultivation, economies of scale are hardly possible, let alone the development of any sort of agri-business (although this position is now rapidly changing).

It is not to be wondered at that the basic unit, or *ta*, was farmed by a single family household, that is the *ie*. As an economic unit, the *ie* was not only concerned with rice, although this was almost always the basic activity. The cultivation of mulberry bushes, for silkworms, could in many areas be carried on at the same time, so that the actual house became a small workshop, with the women busily engaged in the production of silk. With rice and other agricultural products being intended only for domestic consumption, this often provided the *ie*'s only economic tie with the outside world, and it is worth noting how important, even in the twentieth century, the export of silk was for Japan's foreign trade. (At the same time the *ie* was always subject to a very heavy burden of rent and taxation, traditionally paid in rice.)

The *ie* could never stand alone: its members were tied to those of every other *ie* in the village, and the village government not only provided for such public services as a communal bath (of considerable importance where the local religion sets great store by cleanliness and purity), but also regulated the whole cycle of irrigation which is essential to wet-rice cultivation.

The point is simple, though somewhat paradoxical. Where the actual units of production allow no economies of scale, they rely on a man-made infrastructure which represents a joint capital investment for the whole community. A terrace for the cultivation of rice cannot exist in isolation, but must be part of a complex whole, of which only the individual components are allocated to single proprietors. The typical Japanese village (in which each *ie* is a detached residence in its own precinct) is dominated by hillsides, in which the terraces ascend in a series of steps. The normal word for this, *dandanbatake*, literally 'step fields', evokes this pattern. The actual construction may well go back far beyond living memory, but the continual maintenance of the whole complex will be an unremitting task for the entire community, which may well explain the group-mentality so often attributed to the Japanese. In this sort of set-up there is no room for an odd man out.

The annual cycle of cultivation requires even closer co-operation and co-ordination. The wet-rice system requires the supply of water to be regulated for every individual *ta*, in conjunction with all the others. Significantly, the word generally used is not *ta*, but *suiden*, which combines the character 田 with 水, for water. Unless the level of water is right, the rice will not grow.

This poses a mathematical problem of the first order. The solution is not a rule of thumb but ritual. It is no coincidence that the great rice-growing areas of the world largely coincide with the domain of Buddhism, a religion suffused with mystic numbers and obsessed with the calendar. In Japan the series of rites taking place in the first part of the year, when the rice is growing, have largely been taken over by Shinto, but their practical purpose is unchanged. (The cultivation of rice may only have reached Japan with Buddhism, in which case the original association of the *daijōsai* with rice becomes somewhat problematical.) The rites provide a whole series of signals, each opening the way for the next stage in the irrigation process, which involves the constant opening and closing of conduits, so that in every *suiden* the level of water is just right. With this background it is no wonder that the Japanese set such store by virtues, such as punctuality, which are based upon accuracy. The single character, 正, in various readings (all of which have positive mystical connotations) can mean any form of correctness.

Although every village accepts the mystical correctness of the ritual calendar, it would be no use as a guide unless it accorded quite closely with the local topology and climate, which can vary from one mountain valley to another. The calendar, then, must ideally be a local calendar, and that is much more easily achieved with a religion such as Shinto, where every village, and even every household, has its own *kami*. The model may originally have been Buddhist, and Buddhism still maintains its own calendar, even in Japan, so that the ritual year comprises elements of both Shinto and Buddhism; the same is true of the life cycle of every single Japanese.

According to the doctrines of State Shinto as it was established in the Meiji era (which have now become the popular belief at the present day), the emperor is an exception to this rule: only Shinto governs his ritual calendar. In spite of all his disclaimers to divine status, the Showa Emperor, as late as 1968, is recorded as conducting, personally or privately, some thirty Shinto rites every year. For this there are three shrines within the Imperial Precinct in Tokyo: the most important is the *kashikodokoro*, where the copy of the *yata kagami*, the sacred mirror used for the accession ceremony, is kept, but there are also the Shinden (for the earthly and heavenly *kami*) and the Koreiden (for the souls of the imperial ancestors).

True, these imperial rites are not tied to the harvest cycle in the same way as the proliferation of local rites, but they are concentrated in the first part of the year, as the Shinto rites are at village level, so as to maintain a ritual timetable within the imperial household which is echoed in every *ie* in the country. This is a critical point in allowing the humblest household to identify itself with that of the emperor, but of course with the decline of village life, it is one which means much less than it did in the Japan of a hundred years ago.

The Japanese are acutely conscious of the possibility of the adverse intervention of fate in daily life. The agricultural system just described, however perfectly it may be regulated by the ritual calendar, is nevertheless an ideal model. In its actual working it is subject to any number of disturbances, both over the short and the long term.

Over the short term, one must constantly reckon with the *sansai*, the three calamities of fire, flood and storm. As to the first of these, particularly at times of drought, damage by fire, both to crops and buildings, can be catastrophic in a country where almost everything made or produced by man is combustible. Tokyo learnt this lesson well enough in the last year of the Pacific War, when American incendiary bombs destroyed hundreds of thousands of buildings, great and small. Not even the imperial family can escape from this risk: the present emperor, as an adolescent, lost his own private home by fire.

If the shortage of water brings the risk of fire, too great an abundance brings the equally devastating risk of flood, which along the coast can also be caused by the tidal waves known as *tsunami*. Although rice cannot grow on the *suiden* without water (as the word itself clearly implies) the supply of water must be capable of being controlled within certain tolerances, and the weather cannot always be relied upon to respect them. What is true of flood is true also of storm, and other natural disasters, such as volcanic eruptions, which can well be the cause of flood and storm. A religion such as Shinto, with a multiplicity of gods, allows almost endless scope for petitions to prevent the damage caused by the elements. There is also unlimited scope for oracular messages, whose impact does not necessarily spare the imperial house.

Shinto is therefore a religion of fragmentation, of concern for happenings which, however drastic they may be at the time they occur, only very occasionally alter the course of history. But if Shinto is a religion without cosmic pretensions, the opposite is true of Buddhism, which has played a key role in Japanese life for some 1,400 years. The two religions exist side by side, as do the shrines of the one and the temples of the other. The form of Buddhism in Japan is essentially syncretist, as it is to a degree wherever it is established. In the composite religion of modern Japan it is not always easy to separate the strands of the two components. Following the Meiji restoration it was the policy of the government to identify Shinto with the emperor, denying him at the same time any role in Buddhism.

Historically this is quite unjustifiable. The court has consistently provided the most important and powerful patrons of Buddhism, starting with Prince Shotoku, whose role in Japanese history may be compared with that of the Emperor Constantine in the Roman Empire. There is, however, an important difference. The establishment of Christianity in the West divided the world into two quite distinct classes, Christians and pagans. With the spread of Buddhism, not only in Japan, native gods were readily accepted as avatars, that is, subordinate manifestations of the archetypal Buddhas. The distinction is one more of principle than of practice, for all kinds of pagan institutions were in fact incorporated into Christianity. The example of Christmas is sufficient to prove the point.

Historically Buddhism never needed to fight against Shinto: it did not come to Japan as a crusade, in any sense of the word. It operated by means of a principle known in Japanese as *honji-suijaku*, whereby local institutions can be treated as manifestations of a general principle, which leads in the end to a state of affairs known as *shinbutsu-shūgō*, in which *kami* and Buddhas are merged into a single concept. The result is a syncretic universe in which the distinction between Buddhist temples and Shinto shrines becomes blurred, so that there is no longer any clear demarcation of functions. Such ambiguity, which is typically Japanese, never meant that the characteristic institutions of the two religions lost all identity: what it did mean was simply that any Japanese, in his journey through life, would not only be committed to both sides, but also have to choose his own interpretation, and its practical implementation.

The Japanese emperors were not only involved in these developments, but played a major part in bringing them about. The idea that the emperor is only concerned with Shinto is the result of policy following the Meiji restoration, and is hardly more than a hundred years old. The truth is that Buddhism would have achieved nothing in Japan if it had not actively been promoted by the court, and that in a period, more than 1,000 years ago, when the court was at the height of its power. The great Buddhist temple in the old capital of Nara, known as the Todaiji, which still stands as the largest wooden building in the world, may be seen as the *uji-dera*, or 'clan temple' of the imperial house. As such it is the *honji* to the *suijaku* represented by the inner shrine at Ise, so that by the principle of *shinbutsu-shūgō*, the Vairochana Buddha, housed in the Todaiji in the form of a vast bronze statue, is to be equated with the sun-goddess, Amaterasu Omikami.

If the syncretic process was so successful, the question to be asked is, what is the distinctive and lasting contribution of Buddhism to the final result? The whole religious history of Japan is involved in working out an answer to this question, but, to simplify matters, a three-fold reply is sufficient. Once again, because Buddhism came to Japan from China, its place in Japanese history is largely defined by three institutions adopted from China.

The first of these is that of a religion with a political, or even bureaucratic establishment. According to the definition proposed by the German sociologist, Max Weber, Buddhism, in Japan, was a Church, just as Christianity became, in the same sense, a Church after the time of Constantine. In Japan the interaction between Church and State ran a course parallel to that of medieval Europe, with both sides involved, sometimes in conflict, and sometimes in collaboration, in government. The political history of medieval Japan can only be understood in terms of this interaction, so that – to take one instance – when the Buddhist temples became too powerful in Nara in the course of the eighth century, the State was forced to retrieve its position by moving its capital to Kyoto in the year 794, where it was to remain for more than a thousand years. At the same time the increasingly bureaucratic constitution of Buddhism was paralleled by that known to Japanese historians as the *ritsu-ryō* system which governed the court. In the end, in the sixteenth century, at a time when the court had become very weak and the whole country was plunged into a Japanese equivalent to the Wars of the Roses in fifteenth-century England, the Buddhist temples lost their political and economic power. If their public role thereafter was subordinated to State policy, the temples were by no means eclipsed as a public insitution playing a major part in the lives of the ordinary people. Since this is still true today, what is the secret of survival?

The answer is to be found in the two institutions of Chinese origin yet to be considered. Of these, one, the calendar, has already been introduced in Chapter 1. Although the unification process of *shinbutsu-shūgō* has long meant that the feasts, or *matsuri*, of the Shinto calendar are as numerous and important as those of Buddhism, to which they are, of course, complementary, the underlying idea, representing *honji*, is Buddhist, where the Shinto principle, representing *suijaku*, is derivative. Once again, separating the strands is not easy, and for the Japanese it is not even necessary. The ritual calendar is a conflation of quite disparate elements, so that almost every day there is something to celebrate, whether Buddhist or Shinto, as the list of *matsuri* printed in the daily newspapers makes clear. The majority of festivals are of no interest to most Japanese, so that, for example, *shichi-go-san* (or 7-5-3), a Shinto festival which takes place on 15 November, will be completely disregarded by all except the parents of boys of five, or girls of three or seven. A few festivals are however observed by nearly all Japanese. In Shinto the most important is that which celebrates the New Year, while in Buddhism it is *bon*, a festival of requital to the ancestors and to the souls of the dead; these two festivals may be seen as complementary, in spite of quite different origins.

It is the worship of the ancestors which is the third, and much the most interesting, Japanese institution of Buddhist origin. Ancestor worship is as Japanese as blueberry pie is American. Whatever the status of Buddhism or Shinto in Japan, they cannot be separated from it. In the case of Buddhism, this would be nothing in Japan today without ancestor worship. In the context of Shinto, the whole cult of the emperor depends upon the same principles. Throughout Japanese history, ancestor worship has been maintained in the interests of any number of political and private causes, whether it be the suppression of Christianity in the seventeenth century, the restoration of imperial power in the nineteenth, or the promotion of new Buddhist sects, such as the enormously successful Risshō Kōseikai, in the twentieth.

The changing social configuration of Japan poses a radical and unprecedented threat to ancestor worship, with imponderable consequences when it comes to the popular veneration of the emperor. To understand why this is so, one must return to the traditional Japanese village, with its rice fields, and the households which cultivate them. The successful cultivation of rice, as an operation of the entire village, depends upon the villages being constituted by a more or less constant number of separate household units. This means that the household, or *ie*, must operate as a corporation which itself endures, even though its members change from one generation to another. At any one time, therefore, the head of an *ie* – almost always a man – will be the successor to a long line of predecessors, most of whom will be dead. At the same time the head must provide in turn for his successor, for he will not live for ever, and the *ie* must endure. It is quite normal for the head to retire, often when he enters his sixty-first year and celebrates *kanreki*, and simply to continue living, with his wife, as a supernumerary member of the household. Just as in the case of the imperial household, there will generally be an already recognized successor.

The ideal rule for succession is simply for the head to take a wife and produce a son, but although a wife can always be found, the son is more problematical. No matter, a son-in-law or an adopted son are quite acceptable alternatives – and there are also other possibilities – for the survival of the *ie* is more important than adherence to any cast-iron rule of succession. In whatever way the succession is provided for, the *ie* comprises not only its living members, who in most cases will all be quite closely related to the head and his wife, but also such of its former members for whom the final funeral rites, which take place anything up to fifty years after the death, have not been performed. Since in the allocation of functions between Shinto and Buddhism, the protracted mortuary rites belong to the latter, it is only to be expected that the tablets (known as *ihai*) commemorating deceased members of the *ie* are kept on the *butsudan*, the domestic altar required by Buddhist tradition, and still to be found in the majority of Japanese households.

These deceased members are known simply as *senzo*, or ancestors, even though some may never have survived their childhood. The ancestors, then, are simply a category of dead who relate in some mystical way to the living members of the *ie*, or of some other recognized social group – which may even be the whole nation. Just what rites are performed, and with what end in view, are questions with no definitive answer: the interpretation and performance of the rites may vary from one household to another, or even within a single household. The *bon* festival in August, which few families fail to observe, is seen as the time when ancestral spirits return to their homes, but they are also felt to be in some way present during the rest of the year.

Concern for the ancestors can take two basic forms: the first depends upon the way in which they can influence the fortunes of the living members of the *ie*; the second on the way these living members can intercede for the departed. Ancestors, in the true sense of the word, which means in most cases previous heads of the *ie*, are generally seen as belonging to the first category. Their continuing good offices are seen as desirable, even if not essential, for the prosperity of the *ie*. The second category will include collaterals who were never head of the *ie* and, even more, children who died young.

Ancestors of any category will have received a new name, probably bestowed at a Buddhist temple in the first stage of the funeral rites, which will then be commemorated on the *ihai* kept on the *butsudan*. These may vary in size according to the importance of the ancestor commemorated, and there may now also be a photograph of the most recently deceased head of the *ie*, with his *ihai* placed in front of it. Each family may also be represented by its own *ihai* in the local temple.

The presence of a *butsudan*, with *ihai* placed upon it, is the hallmark of an established household: the ideal village may be seen to comprise a fixed number of such households, each with its continuing identity over a period far longer than a single lifetime. The ancestors commemorated may go back for several generations, and the living members may no longer know who they are. It is, however, common practice to remove tablets of forgotten or remote ancestors, perhaps on the occasion of the final funeral rites, thirty-three or sometimes even fifty years after the death.

This system may be all very well for a village with a stable population, which cultivates rice on the same complex of terraces from one generation to another, but what about the millions of Japanese, not always younger sons with little prospect of succession, who, particularly in the course of the present century, have migrated to the big cities? A young man leaving for a job in a large corporation may first find himself lodged in a hall of residence, or dormitory, which he may only leave when he finds a wife, with whom to set up his own household. With a space of only two *tatami* mats to lay down his bedding at the end of the day, and a cupboard with sliding doors for keeping it in, together with his other possessions, such a young man can hardly set up an altar, and even if he could, how would he have any tablets to place upon it?

The problem can be solved in a small flat set up as a matrimonial home by using copies of the *ihai* in the household of one's childhood, but not suprisingly many young families, setting up home in the large cities, do not adopt this expedient. Such families may still celebrate *bon*, and they can hardly fail to celebrate the New Year, but this level of observance reflects only the most nominal adherence to Buddhism or Shinto. A survey of any large new housing complex in Tokyo would reveal remarkably few *butsudan*, and surprisingly many residents who would have no difficulty in admitting that they are agnostics: these are precisely the people who, in the two days following the death of the Showa Emperor, rented the whole supply of video cassettes to enable them to pass away the time declared for official mourning.

Returning to the ancestors, the final problem is one of eschatology. What, in the end, is the destiny of the ancestors, particularly those who, in the course of 2,000 years of history, have passed into oblivion? The answer is simple, but according to any normal Buddhist canons, staggeringly heterodox. In Japan the dead simply become *hotoke*, that is, Buddhas. It is as if Christianity was to give up any notion of purgatory, let alone hell, and admit everyone to heaven, including Judas Iscariot. (The Japanese, after all, have chosen to commemorate General Tojo, executed as a convicted war criminal, in the national Yasukuni shrine in Tokyo – a matter I consider further in Chapter 11.) In the context of Buddhism the principle makes hay of any orthodox doctrine of reincarnation. Moreover, at the end of the nineteenth century, it came to be extended to Shinto, when the government promoted the idea that the Japanese should revere their ancestors as *kami*. This application of the principle of *honji-suijaku* would appear to give the Japanese the best of all possible worlds. In this life prosperity is assured by the beneficent intervention of ancestral *kami*: in the next the certainty of becoming a *hotoke* ensures perpetual enlightenment. No wonder the Japanese are sometimes confused about religious matters. As Groucho Marx might have said, 'I have seen syncretism, but this is ridiculous.'

Where does the emperor come into all this? The answer is to be found in the traditional structure of the *ie*, and its relation to the imperial household. It must now be obvious enough that the latter is the former writ large. The preoccupation with succession and continuity, characteristic of the *ie*, becomes, in the case of the imperial household, an obsession. There is a recognized procedure for dealing with an *ie* which dies out, and is then known as a *zekke*: the tablets on the altar are distributed among collateral branches of the family, and may even assist the setting up of a new *ie*. It is unthinkable that this should ever be the fate of the imperial household, for such an event would undermine the whole principle by which all the *ie*'s in Japan are seen as derivative from and subordinate to that of which the emperor is the head for the time being.

The continued existence of the imperial household, over some 2,000 years of history, has so far been assured by a rule that makes it extremely easy to create an abundance of possible successors in the male line. Although the core of the imperial household is constituted by the emperor and his wife, the empress, or *kōgō*, does not need to be, and seldom is, the mother of all the male children who may be named as successor, although she may well adopt potential heirs to the throne. Even in the case of the recently departed Showa Emperor, when the first four children born of his marriage to the Empress Nagako were girls, his courtiers did not hesitate to make clear to him how the situation could be remedied, and indeed willingly offered their help in making the necessary arrangements. Fortunately the emperor remained faithful to his wife, and the fifth child to be born was a son, who is now the present emperor. In this matter the Showa Emperor was hardly true to the life-style of his father, the Emperor Taisho, let alone to that of his grandfather, the Emperor Meiji, who fathered some fourteen children, born of several different mothers. For the time being the future of the imperial line is assured not only by the two sons of the present emperor (of whom the older will almost certainly be named as Crown Prince), but also by any number of collaterals, who qualify by their descent in the male line from a former emperor.

Historically the problem was not so much that there were too few possible successors, but that there were too many. It is this factor, indeed, which has ensured the unbroken line of succession, proclaimed as dogma in the Meiji constitution of 1889. In practice the size of the imperial family was kept within bounds by providing for the exclusion of collaterals, in the male line, whose kinship with the reigning emperor had become too remote. If one goes back to the first emperor, Jimmu, the number of his descendants in the male line is legion, and the great majority of them are not only excluded from succession, but must be quite unable to establish their descent. On one view the greater part of the population may be reckoned as descendants of Jimmu.

In the Edo period (1600–1868) the families attached to the court, known as *kuge*, not only included many collateral members of the imperial family excluded from succession, but also provided the consorts who would produce potential heirs to the throne. At the same time, those for whom no such role was available would be appointed as *gomonzeki*, that is, as heads of Buddhist temples, monasteries and nunneries, in the Kyoto area, over which the court enjoyed rights of patronage.

As to the actual succession, before the beginning of the modern era in 1868 this generally followed the abdication, rather than the death of an emperor, in which case a single ceremony known as *juzen* was sufficient. This practice had several advantages. First, the absence of any gap between reigns assured the unbroken line of succession. Second, the emperor who abdicated had some chance to escape from the constricting life of the court, to play – in so far as this was possible in an institution which was essentially powerless – the role of a power behind the throne. Third, it made it possible for those who did have real power to ensure that an unacceptable emperor could be replaced. The few powerful families who ruled medieval Japan (and which often provided the *kōgō*) took this practice so far as to have as emperor a minor, who would be pressed upon to abdicate as soon as he began to have any mind of his own. Fourth, abdication avoided any problem about the mortuary rituals for a deceased emperor, a question which became acute when the Showa Emperor died at the beginning of 1989.

Where at the beginning of the seventh century Prince Shotoku established Buddhism in the mainstream of Japanese life, some 1,000 years later the Tokugawa Shoguns, whose regime may be taken to have begun with the victory of Tokugawa Ieyasu at the battle of Sekigahara in the year 1600, adopted Confucianism as the basic principle of their government.

Like Buddhism, Confucianism had played a part in Japanese life during the whole period, beginning before the time of Prince Shotoku, in which the country was open to Chinese cultural influence. Throughout this period Japanese Confucianism continuously adapted to doctrinal changes emanating from China. But what is Confucianism, and what was its appeal to the Tokugawa Shoguns?

Confucianism was certainly never a church in the Weberian sense, and many are reluctant to acknowledge it even as a religion. It may be compared to an élite philosophical school of the ancient world, in which an ethical doctrine was transmitted from teacher to pupil. In the 268 years of the Tokugawa era, during which Japan was largely at peace, Confucianism particularly appealed to the literate *samurai*, for they were then hardly concerned with their traditional military obligations to their feudal lords, or *daimyō*, who constituted the effective government of Japan. Appealing once more to Weber, Confucianism may be seen as a sort of oriental 'Protestant ethic', propagated by the ruling classes, and providing the ethical basis of both Buddhism and Shinto. Its ethic is something like team spirit or group loyalty in the West.

In relation to the emperor, or rather the State of which he was the nominal head, the two most important concepts of Japanese Confucianism were *chū*, loyalty, and *kō*, filial piety. If then the imperial household is the *ie* writ large, upon which every other *ie* depends, *chū* and *kō* may be seen as equivalent, and in fact the two words are conflated to form *chūkō*, which embodies the meaning common to both of them.

The Tokugawa Shoguns were not so interested in *chūkō* being directed to the emperor as such, but in its providing the ethical basis of *bushidō*, which means the 'way of the *bushi*', or *samurai*, just as Shinto is the way of the gods. The blind loyalty of the *samurai*, in Japanese tradition a hereditary class of warriors, was the essential power base of the Shoguns. The loyalty was not directly due to the Shogun, but to the *daimyō*, the feudal lord of the fief, or *han*, to which the *samurai* belonged. *Bushidō*, therefore, is the status ethic of the *samurai* class: in the extreme case it is carried to the point of *seppuku*, ritual suicide committed out of loyalty to one's master. (At the end of the Pacific War the *kamikaze* pilots were committed to the performance of this ritual in achieving their mission.)

The idea behind *chūkō* is the basis of the Japanese obsession with hierarchy. The principle of hierarchy means that in any dyadic relationship, whether its basis is two individuals, two households, or two of any other sort of social entity, one side is recognized as *senpai*, or senior, and the other as *kōhai*, or junior. The application of this principle is part of everyday conversation, for the form of language used by the *senpai* will be different to that used by the *kōhai*. (This is why women in Japan are said to have their own language: their status defines them as essentially, and irretrievably, *kōhai*. In modern Japan the announcements made by the stewardesses in the course of JAL flights are models of such speech.) The hierarchical ordering proceeds first on the basis of time, although in most cases this will be implicit rather than explicit. *Qui prior est tempore, potior est jure.*

The principle can be extended to establish a unique order of rank in any social configuration, however many units may comprise it, provided that there is a rule to determine, in every single instance, which side is *senpai* and which side *kōhai*. At the level of the village, although the component *ie* have considerable historical depth, every single one of them, in principle, must have been founded, originally, as the household of a junior branch of an existing *ie*. It does not matter that this leads back to a founding *ie* in every village, for this can then be seen as *kōhai* to an *ie* from another, and older, village. The *ie* cannot simply be assumed to go back to time immemorial, because in Japan there is a beginning of time, defined by the accession of the Emperor Jimmu, before which, *a fortiori*, no *ie* existed. The logical application of the *senpai-kōhai* principle must lead back to the imperial household, so that it is entirely correct to equate *chū* with *kō*, or loyalty with filial piety. This explains, also, the respect due to the ancestral heads of the household: they are by definition *senpai* to all their successors.

The dyad, *senpai-kōhai*, corresponds to an ethical dyad, *on-hōon*, which was originally Buddhist. *Hōon* is the indebtedness (which can never be repaid) due in return for kindness, represented by *on*. *Arigatō*, the Japanese word for 'thank you', expresses this concept very well, for in its original meaning (clear from the Chinese characters used in the written version), it connotes the difficulty of repaying a kindness. Translated to the context of Japanese religion, *on* represents the blessings bestowed by deity, in whatever form, and *hōon*, the obligation of the recipient to repay them.

Applying this principle to the role of the emperor in relation to the people of Japan, he is the recipient of *on* from his divine ancestors, which he must repay by means of *hōon*, while the people receive *on* from him, which they in turn must repay by the same means. Put another way, the emperor stands in the same relationship to the sun-goddess as his people stand in relation to him. The status of the emperor is then that of an *ikigami*, or living god, and as such he represents the founding ancestress of the imperial line, the sun-goddess. In Tokugawa Japan almost every home had a piece of her shrine at Ise, which would be among the objects worshipped at the household altar.

Tokugawa religion was true to the Japanese syncretic tradition. Its three component elements, Shinto, Buddhism and Confucianism, had all been established for more than a thousand years. What the political establishment achieved was a shift of emphasis from Buddhism to Confucianism: the reasons for it were political rather than religious. Buddhism had been a major, and largely independent, political force, almost from the time of Prince Shotoku, and it was only in the wars of the sixteenth century, ending in 1600 with the Tokugawa victory, that it was finally defeated. From then on the palace castles built for the *daimyō* replaced the Buddhist temples as the focus of power: the most imposing of these, in Edo, was the home of the Shogun, and it is now, in a city renamed Tokyo, the home of the emperor.

Buddhism, if defeated politically, still survived as a religious force. In the seventeenth century the Shoguns even required all Japanese to be registered at their local temple, but this was the result of policy directed to suppressing Christianity. For ordinary Japanese, the most important function of the Buddhist priesthood was to preside at funerals, and this is still true for many even today.

Shinto was the religion of daily life, although the popularity of pilgrimages to Ise (which provided the average Japanese with the only opportunity for travel) linked it with the emperor whom they would never see in person.

Confucianism justified the political ethic of the ruling classes, and as such was important in a system of government in which the effective ruler had no religious standing.

The year 1868 brought an end to the particular form of syncretism which had developed under the Tokugawa Shoguns, but its historical components survive to this day. Chapter 4 begins the story of what happened in the 121 years of the modern era, but before this Chapter 3 is necessary to explain, in some detail, another principle which gives

Japanese society its distinctive form. Once again it is a question of a dyadic relationship, that between outside and inside, or in Japanese, *soto* and *uchi*.

3

Outside and inside

THE distinction between outside and inside or, in Japanese, *soto* and *uchi*, provides a main key to understanding the terms in which the Japanese think of the world they inhabit. The same two Chinese characters have the alternative readings *gai* and *nai*, which generally occur as a prefix, but with much the same meaning. The foreigner does not need to stay long in Japan before he comes to realize that he is inescapably a *gaijin*, literally an outsider. The inner shrine at Ise, the home of the sun-goddess, and known as *naigū*, is the most inside place in Japan, where *gaijin* certainly are never allowed to enter, although they may discern the outside of the *naigū* through a wooden stockade.

The distinction between *soto* and *uchi* is that between a concept whose connotations are mainly negative and one whose connotations are mainly positive. *Soto* is chaos, unknown, unbounded and uncontrollable, where *uchi* is order, familiar, definite and manageable. It is not then surprising that *uchi* also means a house, where everything is controlled by the regime of the *ie* whose home it is.

The distinction in meaning depends on context: where the household is *uchi* in its relation to the world outside, including the rest of Japan (and particularly those parts of it which are still the realm of nature), Japan, as a nation, is *uchi* to the rest of the world – which is where the *gaijin* come from.

In the present context, which for the moment is concerned only with Japan (without any consideration of its place in the outside world), the imperial court is taken to be the epitome of *uchi*. Certainly this has been the image presented to the outside world for hundreds of years.

Where in other countries the Head of State is seen as living in a building, central and imposing in the capital city, in Japan he lives behind a wall, and ideally he is not seen at all.

This contrast can best be appreciated by comparing the White House in Washington with the Kōkyo in Tokyo. The former as its name implies is a house, clearly visible to any visitor to Washington, with at its head a man who is, by virtue of his office, a public figure. It is the home of the President. The Kōkyo is a rampart, some forty feet high, surrounded by a moat, and enclosing a compound, where somewhere must be the house, or *uchi*, of the emperor, who by virtue of his office, as defined by tradition, is a very private person. The less seen of him the better.

In modern Japan the Kōkyo is not always closed to the public. Outsiders are admitted on the occasion of the emperor's birthday, so there is some general idea of the architectural layout within the precinct. What is to be found on the inside of the ramparts as a focal point is not so much a palace but a small city, containing not only all the amenities which its undoubtedly privileged inhabitants might desire, but also such buildings – for instance the three Shinto shrines, *Kashikodokoro*, *Shinden* and *Koreiden* – as are essential to the emperor for carrying out his ritual duties. The emperor's actual home is not nearly so imposing as the British Embassy opposite the north gate. The impression to be gained from actually living inside the precinct would be that it was entirely self-contained, and that it related little to the world outside. Whatever role the central figure must play, it was not one which needed be visible. The French philosopher, Roland Barthes, in his book about Japan, writes of *'un empereur qu'on ne voit jamais'*.

In fact the Kōkyo has only been the home of the emperor since 1868: before then it was the palace castle of the Tokugawa Shoguns, who had far more pretensions to being actual rulers of Japan than any emperor in the last thousand years. The moat and the ramparts were built to surround the castle of a successful warlord: the message they convey is that the man who shelters behind them is concerned with real power. But in contrast to the magnificent castles built for the *daimyō* in Himeji or Kanazawa, which still dominate these cities, no imperial building in Tokyo makes anything like the same impression. The defensive ramparts of the Kōkyo can be seen therefore as no more than a modern version of the walls which surrounded the Imperial

Precinct in Kyoto, where until 1868 the emperor really did live the life of a hermit, quite invisible to any of his subjects outside the immediate court.

Before his death in 1616, Tokugawa Ieyasu, the first of the Shoguns of the line which would rule Japan until 1868, succeeded in imposing upon the imperial institution the form which it would have for more than 250 years. The underlying principle was that the emperor should be a prisoner within the *kindairi*, that is, the imperial compound in Kyoto. The Shogun was represented in Kyoto by his own deputy, known as the *shōshidai*. His duties were twofold. First he imposed whatever physical restraints were necessary to maintain order within the *kindairi*: this could not have been too demanding seeing the precinct had few entrances, and was guarded on all sides by soldiers responsible to the Shogun. Second, and more important, the *shōshidai* represented the Shogun in all dealings with the court: this was an essential role, since the formal assent of the emperor was needed for many acts of government. The Shogun himself had his own base in Kyoto, the Nijo Castle, not far distant from the *kindairi*, but since no Shogun visited the capital between 1634 and 1863 (in which period of course no emperor could leave it), it is clear that all important dealings with the court were left to the *shōshidai*. But in fact the court was left to itself, and one is left to ask how it was constituted, and what it did with its time. The answers to these questions are entirely surrealist.

The *kindairi*, which contained the separate households of the different members of the imperial family (who were not allowed, even as children, to live together), was an enclave in the centre of a much larger enclosure, known as the *gyoen*, or imperial garden. The *gyoen*, whose access to the outside world was also severely limited, contained the houses of the members of the court, known as *kuge*, literally 'public families'.

In the Tokugawa era, there were something over a hundred *kuge*, which constituted a hereditary nobility, entitled to a whole complex of ranks determining their order of seniority. With only very few exceptions they were descended from no more than five of the great clans of medieval Japan: some 70 per cent were descended from the Fujiwara clan, which for centuries had provided the emperor's official consort, or *kōgō*, and had been long before the time of the Tokugawas the power behind the Japanese throne. The highest rank of the nobility comprised but five houses, known as the *go-sekke*, all of them Fujiwara. Even in modern Japan, one of these, the house of Konoye, provided not only the most important of the Prime Ministers in the years immediately before the Pacific War, the Prince Konoye Fujimamo (whose career I look at more closely in Chapters 7 and 8), but also the husband for the daughter of Prince Mikasa, the only surviving brother of the Showa Emperor.

The *kuge* families were supported, economically, by endowments assured by the Tokugawa Shoguns, represented by an income in rice, measured in a unit called *koku*. This income was derived from lands in the *tenryō*, the part of Japan (which included Kyoto) directly governed by the Shoguns. The *go-sekke* all enjoyed an income of more than 1,500 *koku*, which could readily be supplemented from other sources, whereas the poorest of the *kuge* had to be content with less than 100 *koku* (which was still a very large income measured by the standards of the ordinary peasant household). The standing of the *go-sekke* was on the level of that of the junior branches of the imperial family, and most of the other *kuge* depended upon one or other of the *go-sekke*, in much the same way as the latter depended directly upon the imperial house. While the *go-sekke* provided the *kōgō*, or official consorts for the emperor, they also had the right to have younger sons nominated as *gomonzeki*, or abbots of the Buddhist monasteries in the Kyoto neighbourhood under imperial patronage.

The organization of the court and *kuge* can be seen in terms of a series of concentric circles, with the highest ranking families being closest to the emperor, and the lowest ranking closest to the outside world. This was reflected in the actual geography of the *gyoen*, with the estates of the *go-sekke* being located immediately outside the walls of the *kindairi*. Within the *kindairi*, the emperor's own quarters were to be found at the centre, with those of his immediate family around them. The total enclosure of the *kindairi*, about the size of football field, was not large, considering all the households it contained, to say nothing of the shrines required by the unending imperial ritual.

The buildings both within and without the *kindairi* were laid out on the pattern of the rectangular grid which had been adopted for the whole city of Kyoto at the time of its foundation. (This, an essentially Chinese model of town planning, even today makes finding one's way in Kyoto much easier than in any other Japanese city, including Tokyo, which is chaotic in comparison.) The buildings were not particularly impressive and, being of wood, were liable to destruction by fire – which provided about the only reason for the emperor ever being allowed to leave. In this setting the life of the court was characterized by its isolation and its confinement, with the emperor at its centre, living apart even from his family, as the loneliest figure of all.

Judged according to their contribution to the economic and political life of Japan, the *kuge* and the court counted for next to nothing. Were it not for their contribution to the ritual and aesthetic life of the country, they would have to be judged as being purely parasitical. As it was, the members of the *kuge* spent their time in governing their own small, but extremely complex community, engaging in court ceremonial, and, by way of leisure, pursuing and patronizing traditional arts and crafts. Without them the cultural and intellectual life of the country would have been nowhere. The magnificent art of the Edo period, displayed in the Great Japan Exhibition held in London in 1981–82, would not have existed without the inspiration and patronage of the court.

The emperor divided up his time in much the same way as did the members of his court, but the burden of ceremonial resting upon him was far heavier. Throughout the Edo period it became more and more complex, and with one or two exceptions it came to comprise the whole official work of the emperor. In the end there were in every year nearly two hundred separate events, each with its elaborate ritual and its own place in the calendar.

Nothing in all this ritual had any administrative importance. The only activity with any outside significance was the regulation of the calendar, but this did no more than follow established mathematical formulae. The problem was simple enough. The civil year was based on twelve lunar months of twenty-nine or thirty days, the actual length of each successive month being determined in advance. This made the year about ten days too short according to the solar calendar, which according to the demands of nature must govern the agricultural cycle. The ascendancy of the stars in the Chinese zodiac (which is essential also for the *kanshi* system explained in Chapter 1) divides the solar year into twelve equal periods, each slightly longer than the lunar month. The result is that about one month out of thirty does not contain a zodiacal point: this was then designated in advance as an intercalary month, bearing the same name as the month preceding it, but so that none of the calendric ritual was repeated. (This must have provided the emperor with a welcome respite every two or three years.)

In spite of this system of built-in adjustment, corrections to the calendar were required four times in the Tokugawa period. These, although traditionally an imperial prerogative, were still decided upon by the Shoguns, and the same is true of the numerous decisions, known as *kaigen*, to start a new calendrical era. None the less the association of the calendar with the imperial court did have consequences for every *ie* in Japan, even though it may not always have been realized, when a new calendar was announced, that it came from the emperor. The fact that the emperor was to all intents and purposes a prisoner of the Shogun, with far less freedom to move about than the poorest of his subjects, would not be so well known. The documentation of court life was a closed book to all except the *kuge* officials charged with keeping records of all the numerous ceremonies, grist to the mill for the twentieth-century historians who now have access to all this material. Tokugawa Japan was a land of enclosed communities, which, if not entirely isolated from outside influences, had only a limited understanding of the institutions which governed them. The local effects of these institutitions were real enough (such as the heavy burden of taxation imposed by the *daimyō*), but they were more often than not accepted with resignation and unquestioningly, an attitude of mind characteristic of Japan to this day.

The court and the *kuge* formed one of these communities, but it was one charged with the production of ritual rather than rice. The ritual functions were extremely diverse, so that there was a much greater division of labour than in any normal Japanese community, but this imperial institution was none the less a model for the whole country. The basic structure was still that of the interdependent *ie*, with succession based ideally (though not always in practice) on descent through the male line. One family of hereditary priests, the Fujinami, provided the link between the court and the *naigū* at Ise, but these were not the only hereditary priests among the *kuge*. Other families provided hereditary specialists on Shinto lore, the Chinese calendar or the history of the court itself. The *kuge*, if the cultural élite of the whole country, were still ready to transmit their knowledge to outsiders, so long as they were paid for doing so (for many of them felt very hard up).

This process of diffusion was the court's most important cultural contribution to the whole country. If first it was the *daimyō* and their *samurai* retainers who absorbed the civilization of the court, in the end the process reached the remotest corners of Japan. Less palpable perhaps than the calendar, this was still something originating in the court which could be noticed at the level of the Japanese village.

The preceding description of the court and the *kuge* describes an institutional complex which is the quintessence of *uchi*. The emperor's own house, where he lived alone at the centre of the *kindairi*, is the *uchi par excellence*. In relation to this, even the rest of the *kindairi* was *soto*, but for the court the *kindairi* was *uchi*, with *soto* being the world outside the walls which enclosed it. Even then another cordon sanitaire, defined by the boundaries of the *gyoen*, enclosed another space, social as much as geographical, where the *kuge* and other retainers lived. The model is like a series of Chinese boxes, each one being enclosed in the next, one size larger, so that the centre can only be reached by passing through all of them in descending order of size.

The model is constricting at every level: the closer to the centre, the greater the confinement, so that the emperor himself is a virtual prisoner. Even on the periphery there is hardly more freedom. The peasant is tied to his *ie*, his rice fields, his village by an oppressive system where the centre represents a burden of taxation which is almost intolerable. True this centre is not that of the court in Kyoto, but that of the castle of the Tokugawa in Edo, or, more directly, the castle of the local *daimyō*, the feudal lord of the *han* to which the village belongs. This division of function between the emperor and the Shogun assured the emperor of a benign image. The calendar, and the rituals it defines, together with the impact of court civilization, are seen as *imperial* blessings.

The history of the court will be taken up again in Chapter 4, which will show how the model introduced in this chapter was adapted when the capital moved from Kyoto to Tokyo after the accession of the Emperor Meiji. The analysis on the basis of *soto* and *uchi* will now be applied to a different cultural domain, defined by the way the Japanese use and understand their own language. The essential point is that the language is seen as a unique and exclusive cultural heritage belonging to the Japanese people: the Japanese, in mastering the language, acquire a skill unattainable by any *gaijin*, even one born and brought up in Japan. If the science of linguistics now accepts Japanese as a member of the Altaic family of languages, the relationship is a distant one, of no significance to the Japanese themselves, and of no help to *gaijin* who want to learn Japanese. One may take it, at least as a starting point, that Japanese is a language isolated from all others.

The historical problem is that anything that can be known about the development of Japanese, over a period not much less than 2,000 years, can only be discovered by means of records written in Chinese characters. In the beginning, when the written culture of China first came to Japan, some time before the reign of Prince Shotoku, it was adopted in a form known as *kanbun*, as opposed to *wabun*, the name given to the autochthonous Japanese language. This led to a process of assimilation, whose final result, in the shape of modern Japanese, is a language which incorporates a vast Chinese vocabulary, particularly for abstract nouns, but still retains a grammar and syntax which is essentially *wabun*. This may be seen as the grass-roots language of the common people, before there was any question of literacy at this level. *Kanbun* was the language of the literate élite, particularly as represented by the court and the *kuge*. Given the almost complete isolation of the latter, it is not surprising that they developed, even for daily use, a form of language scarcely intelligible to the outside world. This was particularly true of the emperor himself, who had no contacts whatever beyond the top ranks of the *kuge*. The result, in 1945, was that when the Showa Emperor came to broadcast to the Japanese people the decision to accept the terms of surrender imposed by the allied powers, victorious in the Pacific War, he did so in a language which few could understand. This, the most momentous event in some two thousand years of history, had to be made intelligible by a general acting as interpreter.

If, from the time of their very first contacts with the written culture of China in the course of the sixth century, the Japanese court recognized the need to dispose of its own written language, it was well over a hundred years before any authentically Japanese texts, incorporating *wabun*, began to appear. Before this happened it was simpler to use *kanbun* in all contexts having anything to do with the written language, so that *kanbun* had something of the status of Latin in early medieval Europe. It is this status which it retained, within the court and bureaucracy, until well into the twentieth century.

The heart of the problem was simply that Chinese could only be written by means of thousands of separate and often very complicated characters, each of which had its own meaning and pronunciation. This system survived in China not only because no one ever got as far as developing an alternative, phonetic system of writing, but also because the grammar and syntax of the language were uniquely compatible with its traditional written form. It was of no concern to the Chinese that their characters could not readily be adapted to quite unrelated languages, such as Japanese. This was a problem for the Japanese themselves to solve, if they had a mind to do so.

The Japanese have been wrestling with this problem for more than 1,200 years. The main outlines of the solution to it were established by Buddhist monks at a very early period. First, it came to be accepted that a Chinese character, or *kanji*, could represent not only a Chinese, or *kanbun* word, but also a Japanese, or *wabun* word with a similar meaning. The Chinese reading is known as *on* (or sound), the Japanese reading as *kun* (or explanation). Applying this to *soto* and *uchi*, *soto* is the *kun*-reading equivalent to the *on*-reading, *gai*, where *uchi (kun)* corresponds to *nai (on)*. Put another way, *soto* and *uchi* explain in *wabun*, the *kanbun* words pronounced *gai* and *nai*.

The second part of the solution is provided by the two so-called *kana* syllabaries. These are based on the *gojuon*, literally fifty sounds, represented in each syllabary by fifty distinctive characters. Both syllabaries, *hiragana* and *katakana*, are phonetic, and represent the spoken language orthographically, as do also the countless alphabetical systems developed in the rest of the world. The only difference is that each character represents an entire syllable, so that more are needed than in an alphabet whose letters, representing both consonants and vowels, must be combined to form syllables. It is remarkable that written Japanese can get by with some fifty-odd *kana*: a language like English, with a much more complicated phonology, would require several hundred.

Even more remarkable is the fact that the Japanese, having developed an orthography, failed to abandon the older logographic system of *kanji*, from which the *kana* syllabaries derived, but preferred to use a mixed system, in which *kana* and *kanji* would alternate, in any text, both according to context and to the predilections of the writer. This form, known now as *kana majiri bun*, is that of any normal modern Japanese publication. In fact both the *kana* syllabaries are sufficient for writing down anything spoken in Japanese, just as the Latin alphabet is sufficient for doing the same with spoken English. Children learn first to write Japanese in *hiragana*, and then as they go through school they work their way through thousands of *kanji*, a process which, strictly speaking, is completely unnecessary. Historically, when women were excluded from the male world of *kanbun*, they wrote in *hiragana*, which became known as *onna no te*, or women's hand. This is the written language of *The Tale of Genji*, the best-known work in Japanese literature, whose author, the Lady Murasaki, was a member of the court nearly a thousand years ago.

The process of learning *kanji*, according to the syllabus laid down by the Ministry of Education, leads in the end to the mastery of a standard repertoire of something under 2,000 so-called *jōyō* or 'everyday' *kanji*. This is but a fraction of the *kanji* occurring in recorded texts: of these, many, quite outside the list of *jōyō kanji*, will be known to the Japanese intelligentsia, of which the hard core, historically, was to be found in the court of Kyoto. The Showa Emperor was doubtless never tested on his *kanji* repertoire, but one can be certain that it went far beyond the level of the *jōyō kanji* – a list which originated (under another name) some forty years ago. Indeed the court use of *kanbun* takes for granted an exceptional command over *kanji*.

Once again, the *kanji* are an instance of a uniquely Japanese institution which provides the means for ranking individuals in a hierarchy, in which the court – at least historically – stands at the top. There are private institutions which test their members on *kanji* proficiency, so that they can be ranked on the *dan*, or 'step' system, used in any number of competitive activities, whether they be *jūdō*, *go* or *ikebana* flower arranging. When it comes to the court, however, there is a decisive change in content: it is not so much that the court has its own distinctive vocabulary (derived from that which the court ladies used in fifteenth-century Kyoto for everyday conversation), but that in writing about the court, hundreds of words are used which cannot occur in any other context.

The point is not immediately transparent. In English a list could be made of perhaps up to a dozen words which generally only refer to matters connected with the royal family. It would be difficult to add many more words to a list including king, queen, prince, royal, highness, crown, majesty, equerry, lady-in-waiting, without going on to proper names such as Windsor, Balmoral, Sandringham and so on, and even then the list would quite soon be closed. In the United States the list relating to the presidential office would be even shorter. In Japanese the list seems to be almost endless, particularly in relation to terms referring to different aspects of the imperial *rites de passage*. The death of the Showa Emperor led to any number of such words being used, for which the *kanji*, in particular, were quite forgotten by even educated Japanese, if they had known them in the first place. The announcement of the death in a standard form, '*Tennō Heika Hōgyo*', included not only *tenno*, the familiar word used to refer to the emperor, and the somewhat less familiar *heika*, meaning 'majesty', but the special word *hōgyo*, which, although meaning 'death', can only refer to the death of an emperor.

The newspaper reports of the mortuary rites, protracted over a seven-week period following the death of the old emperor, continually caused problems for readers unfamiliar with the special *kanji* and *kanji*-combinations, used. From the very beginning, when the body of the emperor was transferred to the *hinkyū* (listed in Nelson's Japanese-English Character Dictionary with the translation 'temporary imperial mortuary'), Japanese readers had to reckon with the obscure *kanji* for *hin*, which had hardly been seen in a newspaper since the death of the Taisho Emperor sixty-two years earlier. And how many would then have realized that *hin*, an *on*-reading, corresponded to the *kun*-reading, *mogari*, meaning the intermediate state of an emperor between this world and the next? This was just the beginning: on 24 February, the word *rensō*, used to refer to the combined funeral and entombment, was just as obscure. All these words, and more, were used, without translation, in the English instructions sent out by the *kunaichō*, that is the Imperial Household Office, to the diplomatic representatives in Tokyo: the diplomats can hardly have realized that their meaning was no less obscure to the Japanese man in the street. Even the mandarins in the *kunaichō* had probably had to do some homework to get them all in order.

Language, as it is used both in and about the Japanese court, is the epitome of *uchi*. In the Japanese tradition it provides a cultural barrier, separating the emperor from his people, which historically, at least, was no easier to surmount than the social and physical barriers. But just as the language is used to isolate the emperor and his court, so also, if in a quite different direction, it is used to identify and neutralize intrusive outside, or *soto*, elements in Japanese popular culture. This is a function not only of *katakana*, the second *kana* syllabary, but also of *rōmaji*, as the Japanese refer to the Latin alphabet.

In principle there is no need for *katakana*: every character corresponds to one already comprised in *hiragana*, so that a quite elementary word processor can switch from one to the other without any difficulty. In practice *katakana* are used to mark words which need some special emphasis: this is roughly equivalent to using italics in an English text. In particular *katakana* is used in this way to indicate words adopted from languages other than Japanese and Chinese. The six-year-old must learn to write 'panda' and 'koala' in *katakana* where *hiragana* is correct for '*tora*' and '*zo*', meaning, respectively, tiger and elephant. The Japanese child must go to a zoo to see any of these animals: *tora* and *zo* are privileged only because the former is a *kun-* and the latter an *on-*reading of recognized *kanji*. If after the zoo he is taken by *takushi* (taxi) to a *hoteru* (hotel), he is in the realm of *katakana*, while if he goes by *jidōsha* (car) to a *ryokan* (inn), he is safe in that of *hiragana*, which as he grows older, will be translated into *kanji*.

Rōmaji go beyond the use of *katakana* into a world culture whose components are essentially alien, or *soto*, however familiar, if not essential, they may be in Japanese daily life. This world is dominated by the names given to such products as cigarettes, whisky, cars and computers, which even if Japanese in origin – such as Toyota – will still be presented in *rōmaji*. In some cases a choice of a Japanese name is unthinkable: cigarettes all have such names as Peace or Mild Seven, perhaps because they are seen as polluting, a risk inherent in any contact with the outside.

Force of circumstance often necessitates the use of *rōmaji*, or of their numerical equivalent, the *arabiya sūji*, or arabic numerals. In a senior high school, the equations written on the blackboard by the maths teacher will be in a form no different from that which would be used in a Western classroom, and at university level standard Western textbooks would be used as well. The old emperor, in his work as a marine biologist, would have been thoroughly familiar with such material, and may well have reflected that it was the cultural product of a world in which the descent of man was determined according to the principles first established by Darwin (of whom he kept a bust in his own study), and which had no place for a sun-goddess who some 2,600 years previously had hidden herself in a cave in a remote corner of the empire over which he reigned by right of direct descent from her.

Many Japanese see *rōmaji* and words of Western origin written in *katakana* as a sort of cultural Trojan horse. *Rōmaji*, and to a lesser extent *katakana*, have the merit of identifying the threat to Japanese

[47]

cultural identity, and naming one's enemy is the first step towards an effective defence. But even inside Japan certain categories of the population are regarded as essentially *soto*, although they are never seen as *gaijin*. Ironically enough, a people called Ainu, descended from the earliest known settlers in the Japanese islands, are seen in this way. The remote ancestors of the present-day Japanese, who began to arrive, some two or three thousand years ago, from the Asian mainland, and perhaps also from the many islands scattered across the Pacific Ocean, found the Ainu in many different parts of the country. Even today many place names, including that of Mount Fuji, are of Ainu origin, but the Ainu people themselves are now confined to a few communities on the northernmost island of Hokkaido, where they have been largely absorbed into the mainstream of Japanese culture. If their ancient language hardly survives, they still maintain, precariously, their own cultural identity, which is in no way compatible with any of the pretensions of Shinto.

After the death of the Showa Emperor, Kiyoko Kitahara, speaking for the Ainu, claimed that 'the emperor system is the source of all kinds of discrimination, including that against the Ainu', and saw the abolition of the system as an essential step in achieving an egalitarian society. The Ainu are tolerated by the Japanese, but their chances of finding a livelihood outside their traditional and ill-paid farming and fishing are restricted. Given the decline in numbers, even the survival of the Ainu is uncertain.

The *burakumin*, descendants of former outcasts, are a problem of a quite different order. They number nearly three million, and far from being hidden away in the remoter corners of Hokkaido, they are concentrated on the great cities of the Kansai – Osaka, Kobe and Kyoto. Although they are not subject to any formal legal disabilities, the level of actual discrimination is very high, so that employers often go to great lengths in checking that job applicants are not *burakumin*. The result is that the *burakumin* continue to live in their own run-down areas of the great cities, performing only the most menial tasks, and denied any normal social contacts. One of the most painful aspects of the Recruit Cosmos scandal, in which almost every leading Japanese politician seemed to be involved during the period of mourning for the Showa Emperor, is that Hiromasa Ezoe, who started it all off, is a *burakumin*. Pollution, the very essence of *soto*, had penetrated the *uchi* of the Japanese establishment.

[48]

Some million Japanese-born Koreans are subject to similar disabilities, but have probably been better able to surmount them. Particularly in Osaka they have found their own economic niche, largely in catering, and few have become very fat cats indeed. The Korean shamans, or ritual faith-healers, are well-known and are not short of Japanese clients.

To the Japanese themselves the most romantic of the marginal groups are the 100,000-odd gangsters known as *yakuza*. Operating in tightly knit syndicates, characterized by intensive group solidarity and absolute loyalty, the *yakuza* represent the *samurai* ethic, in a form which appeals to millions of Japanese television viewers. The image, then, is much more *uchi* than *soto*, but if the broadcast dramas often portray the *yakuza* as champions of the poor, they are in fact synonymous with organized crime in Japan, and any number of poor people have seen their lives ruined when *yakuza* come in the door as debt collectors and loan sharks. It may be a merit of the *yakuza* (although one which they prefer not to advertise) that they welcome *burakumin* and Koreans as members, but if so, it is a sad comment on Japanese society that these underprivileged classes find their best opportunities in the service of crime.

If the moral status of the *yakuza*, judged according to traditional Japanese canons of loyalty, is ambiguous, that of the right-wing groups known under the generic title of *uyoku* is, by their own lights, not open to question. There are hundreds of *uyoku* groups, and with their armoured cars and sound-trucks, they are as conspicuous as any broad-shouldered *yakuza* in their dark blue suits, white ties and sunglasses. Both the *uyoku* and the *yakuza* are tied to politics in much the same way, and can rely on the authorities turning a blind eye to such activities as strike breaking, or harassing left-wing demonstrators. The distinction is that where the main concern of the *uyoku* is politics, that of the *yakuza* is strictly business. But then of course there is no sharp dividing line between the two, particularly in Japan.

Another category of ambiguous moral status, judged according to the canon of *soto-uchi*, is defined by the 'new religions', or *shinkō shūkyō*, which have proliferated in the years since the Pacific War. Although some of these are highly deviant, most depend upon a re-interpretation of some ancient Japanese tradition, such as that of Nichiren Buddhism, originating in the thirteenth century. One example is Risshō Kōseikai which emphasizes the importance of that quintessentially Japanese institution, ancestor worship. This is a lay movement appealing particularly to lonely housewives, one of the marginal categories left out of the mainstream of Japanese life. Given its appeal to tradition, one wonders why its moral status is in doubt. The answer is that it offers an escape from and an alternative to entrenched authority, as represented traditionally by the head of the *ie*. The ambitious young man in a big firm will not join Risshō Kōseikai, or any other movement like it, and would rather that his wife followed his example. His wife, on the other hand, tied to the monotony of the home by young children, could be emancipated by joining Risshō Kōseikai, where, with a new name, she could share part of her life with others like her. This is not the *uchi*-ethic at all.

Christianity, permitted in Japan since the Meiji era, and even encouraged during the period of the allied occupation (1945–52), is by definition *soto*. A Japanese Christian is seen as mildly deviant, but not as threatening to any essential system. The fact is that Christianity seems to have little appeal to the Japanese. Measured in terms of numbers, it is not nearly as successful as any of the main Japanese sects, such as Risshō Kōseikai. The present situation, judged historically, seems paradoxical, for the regime of the Tokugawa Shoguns, with the emperors confined in Kyoto, derived much of its force from the declared need to eliminate Christianity from Japan, following the activities of Spanish and Portuguese missionaries in the sixteenth century. Before the year 1637, when Christianity was finally suppressed, thousands of Japanese Christians had died for their faith, often in the most appalling circumstances. In this final year 37,000 Christians defended a castle on the Shimabara peninsula against the forces of the Shogun in the last battle in which the *samurai* were ever to see active service. For the next 240 years only the Dutch were allowed to maintain a small trading station on the island of Deshima in the remote harbour of Nagasaki, having convinced the Shoguns that their version of Christianity was much more innocuous than that of the Portuguese Jesuits in the previous century. When at the end of the Tokugawa era, the opposition to the Shoguns rallied under the slogan '*sonnō jōi*' – 'Respect the emperor, expel the barbarians' – no one doubted that the latter were synonymous with Christians. Ideologically, therefore, the emperor, confined in Kyoto, still represented the essence of *uchi*, while the Christians, banished beyond the seas, still represented that of *soto*. The paradox, quite simply, is that so many Japanese were ready, 350 years ago, to die for a faith, which, at the present day, is regarded as almost completely anodyne – and this in spite of the fact that the great victor in the Pacific War, General MacArthur, declared himself a Christian. As it is, Christianity now provides for many Japanese the most attractive rites for a wedding ceremony, which, by tradition, belongs to Shinto. Not even the *uyoku* are much disturbed by this development.

In the context of *soto-uchi* the most interesting category is one which was hardly recognized a generation ago. It is defined by the children of Japanese parents who have worked for long periods abroad. These are known as *kikoku shijo*. The first word, *kikoku*, means 'returning to one's own country' (by implication always Japan), and the second word, *shijo*, simply 'children'. The two words generally occur in combination with a third, *mondai*, which means 'problem, question, issue', or even 'trouble', so that one sees constant references to the *kikoku shijo mondai*. There is no doubt that for those who govern Japan, it really is a *mondai*.

The problem is simple enough to understand, so long as one bears firmly in mind that Japan is *uchi*, where the rest of the world is *soto*, with all the dangers that this entails. Now the category of *soto*, in any cultural or social context, relates primarily to people who can be regarded as marginal. The heart of the *kikoku shijo mondai* is that the success of Japan, internationally, depends upon long periods being spent abroad by thousands of Japanese who, far from being marginal, are recruited from the highest levels of government, business and science. If such representatives of Japanese culture can be relied upon to be more or less immune from contamination – a result often achieved simply by keeping each other's company – the same assurance is not possible with their children, despite the quite large number of Japanese schools now to be found outside Japan. What is more, the influential and articulate parents are no more willing to accept a marginal status for their children than they are for themselves.

Take the case of a Japanese professor of physics, on a temporary three-year attachment to a laboratory at the University of Illinois. Since Urbana is hundreds of miles from the nearest Japanese school, the professor's teenage son must go to the local junior high school, where he will soon become proficient in English, and at the same time imbibe the open, tolerant and inquiring atmosphere which such a school takes for granted. He will hardly miss the Japanese school uniform of black serge and brass buttons, nor the daily grind imposed by the need to master thousands of Chinese characters.

The return home, to Japan, will be traumatic, not only for the child and his parents, but also for his new Japanese school. The child, for one thing, will soon discover not only that he has the greatest difficulty in reading Japanese, but also that the English master can hardly speak a word of English. If he is accepted by his class-mates, he may be able to convince them that there are alternatives to the Japanese school system which pay much more attention to the welfare of the child and much less to indoctrination into an approach to life promulgated by bureaucrats who are never seen in person. It is not surprising that the Japanese run special schools for the *kikoku shijo*, to deny them any chance of contaminating their fellows who have never been abroad. But given the role that Japan has chosen to play on the international scene, such children, with their easy command of a European language – generally English – and their familiarity with foreign ways, are for the State an invaluable intellectual resource. On the other hand they already know too much for the peace of mind of those who govern Japan from the inside. No wonder, then, that the *kikoku shijo* are a *mondai*.

All this relates to the new emperor, who in his own school days, just after the end of the Pacific War, was taught for four years by an extraordinarily gifted American teacher, Elizabeth Gray Vining, who even after the end of this period was to remain a close friend of the imperial family. For the book she wrote about her time in Japan, Mrs Vining chose the significant title *Windows for the Crown Prince*. If you are in a house, *uchi*, what you see through the windows is outside, *soto*: there is no question but that Mrs Vining knew what she was writing about. Now, more than forty years later, the Crown Prince, since 8 January 1989 Emperor of Japan, has sent his two sons to Oxford. Whatever may be the case elsewhere, the problems of the *kikoku shijo* will find a sympathetic understanding in the imperial household.

It is to be noted that *soto* and *uchi* define not only categories of people, but also contexts. In the case of the emperor, who may be seen as the ideal representation of *uchi*, one notes that it is in the context of *soto* that he becomes a public figure. It is the fact that this context was never part of the emperor's life that makes the regime of the *kindairi*, described at the beginning of this chapter, so significant. But although the emperor left Kyoto more than a hundred years ago, this regime still represents the ideal for many self-appointed guardians of the imperial institution.

The conflict between *soto* and *uchi* is reflected in the alternative policies of *kaikoku* and *sakoku*, which have dominated Japanese thinking about the place of their country in the world for well over 300 years. The former means simply 'opening the country', and although in practical terms it must have its place in Japanese politics, it still meets considerable psychological resistance. *Sakoku* is the policy of national isolation always associated with the Tokugawa Shoguns. The first character in its written form has an alternative *kun*-reading, *kusari*, which is the Japanese word for chain, such as one would use for a dog or a prisoner. The implications, therefore, of *sakoku* are much more drastic than simply 'closing the country', which could have been expressed by the alternative phrase *heikoku*. *Sakoku* can be seen simply as a term of art referring to the extreme instance of this policy adopted in 1639 when the government of the Shogun decreed that, with immediate effect, Portuguese ships coming to Japan were to be burnt with all their cargo, and their crews executed. This meant that for more than 200 years, the only Westerners allowed in Japan would be the Dutch in their small enclave of Deshima, a base from which they would send once a year an embassy to the Shogun in Edo, more than 1,000 miles away.

Against this historical background, it is not surprising that Showa, in 1971, was the first *emperor* ever to leave the shores of Japan; now his successor, the Emperor Akihito, is a man who speaks nearly perfect English and has visited more than fifty foreign countries. To the end of his life the old emperor still spoke of his visit to Europe in 1921 when he was the Crown Prince. Even to this day the context of *soto* allows the taboos relating to the emperor's life to be lifted, so that a quite disproportionate amount of the archive material published after the death of the Showa Emperor recorded incidents occurring during his visits abroad.

The context of *soto* is also part and parcel of the life of any Japanese travelling away from home. *Uchi* in any context is always defined by boundaries: even a house has walls. Travel is a matter of crossing boundaries, in traditional Japan a somewhat momentous operation. Now, with the *shinkansen* taking hardly three hours to cover the 350-odd miles between Tokyo and Osaka, the passengers can hardly be conscious of crossing any boundaries at all. None the less their standard of behaviour is often decidedly *soto*: the traveller forgets the demands of *uchi* etiquette. In old Japan, with an emperor who hardly moved a stone's throw from his palace, the lowest classes were defined as those who travelled, pedlars, actors, jugglers, musicians – all unmistakably *soto*, but still the source of colour and variety in the humdrum of a hard life. In medieval Japan, the privilege of unfettered travel, essential to the way of life of such people, was seen as being granted by the emperor himself, who directly controlled all boundary areas.

4

The Empire of Meiji

A book by Leonard Mosley, published in 1966 and entitled *Hirohito Emperor of Japan*, includes a photograph of an imposing Edwardian figure with the caption 'Emperor Meiji, grandfather of Hirohito, and the architect of Modern Japan'. If the first five words of this caption state no more than the familiar historical record, the last five are tendentious. The word is chosen deliberately. Tendentious, according to the Concise Oxford Dictionary, means 'having an underlying purpose, calculated to advance a cause'. The purpose, or the cause, in this case was not so much Leonard Mosley's, but one he adopted, unwittingly perhaps, from an accepted, and officially encouraged, Japanese view of history which projects the Emperor Meiji as the man responsible for bringing Japan into the modern world.

I have already shown, in Chapter 1, how the 120-odd years of modern Japan can be seen from the perspective of but two historical figures, Meiji and his grandson, Showa, both Emperors of Japan. Although the focus of this book is the Showa Emperor, his grandfather, Meiji, is always behind him, in a sense looking over his shoulder. One single instance illustrates this point. On 6 September 1941, when the Japanese government was already well set on the course which would lead to the Pacific War, the Cabinet, the Chiefs of Staff, the President of the Privy Council, together with a number of supporting officials, were summoned to a meeting in the east wing of the imperial palace over which the emperor would preside. It was almost his last chance to turn back the course of events, and after he had listened to the question of war or peace as it was being presented to him, he paused for a moment, and then said, 'As for myself I have no doubt of the answer. I would like to read you a poem which was written by my grandfather, the great Meiji Emperor,' and then, after reading a *tanka*, a traditional form of poem with five lines and thirty-one syllables and almost always highly allusive in the meaning it conveys, he added, 'This is a poem which has always been one of my favourites, for it expresses what is in my heart and was in my grandfather's when he wrote it – his great love of peace.'

The question could hardly be more important for understanding modern Japan: who was the Emperor Meiji? And what did he represent?

The textbook answer is simple. Until 1868 Japan was a country which, for more than 250 years, had enjoyed peace under the feudal regime of the Tokugawa Shoguns, quite undisturbed by any foreign influence. From the beginning of the nineteenth century this idyllic state was threatened by increasing interference by the United States and a number of European powers in the politics of the Far East, which took a decisive turn for Japan when, in the summer of 1853, the American Commodore Perry sailed with his fleet of iron-clads into Edo bay. In the end Japan had no choice but to admit representatives of the great powers, allowing them much the same privileges as they had obtained in China in 1842, by their victory in the Opium War. The government of the Shoguns, which had never countenanced any change, was quite unable to cope. Then, for first time in the whole Edo period, the court in Kyoto began to take political initiatives, with the support of *daimyō* from a number of outlying regions, such as Chōshū and Satsuma. Finally, at the beginning of 1868, the regime of the Shoguns surrendered its power to a new government, led by the Emperor Meiji, who established himself in the Shoguns' own palace in Edo, which thereupon became the new capital of Tokyo.

The Meiji government realized, almost from the very beginning, that if Japan was to survive, it would have to become powerful enough to deal with the Western powers on its own terms. To achieve this result selected Japanese were sent abroad to master not only Western industrial technology, but also Western forms of government. Within twenty years the entire government of Japan had been reconstructed: the Shoguns had disappeared from the scene, almost without trace, taking the whole complex of feudal Japan with them. A cabinet form of government was constituted, with standing armed forces, commanded by career officers and equipped with modern weapons.

The climax to the whole process was the Constitution granted by the emperor himself in 1889, and followed by the Rescript on Education a year later.

This is the sort of answer which would earn 'straight As' for a Japanese high-school graduate. The presentation of Meiji as a sort of latter-day Peter the Great, or 'the architect of Modern Japan', is, however, truly tendentious. The only aspect of the story which still rings true is the breathless pace of events. B. H. Chamberlain, an eminent British historian and eye-witness to the events of the Meiji era, wrote in 1908:

> To have lived through the transition stage of modern Japan makes a man feel preternaturally old; for here he is in modern times, with the air full of talk about bicycles and bacilli and 'spheres of influence', and yet he can himself distinctly remember the Middle Ages. The dear old Samurai who first initiated the present writer into the mysteries of the Japanese language, wore a queue and two swords. This relic of feudalism now sleeps in Nirvana. His modern successor . . . might almost be a European . . . Old things pass away between a night and a morning. The Japanese boast that they have done in thirty or forty years what it took Europe half as many centuries to accomplish.

To attribute all this to the drive and initiative of Meiji is really going too far. It is the Meiji era that counts, not the Meiji Emperor, who, far from resembling Peter the Great, was much closer to his contemporary, the King Emperor, Edward VII. To see why the Meiji Emperor was the creature and not the master of circumstance, it is necessary to look more closely at the historical record – a process which must start with the Tokugawa Shoguns.

The basis of the Tokugawa regime was feudal. Japan was divided into a number of districts, known as *han*, which were governed from the castle of the feudal lord, or *daimyō* – literally 'great name'. The *han* varied greatly in size, power and distance from the seat of the Shogun's power in Edo. According to these factors the *daimyō* divided into two recognized groups, the *fudai* on the one hand, and the *tozama* on the other. The former were directly subordinate to the Shogun, where the latter, by force of circumstance, were able to retain considerable political independence. In the land as a whole, there was, besides the *fudai* and *tozama han*, a domain known as the *tenryō* directly administered by the Shogun. (The *tenryō* was the source of the endowments for the *kuge*, considered in Chapter 3.)

The *samurai* were a hereditary class of warriors directly dependent upon the *daimyō* who, in principle, were obliged to maintain them – an obligation which could not always be fulfilled in practice. There were two classes of *samurai*, with very little mobility between the two. The upper *samurai* provided the top officials, intelligentsia, professional élite and personal retainers for the *daimyō*. The much more numerous lower *samurai* were divided among an even greater number of separate occupations, and it is here that one finds the military role, as exemplified by that of the *ashigari*, or common foot soldiers. This is the basis of the popular conception of the *samurai* ethic, as presented even in Western television series (such as *Shogun*), where the *samurai* is loyal to his master, even unto death, if necessary by *harakiri* (which is generally known in Japan by the alternative *on*-reading, *seppuku*). In fact the lower *samurai* had little opportunity for displaying such loyalty; if anything, by becoming competent in arithmetic (which the upper *samurai* despised) they equipped themselves for the lower ranks of the bureaucracy, where they were largely engaged in enforcing upon the peasants the appalling burden of taxation in rice.

Such oppressive taxation, which often took more than half the crop, was indispensable for maintaining the system, particularly in the form imposed by the Tokugawa Shoguns. The model could almost have been the court of Louis XIV at Versailles, which was also established in the seventeenth century. The Shogun required the *daimyō* to reside in Edo every other year, and to keep their families there the whole time. The actual administration of the *han* was left to an official known as the *daikan*, and the office – as one comes to expect in Japan – was generally hereditary.

The one activity which the system, if not its beneficiaries, was bound to encourage was trade, and derivatively, in support of trade, finance. The traders, known as *chōnin*, ranked below the multitude of peasants in the traditional Japanese hierarchy, but their command of the cash economy gave them considerable power, and many a *samurai* only too readily exchanged his high status for the lowly status of a *chōnin*. The point is simple enough. Government finance, with its basis in the feudal structure, could only be based upon rice. The growth of the cities, keeping pace with the expansion of trade, provided a market for rice, which supplied the cash necessary for the Shogun, the *daimyō* and the *samurai*, as well as the court and the *kuge* in Kyoto, to satisfy their demand for conspicuous consumption. It is this process which lies behind all the magnificent arts and crafts of the Edo period.

The process led, inexorably, to the decline of the feudal economy: the *daimyō* as well as the *samurai* incurred debts they could not repay, and the position was exacerbated by the *daimyō* failing to reward the *samurai*. It was no good increasing the burden of taxation on the peasants: they were already squeezed dry, and in bad years famine reigned. Even in the early years of the Tokugawa Shoguns there had been occasional peasant uprisings: by the end of the period these had become much more frequent. The *chōnin*, whatever their formal status, were the only class whose prosperity steadily increased. The system of government, failing to adjust to economic and demographic change, and often deprived of effective leaders, was in increasing measure vulnerable to any substantial challenge to its power.

The challenge came in the end from three sides. The first was the threat originally made palpable by Commodore Perry's arrival in Edo bay in August 1853. The second was the reaction to this threat by some among the *tozama daimyō*, and even more their retainers among the lesser *samurai* from the remote provinces of Chōshū and Satsuma. The third side, perhaps surprisingly, was constituted by the court and certain of the *kuge* in Kyoto, supported by the large trading houses of Osaka, some thirty miles away.

The role of Chōshū and Satsuma can be explained by geographical factors. The former, at the western extreme of the main island of Honshu, and the latter, on the opposite shore on the island of Kyushu, were remote from Edo but close to the busy sea-routes where ships from the Western world were to be seen in ever-increasing numbers. For two centuries and more they had been accustomed to the Dutch trading from their enclave of Deshima, in the harbour of Nagasaki, on the other side of Kyushu, and every year they had witnessed the passage of the embassy sent by the Dutch to the Shogun's court. But by the middle of the nineteenth century it was not only the Dutch who sailed into Japanese waters, and the Shogun's government, located in Edo and remote from the scene of the most intense action, was obviously unable to meet this new threat: they had been unable to keep Commodore Perry away from their own doorstep.

Where Edo had been forced to accommodate the Western powers, those most directly threatened were determined to resist them. Implicit in their policy of *jōi*, that is, 'drive out the barbarians', was the accusation that the government of the Shogun, the so-called *bakufu*, was unable to do its job properly. In 1863 the warriors of Chōshū took the matter into their own hands, and used their shore batteries to fire upon American, French and Dutch ships passing through the narrow straits of Shimonoseki, which separate Honshu from Kyushu. Later in the year it was the British who taught the recalcitrant Japanese a lesson: a naval squadron bombarded Kagoshima, the capital of the Satsuma *han*, and much of it was burnt to the ground. The struggle continued, and it was beyond the powers of the Shogun to control its course.

In the light of history, the really significant development was the combination of *jōi*, with the policy of *sonnō*, that is, 'revere the emperor'. If at first sight *sonnō-jōi* seems an unlikely hybrid, it had none the less a quite definite political rationale, which had been developed in the late Tokugawa era. This was above all the contribution of a number of scholars belonging to the Mito school, of whom the most influential was Aizawa Seishisai (1782–1863). If one realizes that Seishisai was a contemporary of Abraham Lincoln, one sees how much Japan, at this time, lived in a quite different world. In his best-known work, *Tekiihen*, he wrote:

> Barbarians call everybody in the world a friend and fail to distinguish between lord and subject, father and son, husband and wife, older and younger brothers . . . *samurai* and merchants. Those holding official positions engage in overseas trade with other nations. This is so because they are barbarians and have no conception of righteousness and shame. It is their way to concentrate solely on profits. It is different in Japan. Here, there are proper distinctions between *samurai* and merchants. The *samurai* value most highly righteousness and shame. As a result Japan has become the most respectable country in the world. If Japan were to become like other nations, she would lose her most precious aspects, and we would fall to their level and become completely degenerate.

So much for *jōi*: as for the other side of the medal, *sonnō*, Seishisai wrote:

The Emperor, representing the activities of heaven, spreads the deeds of heaven. The Bakufu aids the Imperial Court and governs the whole country. The local rulers are all supporters of the Imperial Court and promulgate the decrees of the Bakufu throughout their provinces. That is why the people who obey the commands of the local *daimyō* are in effect obeying the decrees of the Bakufu and this is precisely the way to revere the Imperial Court and repay one's debt to the heavenly ancestors. The principle is simple and the way is clear.

This establishment version of *sonnō-jōi*, as put forward by Seishisai and many others who followed him, affirmed the feudal government of Japan, according to a policy known as *kōbu gattai*, that is, the union of the court and the *bakufu*. Its basis was the hierarchical ordering of Japanese society, with great masses of the common people kept in permanent subjection. Seishisai made no bones about this: 'many among the people of the country are stupid, only a few are superior. Once the hearts of the stupid begin to lose their balance, it is impossible to govern the country in a stable manner.'

The policy of *kōbu gattai* was doomed to failure for a number of reasons. In the first place the people were not nearly so stupid as Seishisai would have them be. In comparison with the Western world, there was a high level of literacy in Japan, particularly in the last hundred years of the Tokugawa era. Almost from the beginning, there were special schools in the *han* for educating *samurai*, and in increasing measure these admitted a limited number of commoners, often selected on the basis of merit, and known as *shosei*. More important, at the level of the masses, were the *terakoya*, a word meaning, literally, 'temple children room', which even in the remotest villages provided instruction in reading and writing for commoners. Although the name suggests a Buddhist institution, many such schools had lost all formal connection with Buddhism long before the end of the Tokugawa era. By this time as many as half the teachers could also be commoners, with the remainder being either *samurai* or Buddhist, or sometimes even Shinto, priests.

It was the *shosei* who in the end put forward an alternative and historically more successful version of *sonnō-jōi*, which encompassed the overthrow of the *bakufu* and the feudal system. This version succeeded simply because the centre of the *bakufu* system was too weak to impose a strong national policy to counter the threat from outside. Unless the Shogun was powerful in his own right, too much power still remained with the *daimyō*, who in increasing measure were preoccupied with their own local problems. When, in 1858, a commerical treaty was agreed between the *bakufu* and the American envoy, Townsend Harris, it was clear that effective support from the *bakufu* could no longer be relied upon. To make clear the position of the court, the emperor of the day, Meiji's father, Komei, issued a decree severing relations with the American envoy and, by implication, repudiating the policy of the *bakufu*. It is not surprising then that the court, for the first time in nearly 300 years, began to be an important factor in Japanese political life.

This was a welcome development to many of the *kuge*, who had suffered years of frustration by being excluded from public life. In the result the court became a centre of political activity during the reign of the Emperor Komei (1846–66), but he was not to be the head of the new Japan to follow the political reforms known as 'Oseifukko', that is the restoration of imperial rule. Komei died at the age of thirty-five, to be succeeded by his fourteen-year-old son, Mutsuhito, known to history as Meiji – 'the architect of Modern Japan'.

In the same year as Meiji succeeded as emperor, the young Shogun Iemochi died, to be succeeded by his guardian, Keiki. Keiki was immediately confronted by the alliance constituted by the imperial court, the merchant houses of Osaka led by the renowned Mitsui, and the *samurai* zealots of Chōshū and Satsuma, who had been joined by their neighbours, the equally powerful *han* of Tosa and Hizen. The reluctant Keiki, breaking all precedent, came in 1867 to Nijo Castle in Kyoto, and seeing which way the wind was blowing, surrendered all his powers to the fifteen-year-old emperor. The Chōshū and Satsuma faction were already planning a *coup d'état*, and the ex-Shogun left Kyoto by night for Osaka, whence he took ship to Edo. His supporters, in January 1868, made a last desperate attempt to retrieve power, but after a three-day battle on a site lying between the villages of Toba and Fushimi, just outside Kyoto, they were decisively defeated. Keiki, once in Edo, gave orders for its surrender to be negotiated with the imperial forces. By the end of the month the Tokugawa dynasty, whose regime had been in power for 268 years, had passed into oblivion. Keiki lived on into the twentieth century, and at the end of his life he was received by the Emperor Meiji and raised to the rank of prince.

In November 1868 the new emperor visited Edo for the first time, in a scene described as 'the last purely Japanese pageant either Japan or the world is like to see'. In a procession in which the *daimyō* and the *kuge* were in the vanguard, came at last 'the Prince of Bizen, in charge of two square boxes borne high upon men's shoulders . . . covered with a red and yellow damask silk [and] . . . believed to contain the insignia or regalia [for which] . . . small shrines had been erected for their safe custody at all the halting-places along the road . . . and then we saw approaching the Ho-o-ren or phoenix car.

'This is a black lacquered palanquin, about six feet square and with a dome-shaped roof; the front is closed only by curtains, and in the centre of each side is a latticed window, through which it was possible to see that it held no one. The Mikado is supposed to travel in it, but has really a more comfortable palanquin . . . the bearers of the car, which is carried high upon their shoulders and on a frame which raises it six feet from the ground, were . . . all dressed in bright yellow silk . . . There were fully sixty of them immediately surrounding the Ho-o-ren, and the effect of the group, with the brilliant sun lighting up the sheen of the silk and the glitter of the lacquer, was very gorgeous and indescribably strange, comparable to nothing ever seen in any other part of the world. And now a great silence fell upon the people. Far as the eye could see on either side, the roadsides were densely packed with the crouching populace, in their ordinary position when any official of rank passes by . . . As the phoenix car . . . with its halo of glittering attendants came on . . . the people without order or signal turned their faces to the earth . . . no man moved or spoke for a space, and all seemed to hold their breath for very awe, as the mysterious presence, on whom few are privileged to look and live, was passing by.'

In the spring of 1869 the Meiji Emperor returned for good, to establish his court in the castle of the Tokugawa Shoguns. On this second occasion a British regimental band, part of the infantry detachment that guarded the foreign legations in Yokohama, welcomed the emperor's palanquin with 'The British Grenadiers'. So much for the success of *jōi*. The emperor's advance upon Edo (now renamed Tokyo, 'Eastern Capital') was about as triumphant as the progress of William of Orange from Torbay to London in 1688. The time was ripe for change.

Three inter-related policies were then to govern the future development of Japan. The first of these was the abolition of feudalism, the second, the adoption of Western institutions, and the third, the establishment of Shinto as the official State religion.

The abolition of feudalism was hardly a problem, for the system was moribund. The actual government in Tokyo was in the hands of a very able oligarchy of lesser *samurai* from the four western *han* of Chōshū, Satsuma, Tosa and Hizen, but they had been wise enough to win the support of a number of *daimyō* and court nobles, by appointing them to high office, and leaving the *han* intact – for the time being. Then, in March 1869, the *daimyō* of the four western *han* surrendered their fiefs to the emperor, addressing to him a memorial which was also made public. The sense of the memorial is given by the following passages:

> There is no soil within the Empire that does not belong to the Emperor . . . and no inhabitant who is not a subject of the Emperor, though, in the Middle Ages, the Imperial power declined and the military classes rose, taking possession of the land and dividing it among themselves as the prize of their bow and spear. But now that the Imperial power is restored, how can we retain possession of land that belongs to the Emperor and govern people who are his subjects? We therefore reverently offer up all our feudal possessions . . . so that a uniform rule may prevail throughout the Empire. Thus the country will be able to rank equally with the other nations of the world.

This memorial, with its keen sense of *realpolitik*, is a far cry from the obscurantism of Seishisai. The old guard was out-played. It is not surprising that the *han* were formally abolished only two years later, in 1871. In that year some 302 *han* were consolidated into seventy-two prefectures, each with a governor appointed by the central government. The prefectures were further subdivided into *gun, ku, machi* and *mura*, roughly speaking, districts, cities, towns and villages, on the basis of hierarchical ordering characteristic of Japan. At every level the officials were responsible to the central government. The system so established still governs Japan.

In 1872, the process of reform was completed by abolishing the rigid feudal caste system, so that the formal status, at least, of the *daimyō*, *samurai*, peasants and merchants was no longer recognized. This was, however, hardly a step in the direction of an egalitarian democratic society. One hierarchy had replaced another.

The young emperor, if he was the architect of Modern Japan, had much to be proud of by the time he was eighteen. A system of government, which had lasted for getting on for 300 years, was turned on its head, and that by a young man who been brought up in the court life described in Chapter 3. As they say, if you can believe that, you can believe anything. It is necessary to look for an alternative explanation – the more so if one realizes that, in 1868, every emperor for 1,000 years, if he was to count for anything, had had to accept the role that others imposed upon him. On the face of it, was it likely that the new emperor should be any exception to the rule?

Before considering further the modernization of Japan under Meiji, it is worth looking once again at the idea implicit in the term, *ōseifukkō*, which is the essential expression of the idea of restoration. To anyone brought up on English history, restoration can only mean the return of Charles II in 1660, after the eleven years of Oliver Cromwell's Protectorate. Quite simply, the monarchy was restored after a comparatively short interregnum. But what was there to restore in Japan?

It would be quite mistaken to think that the secluded Kyoto court was simply the creation of the Tokugawa Shoguns, and that somehow, in the year 1600, Tokugawa Ieyasu usurped the power of the emperor, moved the centre of government to Edo, and established his own dynasty. It must be clear, for one thing, that the Tokugawas never questioned the legitimacy of the imperial institution. If anything they made it much stronger than it had been in the sixteenth century, when the emperors, powerless and often destitute, had lost all control of events. The key to *ōseifukkō* is that where *ōsei* means simply the monarchical system, *fukkō* means 'to restore antiquity'. In contrast to the England of 1660, the Japan of 1868 was concerned with the restoration of a mythical rather than a historical institution.

The essential point, even today, is that legitimacy in Japan is a question of form rather than substance. The two sometimes coincide, but in 1600 that had not been true of the court for several hundred years. Much more frequently offices were created, and perpetuated (often by being made hereditary), which allowed for the indefinite delegation of substantive power, so that the English historian, George Sansom, in a well-known passage relating to the thirteenth-century Shoguns, noted 'the astonishing spectacle of a state at the head of which stands a titular Emperor whose vestigial functions are usurped by an abdicated Emperor, and whose real power is nominally delegated to an hereditary military dictator but actually wielded by an hereditary adviser of that dictator'.

The truth is that the Meiji restoration restored nothing, for there was nothing to restore. True there had been a golden age, the so-called early Heian period (794–898), during which the emperors were effectively at the head of the government, but this could hardly provide the model for a regime which was established nearly 1,000 years later. The idea of restoration is part of the Meiji mythology: the word *ishin*, which refers, historically, only to the events of 1868, is much less misleading if it is translated simply as a 'new deal' – foreshadowing the politics of President Roosevelt in the United States in the 1930s.

Once the reform of government in Japan had got under way, it soon became clear to the oligarchs in Tokyo that Japan could only confront the West on anything like equal terms by adopting Western methods. As early as the battle of Shimonoseki, two young men from Chōshū, Hirobumi Ito and Kaoru Inouye, left secretly for London on a British ship, and once there they became convinced that Japan would have to live with the foreign barbarians. Later the Marquis Ito was to become one of the leading Japanese statesmen of the late nineteenth century, but even at the time of the restoration his voice was heard, and the oligarchy was persuaded that young representatives from Japan should be sent to Western countries to study almost every aspect of science and industrial technology, finance and commerce, law and government. At the same time Western advisers would be recruited to work in Japan. *Jōi* had been replaced by a policy of 'If you can't beat them, join them'.

Within two decades the face of Japan was transformed. The material culture of the West was adopted lock, stock and barrel. The infrastructure was completely modernized, with the construction of railways, harbours and telegraph lines providing the basis for a modern postal service. Printing presses made mass circulation newspapers available to the new literate classes created by the introduction of universal, public, elementary education. Western habits, such as smoking, were also adopted. From the seclusion of Tokugawa Japan to the new open

Japan of Meiji was a heady transformation for many Japanese. Inouye even advocated the substitution of bread for rice, and suggested that sheep be imported to graze such former *suiden* as were not needed for the cultivation of wheat, oats and barley. Others among the intelligentsia suggested that the language be written henceforth in *rōmaji*, or even abandoned completely in favour of one or other European language.

The institutional reforms were just as radical. A new national conscript army, led by career officers, took over the historical role of the *samurai*, each loyal to his own *daimyō*. A new order of nobility was created, with titles equivalent to the English prince (duke), marquis, count (earl), viscount and baron, to take the place of both the *kuge* and the *daimyō*. The two old orders became known as *kwazoku* (literally 'flower families'), and from this source much of the new nobility was appointed in 1884. This provided the basis for the House of Peers in the new Diet, which was to remain an important political force until its abolition by the 1947 Constitution. (Many of the key figures whom I discuss in later chapters, such as Ito, Saionji, Minobe, Konoye and Kido, were all members of the House of Peers.) At the executive level the government was reorganized on the basis of separate ministries, each with its own departmental responsibilities. Finally, in 1889, the Meiji Emperor promulgated the first modern constitution, which was based upon a Prussian model. From that time on, the emphasis within Japan was more on the consolidation of the gains already made, leaving the way open for an expansionist foreign policy, which was soon to make Japan a country to be reckoned with on the world scene.

The breathless pace of advance was not without cost to the Japanese people. The rapid expansion of the economy could only be financed by taxation and, as in the Tokugawa era, the burden was carried by the peasants. There was little reform of agriculture, but the Meiji government required taxes to be paid in cash and no longer in kind. With a poorly developed marketing structure, this led many of the smaller peasants into debt, secured on their land, and enforced by foreclosure. This led to a concentration of land-holdings, with land-lords being entitled to as much as half the crop as rent, which, by being sold on the market, allowed them to meet the taxes imposed by the government. The burden, needless to say, was passed on to the tenants. It is not suprising that peasant uprisings continued throughout the 1870s, without leading to any improvement.

The old orders of Japanese society also suffered from the reforms. The *daimyō* had the least to complain about, for they received generous compensation for the loss of their fiefs, and were often appointed as the first prefectural governors. The lot of the *samurai* was much more uncertain. True, many had found a place in the new modern bureaucracy, or in the rapidly expanding business world. Many others, however, suffered greatly from their loss of status following the introduction of conscription, accompanied by a rule allowing only the police and members of the armed forces to carry swords.

The peasant uprisings were accompanied by local *samurai* revolts, which culminated in that led by Saigo Takamori in his own home territory of Satsuma. Saigo, as a *samurai* from Satsuma, was an original member of the Tokyo oligarchy. But within four years of the restoration, a crisis arose within the oligarchy, relating to Japanese policy *vis-à-vis* Korea. Saigo was the leader of a minority advocating military intervention in order to force Korea to open its door to Japanese commerce. The majority temporized on the grounds that Japan was not yet strong enough to provoke the outside world by such action. Saigo returned home to Satsuma, where he watched the progress of events with increasing distaste. He became the head of a local faction composed of *samurai* who shared his discontent, and in 1877 he led a rebellion in Satsuma. After several months of bitter fighting, Saigo and his *samurai* were defeated by units of the new conscript army, commanded by a general from Chōshū, who proclaimed his victory with the words, 'The Japanese, whether of the military class or not, originally sprang from the same blood, and, when subjected to regular discipline, could scarcely fail to make soldiers worthy of the renowned bravery of their ancestors.' Some sixty years later the Pacific War was to prove how prophetic a judgement this was.

In all these events, what was the actual role of the Meiji Emperor? In answering this question, the period of his reign can usefully be divided into two periods by the year of the new constitution, 1889. In the early period, the emperor was established as a public figure. Before there was any modern transport, he made in the years from 1872 to 1885 six great circuits, or *kunko*, of Japan, spending not short of a year away from the capital, and travelling by ship, horse and palanquin, staying in the houses of the local notables, and meeting the common people by the roadside. Later on, as the modernization of the country progressed, he would visit shipyards, attend the opening of new railway lines, and appear at the new local schools. By this time the emperor's style had completely changed, as was noted by a witness who had also been present at the time of this first visit to Edo in 1868: 'The next time I witnessed a procession in which the Mikado figured . . . His Majesty dressed in European costume rode in a carriage, free to be gazed on by all beholders; and the people had been notified that the . . . bowing-down would not be enforced.' In this same period the emperor was involved in the deliberations of his ministers, although it cannot be said that he ever showed much interest in governing (which was just as well since the oligarchy never wished him to have any real power).

After the promulgation of the new constitution in 1889, an event over which the emperor presided in a scene of truly imperial splendour, with the nobility, senior members of the government and diplomatic corps clothed in magnificent court uniforms in Western style, and arrayed against an oriental background, not the person of the emperor, but an image was placed before the Japanese public. In 1888 an Italian artist produced an engraved portrait of the Meiji Emperor, in a magnificent uniform, covered with medals and decorations, and showing him with his left hand on the hilt of his sword, and a white-plumed cap on a table by his right hand. For the rest of his reign (which lasted until 1912) photographs of this engraving were sent to government offices, schools and foreign embassies, so that this likeness of the emperor, at least, became known to far more people than had ever been able to see him on his earlier travels.

The moral system over which the new image of the emperor would preside is encapsulated in the Imperial Rescript on Education, issued by the Meiji Emperor shortly before the convening of the first Diet under the constitution of 1889. So extraordinary is this ordinance to Western eyes (particularly in the light of the reverence paid to it in Japan) that it is worth while reproducing it in full:

Our Imperial Ancestors have founded our Empire on a basis broad and everlasting. Our subjects ever united in loyalty and filial piety have from generation to generation illustrated the beauty thereof. This is the glory of the fundamental character of Our Empire, and herein also lies the source of Our Education. Ye, Our Subjects, be filial to your parents, affectionate to your brothers and sisters; as husbands and wives be harmonious; as friends, true. Pursue learning and cultivate arts, and thereby develop intellectual faculties and perfect moral powers; furthermore, advance public good and promote common interests; always respect the Constitution and observe the laws; should emergency arise, offer yourselves courageously to the State; and thus guard and maintain the prosperity of Our Imperial Throne coeval with heaven and earth. So shall ye be not only Our good and faithful subjects, but render illustrious the best traditions of your forefathers.

The Way here set forth is indeed the teaching bequeathed by Our Imperial Ancestors, to be observed alike by Their Descendants and the subjects, infallible for all ages and true in all places. It is Our wish to lay it to heart in all reverence, in common with you, Our subjects, that we may all thus attain to the same virtue.

Although the language is not quite his style, this reads like something that Lord Baden-Powell could have written for the Boy Scout movement. The Imperial Rescript was a deliberate step to counteract liberal political ideas and moral values imported from the West. From the beginning the Ministry of Education made clear that the authority behind the rescript was imperial rather than legal, although the document itself was the product of a committee, which had had some difficult in agreeing its contents.

The actual purpose of the Rescript on Education was not clear at the time of its issue, but it soon became the official basis of *shūshin*, or moral instruction, in all Japanese schools. Schools competed in elaborating the ceremonial surrounding its use for this purpose. A typical school would keep it in a lacquer box, together with the imperial portraits, and they would be produced for special occasions, when the words of the Rescript would be recited, in unison, by the whole school together, led by the principal. Almost from the very beginning, scholarly exegeses began to appear, and the number of books commenting upon and explaining the rescript ran into hundreds. It became the centre of a new cult of the emperor, and it is not surprising that after the defeat of Japan in the Pacific War, some fifty-five years later, the Supreme Command of the Allies in the Pacific (SCAP) insisted on its suppression, much against the wishes of the bureaucrats who still headed the Ministry of Education. Seen historically, the rescript was the culmination of a process which started in the year 1878, when the Meiji Emperor, after one of his provincial tours, had concluded that

Confucian ethics should again be imposed upon the schools, which had gone too far in the direction of Westernization. This represented a sort of cultural *jōi*, which was taken up by the Ministry of Education, with consequences which no one could have foreseen.

Of the three policies which provide the key to understanding the way political institutions developed in the Meiji era, the deliberate reformation of Japan's ancient religion of Shinto is significant for the way it involved the status of the emperor. State Shinto, as the product of this reformation is generally known, is often seen by outside critics as the root of all evil in the historical process which led to the Pacific War. This view led Robert Ballou, an American with Messianic fervour, to publish a book, just after the defeat of the Japanese, with the title, *Shinto: the Unconquered Enemy. Japan's Doctrine of Racial Superiority and World Conquest. With Selections from Japanese Texts.* But what was State Shinto?

The basic canon, which existed long before the Meiji era, consisted of historical works which combined the traditional Shinto mythology with the history of the imperial line. All this was implicit in the day-to-day life of the court in Kyoto in the years before 1868. What Shinto then lacked was any sort of national organization, as well as any theology beyond that based upon the descent of the emperors from the sun-goddess. What then the Meiji government provided was a Church in the Weberian sense, and a politically oriented doctrine, the whole encapsulated in an institution which in its final form was legal, and not religious. This reform involved government investment in Shinto, largely taking the form of establishing a centralized bureaucracy, which from the year 1900 was directed by the Shrine Bureau of the Home Ministry. (In November 1940, at the time of the official celebrations commemorating the first 2,600 years of the imperial line, this was to become a separate office, the Jingi-in: this was abolished by SCAP after the defeat of Japan in 1945.) The priests of this new *legal* version of Shinto were public officials.

As for theology, the Yasukuni shrine in Tokyo, founded by the Meiji Emperor in 1869 (with the actual name being bestowed ten years later) 'for the worship of the divine spirits of those who gave their lives in defence of the Empire of Japan' (to quote from a hand-out given to visitors), may be taken to symbolize all that State Shinto involves. This doctrine can be summed up in the single word *kokutai*, which also expresses an idea developed before the Meiji era. The best literal translation is something like 'the essence of the nation', but as so often in Japan the actual meaning is much less important than the ideological uses to which it is put. *Kokutai* can be seen best as a sort of slogan embodying the ethic behind government policy as it developed in the Meiji era. In principle every nation will have its own *kokutai*, but as the idea developed in the Japan of the 1890s, it came in increasing measure to represent something almost undefinable that was uniquely Japanese.

The practical effect of *kokutai* in the development of State Shinto is not easy to understand. The Meiji era opened with the idea of *saisei itchi*, the 'unity of rites and governance', which meant that the emperor was to retain his historic status within Shinto, and at the same time be Head of State. Very shortly thereafter Shinto was disestablished, largely in response to Western demands for religious freedom, which in the end was guaranteed by the constitution of 1889. If this change of policy had little direct effect on traditional Shinto at village level, which remained a component in the syncretic religion summed up in the phrase *sankyō itchi* (the 'meeting of the three religions' discussed in Chapter 2), it made the position of national Shinto extremely equivocal. The object was to separate rites (*saishi*) from doctrine (*shūkyō*), allowing Shinto to retain its secular function of imperial ritual, while leaving traditional doctrine undisturbed. What this development meant in practice was that the rites attracted their own doctrinal rationale, and this was *kokutai*. Given the context of these events, it is not surprising that *kokutai* came to be identified with the ancestral tradition of the imperial house.

At the same time the status of the emperor, in relation to Shinto, was almost as ambiguous as Shinto itself. If in the eyes of Shinto scholars he was *arahitogami*, a manifest deity representing in this world the divine imperial line, his popular image was more down to earth. This was the image captured by the Italian artist in 1888. He was compared, to their disadvantage, with other earthly rulers, such as Napoleon and Alexander the Great. The ruler who came closest to him was the old German Kaiser Wilhelm I, but he, poor man, never learnt to write poetry, of which the Meiji Emperor was an acknowledged master. The popular press gave details of his equestrian and gastronomic interests, and a lucrative industry grew up to satisfy the public demand for imperial kitsch. The endless Shinto ritual still carried out in private by the emperor was of little public interest. The great transformation of the Meiji era was that for the first time virtually all Japanese became conscious of the emperor's existence.

Returning to the critical years around 1890, when Meiji, as it were, was withdrawn from circulation, one sees the beginning of a process which was to return the emperor 'above the clouds'. His visits, at a time when transport had become much more efficient, were severely limited, and the image presented of him became increasingly surrealist. The American scholar, Carol Gluck, puts the transformation in the following words:

> The phase of the 'Restoration Emperor' which could be said to have begun in 1846 when Emperor Komei was drawn into politics over the foreign issue, ended in 1889 when Emperor Meiji was once again raised above politics by the Constitution, which rendered sovereignty but not government within his powers.

The event which made way for the transformation was the removal, in 1887, of the Marquis Ito – Japan's foremost statesman in the late nineteenth century – from his office as head of the *kunaishō*, the department which governed the Imperial Household. Soon after, the Imperial Household Law established the *kunaishō* as a separate ministry, which was well placed to develop the image of the emperor according to its own policies.

The process went in two directions at once. First, the emperor was credited with every success achieved by his government, but blamed for none of its failures. Considering that before he died in 1912, Japan had not only succeeded in persuading the Western powers to surrender their consular privileges, but also had defeated a major power, Russia, in a war in which world opinion was largely on its side, the final version of the Meiji Emperor was that of an imposing world figure, who had hardly ever put a foot wrong. In 1895 the treaty of Shimonoseki, which ended a successful war against China, gave Japan not only Taiwan, but also a foothold on the Chinese mainland. In 1910 Korea was annexed. The empire of the sun-goddess was extending its frontiers beyond the Japanese islands for almost the first time in history.

The divine, as opposed to the political, image caused problems of a different order, largely because of the ambiguous status which had been imposed upon State Shinto. During his lifetime Meiji was occasionally worshipped as a living god (*ikigami*), but this was irregular, for legally an emperor could only be enshrined after his death. The Meiji Emperor died in July 1912, and his funeral mound in the suburb of Momoyama was to be the last *goryō*, or imperial tomb, in Kyoto. The funeral rites were pure Shinto, where those for all his predecessors, including his own father, Komei, had – at least from the time of Prince Shotoku – been Buddhist. A new shrine was built for Meiji in Tokyo, and he was to be enshrined there in 1920, having already been recognized as a *kami*.

Hardly a year later, the Meiji Emperor's grandson, the Prince Hirohito, became regent for his father (and Meiji's son), Taisho, and after another five years he was himself to succeed to the Chrysanthemum Throne. The stage had been set during the first eleven years in the life of the young prince, when his grandfather was still alive, although no one could then have predicted the course of the drama during the very long life ahead of him. In any case the die had been cast.

5

The Prince Hirohito

IN the morning of 10 May 1900, the Crown Prince Yoshihito, son of the Meiji Emperor, was married to the Lady Sadako, a daughter of the Fujiwara, the family which, more than any other, had for hundreds of years provided imperial consorts. The Crown Prince was twenty years old, and his bride no more than sixteen. Within a year, on 29 April 1901, the first of four sons was born. This was the Prince Hirohito, who was himself to become the Showa Emperor some twenty-five years later.

The young prince was never to have the chance of enjoying a normal childhood. At the age of three months, following the custom which prevailed in the old court in Kyoto, where every prince of the blood had his own household, Hirohito left the home of his own parents to be brought up in that of a retired admiral, the Count Sumiyoshi Kawamura. Unlike the old times in Kyoto, the house where the prince was to live was not within the Imperial Precinct, and nor was that of his parents. No matter, his parents, as well as his grandfather, the emperor, were not far away, and his father in any case was never to show much interest in any of his children.

The regime in the admiral's house, if old-fashioned and austere, was not unkind. It was not to last: when Hirohito was three, the old admiral died and the prince, together with his younger brother, Chichibu, returned to the palace of their father at Akasaka. There they were given their own house in the grounds, where they lived under the tutelage of the Marquis Takamasa Kido, the son of a former *samurai* who had been a member of the oligarchy in the first years after the restoration. To begin with the imperial princes were educated within their own household, where they were taught by a new guardian, Kinsaku Maruo, a stern disciplinarian, only too ready to deny his charges the normal pleasures of childhood. When Hirohito was seven, he was sent to a special class at the Peers' School, Gakushuin, where life became somewhat better. True, the young prince now had to wear the black serge uniform, with its brass buttons, but in this his lot was no different from that of his fellows.

What made all the difference to Hirohito was the personal interest taken in him by the head of the Gakushuin, Count Maresuke Nogi. When Hirohito arrived, Count Nogi was nearly seventy, and so was hardly any younger than the old admiral who had looked after the prince for the first three years of his life. Nogi, born a *samurai*, had by vocation always been a soldier, and his life in action had begun at the battle of Toba and Fushimi, in January 1868, when he had fought on the side of the young Meiji Emperor against the forces of the last of the Tokugawa Shoguns. He ended his military career as the general commanding the Third Japanese Army in the war against Russia, and almost exactly thirty-seven years after his first battle, he accepted the surrender of Port Arthur by the Russians. The Japanese victory had been bought at enormous cost, and both of the general's sons had died in action.

It was with this background that Nogi was appointed principal of the Gakushuin: confronted with his most distinguished pupil, the father who had lost his sons found a boy who had never had a true father. If at first sight the old general, who was quite literally battle-scarred, seems hardly a sympathetic figure for the diffident and pacific Hirohito, it is to be noted that he was also adept at the gentler arts of traditional Japan: calligraphy, *ikebana* flower-arranging, the cultivation of the miniature *bonzai* and the tea ceremony were all part of his life. However it may be, a close relationship grew up between Prince Hirohito and General Nogi.

The curriculum of the school, like that of any other in Japan, was dominated by the need to master the written language. The texts to be studied would have been largely in *kanbun*, the version of Chinese used by the intelligentsia, which formed the basis for the court's own idiosyncratic version of Japanese. The prince spent hours of his time simply learning the Chinese characters required by any well-educated Japanese. In his lessons in calligraphy, he would have learnt the different styles of writing with a brush, and the same techniques would have been applied to *sumi-e*, the traditional Japanese art of drawing in ink. The aesthetic of literary Japanese extended also to the composition of the seventeen-syllable *haiku* and the thirty-one syllable *tanka*, verse forms which the prince, following his grandfather, would use thousands of times in the course of his life. Tradition also governed the teaching of history, which included, inevitably for one who would some day be emperor, the whole story of the divine origins of the imperial line.

The remaining part of the curriculum included not only mathematics, science and geography, but also English, and although Hirohito was never to become proficient, he never lost his interest in English, nor his belief in its importance for Japanese contacts with the outside world. In addition to classroom subjects, time was also given to sports and gymnastics, for which the prince had little aptitude, although he was always a good swimmer.

There was still no question of any normal social or family life. He saw his grandfather, Meiji, three or four times a year, when he enjoyed not only the rare privilege of actually looking the emperor in the face, but also of being touched by him in a familiar grandfatherly sort of way. In this, the final period of the Meiji Emperor's life, there was (as I have shown in Chapter 4) no longer any question of the common touch. The emperor had been kept for many years remote from his people, and now, when he left the imperial palace (which did not happen often), the crowds on the streets bowed their heads, and the shutters were closed on all windows above the ground floor – a regime enforced by the police.

If the political events of the last years of the Meiji Emperor made, at the time, little impression upon his young grandson, they were none the less decisive for the history of Japan at least until the end of the Pacific War. The most devastating, for the imperial household, was the assassination, by a Korean, of the Marquis Ito on the station of Harbin in Manchuria. When this event took place in the summer of 1908, Hirohito was only seven, but he had already been enrolled in the Gakushuin, so the murder of Japan's leading statesman could not have passed unnoticed.

Ito, after his secret visit to England as a young man, had always been a leading figure in the Meiji oligarchy. When, in 1885, the oligarchy recast the Japanese government in modern form, with separate departmental ministries, Ito became the first Prime Minister, an office which he would hold a number of times in the coming years. The constitution of 1889 was largely his work, although by the time it was handed over by the Meiji Emperor, the Count Kuroda had become Prime Minister.

In 1895 it was Ito who signed the treaty of Shimonoseki by which Taiwan was ceded to Japan, but it was in 1900 that he took the most decisive step in his political career, by assuming the leadership of a new political party, the Seiyūkai. Throughout the 1890s the Japanese government had found it difficult to accept the democratic forms incorporated into the 1889 constitution. The House of Representatives, which was the lower of the two houses in the Diet, was an entirely elected body, but suffrage was so restricted that little more than 1 per cent of the population had the right to vote.

Even this limited popular representation was further constricted by the way the government worked in practice. To begin with, the upper house, the House of Peers, whose most important members, such as Ito, had been nominated from the Meiji oligarchy, had the power to block legislation originating in the House of Representatives. What is more, the House of Representatives could be dissolved by the emperor, on the advice of the cabinet, at any time, and the cabinet ministers were responsible only to the emperor.

In spite of all restraints, throughout the 1890s the half-million-odd Japanese with the right to vote did their best to show their political independence. The government consistently failed to win a majority in the lower house, and Ito, and the other Prime Ministers in this period, tried every expedient to control the unruly political parties. The latter were almost always able to make things difficult for the government when it came to passing the annual budget through the Diet, but quite failed to have any of their members included, as of right, in the cabinet. To counter any such possibility, an imperial rescript made clear that 'the appointment or removal of Ministers of State is absolutely at the will of the Sovereign, and no interference whatever is allowed in this matter'. So much for democracy in Meiji Japan.

The most significant act in Ito's political career took place in 1900, the year before Hirohito was born, but none the less it was to affect the character of the Japanese political system throughout almost his whole life. Ito, in the last years of the nineteenth century, had come to the conclusion that the oligarchy could not govern effectively without some political support in the House of Representatives. The need for this concession to democracy was hotly disputed by the Marquis Yamagata, who was, like Ito, by origin a *samurai* from Chōshū.

It was this which led Ito to take the initiative in establishing the Seiyūkai, which was born out of parties already represented in the Diet. In 1900 he became the leader of this party, and by doing so he established two principles that, today, some ninety years later, still determine the way politics work in Japan. The first of these principles goes under the evocative name of *amakudari*, literally 'descending from heaven': it means quite simply that political leaders are best recruited from the top levels of the bureaucracy, and one need only look at the record for the last thirty years to see how often this principle has been applied. The second principle is that the common people must have, or at least appear to have, some say in the way the country is governed. That is, however autocratic the substance of government, the form must be democratic.

The true position was soon made clear by Ito, who stated that the emperor 'retains absolute freedom to select His advisers from whatever quarters He deems proper, be it from among members of political parties or from circles outside those parties'. If Ito was not exactly a Japanese Thomas Jefferson, he must still be reckoned as an influence for good in modern Japanese history. He represented, against Yamagata and many others who supported Yamagata, the principle that the government of Japan was a matter for civilians, and not soldiers. In taking this stand, he was for the last ten years of his life fighting a losing battle, and when he was murdered in the late summer of 1908 he had, to all intents and purposes, already lost it.

The decisive turning point came in 1895, at the time of the war with China, when Yamagata, then Prime Minister, accepted the rule that the ministers for the army and navy should always be serving officers. In practice this was to mean not only that the army and navy could choose their own heads of department, but also that the latter could force a cabinet crisis, simply by resigning, and seeing to it that no successor was available until the crisis was resolved according to their wishes. The position was generally complicated by the fact that the high commands of the two armed services were generally at logger-heads, to the point that a co-ordinated policy was often out of the question.

Within the imperial household it was the Crown Prince, Hirohito's father, who felt the loss of Ito most keenly. Not only was Ito a trusted adviser, but his violent death made the Crown Prince, who had long feared assassination, even more terrified of such a fate. He was not only vain, sadistic and promiscuous, but mentally unstable. The prospect of becoming emperor interested him only for the increasing opportunities it would provide for dressing up in military uniform, aping his idol, the Kaiser Wilhelm II of Germany. After the death of Ito the Crown Prince did not have to wait long before he succeeded his father, Meiji.

On 20 July 1912, the *kunaishō* (the Imperial Household Ministry) announced that the emperor was seriously ill. Every day crowds gathered in the imperial plaza as they would, seventy-six years later, during the final illness of the Showa Emperor, Meiji's grandson. The emperor died on 30 July, just three months after his grandson's eleventh birthday.

The death of the Meiji Emperor had religious consequences which it was impossible to avoid. When his father had died, forty-five years earlier, the rites were performed by Buddhist monks from the Kyoto monastery of Sennyūji, with the abbot (*jogen*) himself officiating at the actual funeral (*taisō no rei*) and entombment (*ryōsho no gi*), which took place thirty-three days after the death. The most significant deviation from normal Buddhist practice was that the body was buried and not cremated. The Meiji government had, in effect, disestablished Buddhism, so that there was no precedent for the funeral rites to be performed on the emperor's death.

The question of Shinto funerals was not one which had much interested the Meiji government. At the time of the Russo-Japanese war, when casualties had been very high, Shinto priests had complained that Buddhists had a monopoly of funerals, and had debated whether or not funerals should be considered 'religious'. The government, however, was content to affirm its support of the Yasukuni shrine (founded by the emperor himself), which in time of war had become much more important: if this policy helped State Shinto, it did nothing to make it a religion in terms of the 1889 constitution. Formally the position was not changed by Meiji's funeral, but given that the rites actually followed included offering ritual meals to the deceased emperor throughout the forty-five days of mourning, and that on the twenty-eighth day after his death his posthumous name (which was of course Meiji) was announced to his spirit (*reizen*), then, if these various acts were not 'religious', one does begin to wonder what the word actually means.

In the end a form was found for all the various rites, as they were carried out from day to day – mostly within the privacy of the court – and a precedent for the *taisō* or 'great mourning' for an emperor was established. This was to be followed not only when Taisho died fourteen years later (in 1926), but also, if somewhat uncertainly, when the Showa Emperor died in 1989. The only difference was that the imperial tomb built for Meiji was in Momoyama, a part of Kyoto far from the *kindairi* but with long associations with the imperial family, whereas Taisho and Showa would be laid to rest in Hachioji, outside Tokyo.

A torrent of publicity relating to the emperor was released in the ten days of his last illness, and the forty-five days of mourning which then followed. A Japanese journalist noted that 'until then court life had been utterly above the clouds, the people given no opportunity to know of it . . . this time they broke with age-old custom and published daily bulletins on His Majesty's condition'. The press published every possible detail of the funeral rites, and extra illustrated supplements related incidents going back to the beginning of the reign. This was really the beginning of photographic journalism in Japan.

Appropriate ceremonies were prescribed for even the smallest villages: the *bon* festival, the major annual event in Buddhist ancestor worship, was to take place two weeks after the emperor died, and the normal drums, dancing and athletic competitions were forbidden. A month later, on the day of the funeral, *yōhaishiki* or 'ceremonies from afar' were held all over the country, presided over by local notables, and complete with representatives from the village assemblies, local associations, schools and the police: these were but the climax to a whole series of local memorial services which had begun immediately after the death, and followed detailed instructions given by both the central government and the prefectures.

At the time of the Emperor Meiji's death, Prince Hirohito, who then became next in line to the throne after his father, the new Emperor Taisho, still attended the Gakushuin. Little is recorded of how the young prince reacted to the change in his status, but the death of his grandfather was to be followed by a quite unexpected event, which must have been traumatic. On the evening before the funeral, he was summoned into the presence of General Nogi. For three hours he sat cross-legged on the floor, while the general examined him first on his day's calligraphy lesson, then going on to cover other parts of his studies.

The general ended the examination with the words, 'I am not dissatisfied with your progress . . . Please remember that my physical presence is not necessary for me to be with you in your work. I shall always be watching and your welfare will always be my concern. Work hard, for your own sake and the sake of Japan.' General Nogi returned to his house where his wife was waiting for him. As a rite of purification they bathed together, and then donned ceremonial kimonos. In the *tokonoma*, the corner reserved in every Japanese home for the household shrine, a picture of the Meiji Emperor had been placed. After he had accepted a cup of sake from his wife, the general, as the two had agreed beforehand, killed her with his ceremonial dagger and then, following the prescribed ritual, himself committed *seppuku*.

The Prince Hirohito betrayed no emotion on hearing of the death of the general and his wife. Had he not taken part, every morning at the Gakushuin, in a ritual in which, after the recital of the Rescript on Education, General Nogi rehearsed the following litany with his young charges:

'What is your dearest ambition?'
'To die for the emperor.'

The message implicit in General Nogi's suicide was disastrous for the future of the imperial institution. *Seppuku* is the ultimate act of loyalty of a *samurai* to his master. General Nogi, like it or not, had imposed the *samurai* ethic of *bushidō* upon the Chrysanthemum Throne. He had made himself the exemplar in years to come of all those who would die for the emperor. Some fifty years later, in the final year of the Pacific War, the *kamikaze* pilots, in their suicidal attacks on allied warships, were following in the same tradition. The emperor was not only *tennō*; he had come to be presented as Shogun, a role without any historical justification. General Nogi, if he had but known it, was not following tradition, but defying it. As early as 1663 the Tokugawa Shogunate had outlawed, as antiquated, *junshi*, the feudal custom of following one's lord into death. This had in any case never been followed out of loyalty to the emperor, who had about as much to do with *bushidō* as the Archbishop of Canterbury with fox-hunting. The Prince Hirohito must have realized the enormity of the general's act almost from the moment he heard the news. And even if it can be said of General Nogi that he practised what he himself had preached, his suicide must be judged as one of the most disastrous single actions in the modern history of Japan.

Whatever the reactions of Hirohito may have been (and it is clear that he kept them to himself), the manner of Nogi's death stirred up the whole country. Within days the press gave far more space to the rights and wrongs of Nogi's suicide than they had to the recently deceased emperor. (The pattern was to repeat itself on the death of the Showa Emperor when the press, even before the funeral, was completely obsessed with the Recruit Cosmos scandal, which in the end led to the fall of the Prime Minister, Takeshita.) The wisest commentators did their best to sit on the fence, as witness the following editorial from the *Tokyo Asahi Shimbun* of 15 September 1912:

> General Nogi's death marked the completion of Japan's *bushidō* of old. And while emotionally we express the greatest respect, rationally we regret we cannot approve. One can only hope that this act will not long blight the future of our national morality. We can appreciate the General's intention; we must not learn from his behaviour.

If, with the death of Meiji, Japan had been united in its reverence for the emperor, with that of Nogi, forty-five days later, it became hopelessly divided in its interpretation of the role of the imperial institution. Before the end of the year this divisiveness had become manifest in riots in Tokyo, in reaction to a government crisis which was born out of a fundamental conflict between the military and the civil rulers of the country.

Prince Saionji, who headed the government at the time of Meiji's death, was a Prime Minister in the tradition of the Marquis Ito. The military, who were represented in the government by General Uehara, the Minister for War, pressed for two extra divisions to strengthen the Japanese position in Korea. Saionji, supported by the entire cabinet except for Uehara, refused this request. Uehara resigned, and since no serving officer would replace him (as the rule established by Yamagata in 1895 required), the government fell.

The new emperor (who had no other choice) asked the Prince

Katsura (who as an army man from Chōshū was allied with Yamagata) to form a government. Katsura, taking into account the obviously weak character of the Taisho Emperor, saw himself as a new Shogun, and to establish his own autocratic rule betrayed Yamagata by temporizing on the army's demands, at the same time agreeing a vast expansion of the navy. (This was inexcusable since the navy was always the concern of Satsuma, the traditional rival to Chōshū.) Not only Yamagata but also the Diet and the press were furious, and the situation was only made worse when Katsura prorogued the Diet. It was then that the rioting started on the streets of Tokyo.

Saionji and Yamagata joined forces, and Katsura was forced to reconvene the Diet, which immediately debated a motion of 'no confidence' in the government. This provided the occasion for an opposition leader, Yukio Ozaki, to ask who was responsible for advising the emperor to make the *mistake* of summoning Katsura to form a government. Such *lèse-majesté* led to immediate uproar among the government supporters, but Ozaki made his position quite clear with the following words:

> There are people who always mouth 'loyalty' and 'patriotism' and who advertise themselves as the sole repositories of these qualities, but what they actually do is hide themselves behind the throne and fire at their political enemies from this secure ambush. The throne is their ambush. Imperial Rescripts are their bullets.

Astonishingly, perhaps, Ozaki survived his reckless outburst, which indeed provoked a rejoinder stating, quite clearly, the defensive position taken by Katsura and his supporters:

> Our Constitution definitely states that the Emperor is divine and superhuman, and the fact of his sanctity cannot of its nature depend on the responsibility of Ministers of State . . . If such imprudent words and immoral actions be left unquestioned, the country will be shaken to its foundations. We appeal with tears to all patriotic hearts and hope they will make earnest efforts for the sake of the country.

Katsura died at the end of the year, completely discredited. Saionji and Yamagata, maintaining their alliance, accepted that no government could rule without the goodwill of the Diet and the press, and the Marquis Okuma, a sort of grand old man of Japanese politics, became Prime Minister. This was the beginning of the era of the so-called 'Taisho Democracy', which could have been a golden age for modern Japan. The good times just about lasted into the Showa era, but then – as I shall show in Chapter 7 – the whole edifice proved to be built on sand.

The enthronement ceremony, known as *daijōsai* (which I describe in full in Chapter 6), was the essential final stage in establishing Taisho as emperor of Japan. The ceremony, which always takes place in Kyoto, requires considerable advance preparation, and the fact that there were still mortuary rites to be performed for the Meiji Emperor made certain that it would not take place in 1913. Then, in April 1914, the Dowager Empress Haruko (widow of Meiji but not the mother of Taisho) died, and the *daijōsai* was postponed, once again, until November 1915.

In the autumn of 1914, Japan entered the First World War as one of the allied powers, and soon defeated a weak German garrison on the Chinese mainland, and occupied Tsingtao. The Taisho Emperor then enjoyed a few months of, for him, exceptional emotional stability, during which he saw more of his oldest son than he had at any other time in his life. At the same time the Empress Sadako, who for nearly ten years had hardly had any contact with her husband, became once more with child. Prince Mikasa (who is now the only survivor of Taisho's four sons) was born in the autumn of 1915. This meant that the empress was unable to take part in the *daijōsai*, which finally began on 10 November. Thereafter the emperor, perhaps exhausted by all the ceremonial (which is extremely demanding), lost his new-found composure and gradually retired from public life. When he came to the Diet to make a farewell speech, he rolled up the paper containing the text, and used it as a telescope to survey the members seated below his throne. For the public this was the final stage in the process of degradation. Taisho retired to a palace on the secluded beach of Hayama, on the coast south of Tokyo, where the Empress Sadako looked after him for the remaining eleven years of his life.

In the meantime Hirohito continued his education in the Takanawa Palace, to which his household had been moved in April 1914. The education was supervised by a special department, the *tōgū-gogakumonsho*, headed by Admiral Togo, who even more than General

Nogi was a hero of the war against Russia. Now that Hirohito was growing up, the regime became even more demanding. The daily grind was mitigated by the presence of two figures in the life of the prince. The first of these was Saionji, who had been asked by Togo to try to overcome the prince's scepticism about his descent from the sun-goddess. Once the prince and Saionji were together, the latter proved to share the former's scepticism, but insisted that the prince should never try to disillusion his subjects on the matter of his divine descent. The loyalty of the Japanese people depended upon their accepting it.

The second important figure was Dr Hirotaro Hattori, the prince's tutor in natural history. Saionji had discovered that this was the subject which most interested the prince, and he arranged for more time to be given to it, and less to the official version of Japanese history. This change of direction allowed the prince, accompanied by Hattori, to spend hours collecting specimens in the hills behind the imperial estates at Hayama, Nikko and Karuizawa. Finally, on the occasion of his weekly visits to his parents at Hayama, the prince went to sea in a small boat and, helped by two pearl-divers from Toba, searched for marine specimens in Sagami Bay. Once back in Tokyo, he worked on the specimens collected in a small laboratory which he and Hattori had set up in the Takanawa Palace. This was the beginning of a lifelong interest, which would lead Hirohito to become a recognized expert in the field of marine biology.

In November 1916, when he was fifteen and a half years old, Hirohito was installed as Crown Prince. This was the official recognition that he was the direct heir to the Chrysanthemum Throne. Henceforth he would no longer be Hirohito, but *tōgū* or *kōtaishi*, just as his father was *tennō*, or his mother, *kōgō*. The die had been cast for the part he would play in the imperial drama. And for this part he would need, sooner rather than later, a wife.

Prince Yamagata, still active behind the scenes, had taken it for granted that a wife would be found from the Chōshū nobility, to which he himself belonged. The empress, who had always resented the way Yamagata had treated her disturbed husband, had other ideas, and in this she was supported by Professor Sugiura, who taught the Crown Prince ethics, and Count Makino, the Lord Privy Seal. The latter, a member of the Satsuma nobility, was related to Prince Kuniyoshi Kuni, whose daughter, the Princess Nagako, won the imperial favour.

To Yamagata's fury, the Crown Prince's engagement to her was announced on 4 February 1918.

For nearly two years it appeared as if the engagement had been accepted by all. Then, in 1920, Yamagata's family physician, Dr Hirai, discovered an article in a medical journal, written by a specialist in heredity, and dealing with colour blindness in the Shimazu family, to which Princess Nagako's mother belonged. Yamagata, on being shown the article, immediately consulted another Chōshū noble, Baron Nakamura, who happened to be head of the *kunaishō*, and the Prime Minister Takasha Hara. To these two men Yamagata proposed a direct appeal to Prince Kuniyoshi's patriotism, so that he would then consent to the engagement being broken off.

Prince Kuniyoshi would hear nothing of this plan, and when the two Chōshū nobles assured him that his financial interests would not be forgotten, his Satsuma pride was doubly insulted. In this he was supported by the ethics professor, Sugiura, who resigned his position at the Gakushuin in December 1920, and let all his old pupils know why he had done so.

Support for Sugiura was immediate, and included Mitsuru Toyama who, at one and the same time, was a fervent patriot and organizer of the Kokuryūkai, Japan's most powerful and effective secret society. Yamagata, who was not only intriguing against the Crown Prince's engagement but was also planning a long foreign tour for him (to get him out of the way), was seen by Toyama as a sworn enemy. On 11 February 1921 (or *kigensetsu*, the public holiday celebrating the birthday of the mythical first emperor, Jimmu) Toyama had his henchmen distribute pamphlets among the crowds on the streets of Tokyo asking for their blessing on the Crown Prince's betrothal, and decrying those who opposed it. At the same time students rushed though the crowds shouting, 'Death to Yamagata' and 'Nakamura insults the emperor.'

Hara, the Prime Minister, reacted immediately and summoned Nakamura to discuss the action to be taken to avert the danger confronting them. The result was that Nakamura sought an immediate audience with the emperor, and laid the case of the Princess Nagako's possible colour blindness before him. The emperor was unmoved, and dismissed Nakamura with the words, 'I hear that even science is fallible.'

Hara and Yamagata knew that their cause was now hopeless, and feared for their own lives – rightly as it proved to be for Hara, who was assassinated before the year was out. Nakamura resigned from being minister in charge of the *kunaishō* 'because of his apprehensions over mistaken manifestations of public indignation towards him'. From the Imperial Palace came official confirmation of the engagement between the Crown Prince and the Princess Nagako. Both the *New York Times* and *The Times* of London gave public opinion the credit for foiling Prince Yamagata's plot. Taisho Democracy had triumphed once again.

Throughout the whole chain of events the Crown Prince was allowed no contact with the Princess Nagako, who was scarcely even informed of what was happening. She was in fact not colour blind (a matter which no one had thought worth investigating), and had from early childhood been a keen painter. In the favourable atmosphere following the official confirmation of the engagement, Yamagata had his way, and the Crown Prince left on his world tour a week earlier than planned (no doubt much to the disgust of Toyama).

Before following the Crown Prince half-way round the world, it is worth a little time to consider why the choice of a wife for him caused such an uproar. Although his marriage to the Princess Nagako, which was to last for well over sixty years, would prove to be a model of faithfulness and devotion (particularly by the standards of the Japanese court), the years which preceded it were no Hollywood romance. In seven years the prince and the princess saw each other only nine times, and outside these contacts there was little communication between them.

The lesson to be learnt is that those who rule Japan simply cannot leave the court alone, and feel almost compelled to involve the court in their own internal struggles. Considering that some fifty years had elapsed from the time of the Meiji restoration when the choice of a wife for Meiji's grandson became an issue, it is remarkable that there had been little change in the political line-up of the early Meiji era. The oligarchy was still dominated by descendants of *samurai* from Chōshū and Satsuma, but the two groups were now antagonistic. One can recall how, in the crisis of the first year of the Taisho Emperor, support for the army's interests came from Chōshū, and for the navy's, from Satsuma. Now, in the politics surrounding the Crown Prince's betrothal, it was the Chōshū faction which tried to force the emperor's hand, so its defeat must be seen as a victory for Satsuma. In all this, little regard was paid to the wishes of the court: indeed the emperor was commonly referred to as *dōgu*, literally 'a tool'. True, in this case the court got its way in the end, but then consider how hard it had to work to achieve this result. The young Crown Prince, as the Showa Emperor, would discover only too soon that, on a matter of real political substance, the will of the court, however expressed, counted for next to nothing.

The prince's grand tour, in 1921, was the most enjoyable period of his life: the happiest time was spent in England, where the king, George V, put him completely at ease. Although the Crown Prince was too shy ever to try and speak English, he was a welcome guest. After visiting both England and Scotland (where he was delighted by the way the Duke of Atholl had received him at Blair Castle), the Crown Prince went on to Holland, France and Italy. In the whole European tour he had been received by eight Heads of State and visited the Pope, Benedict XV. What he most valued was the chance to participate in the normal life of the people: he dined out in restaurants, travelled on the Paris Métro (where, in buying his ticket, he used money for the first time in his life), and danced in night clubs. Invited to a lunch given by the Secretary of State for Foreign Affairs at Carlton House Terrace, the Crown Prince even found Lord Curzon – probably the most frigid character in recent British history – an 'amiable and affable host'. Considering how spontaneously the prince reacted to even the most formal parts of his programme, one gets some idea of how appallingly constricted his life, back home in Japan, must have been.

When the Crown Prince returned to Japan, both the country and the court were in a state of crisis. The economic boom following the First World War was over. Unemployment was increasing, and the unions, steadily gaining recruits, often clashed with the police. Taisho Democracy was too feeble to bring about reforms which would have allowed strikes and union meetings. It also lacked the will to reduce the appalling burden of military expenditure, which reduced many farming communities almost to destitution. Only the Black Dragons of the *kokuryūkai*, still led by Toyama, could stimulate any popular response to the reactionary policies of the government. A secret society which condemned the 'modernism' of the world of entertainment in the West, at the same time encouraging the hatred of all foreigners, the aggrandizement of Japan and the worship of the divine emperor, could hardly expect much sympathy from the Crown Prince who, in the judgement of Prince Saionji, had returned from Europe 'filled with dangerous delusions of liberalism'.

The crisis in the court affected the Crown Prince more directly than that in the government. The emperor was so disturbed, mentally, that he could no longer perform the duties of his office. His health was steadily deteriorating, even though he was barely forty years old. At the end of the year, the Crown Prince, who had already been acting for his father in carrying out official duties, was appointed Prince Regent, so becoming emperor in all but name. He was then twenty: he would be Head of State for more than sixty-seven years, carrying a burden of office without any historical parallel, and that not only in Japan.

The great tragedy of the final years of the Taisho Emperor was that the Prince Regent's two most trusted advisers, Prince Saionji and Count Makino, persuaded him not to push his popular image. In 1922 the Prince of Wales paid a return visit to Japan, and the Prince Regent accompanied him on his public appearances, smiling and waving to the crowds. The idea that the Prince Regent might actually be an ordinary man was anathema both to the armed services and to the *kokuryūkai*. The Prince Regent, against his own inclination, was persuaded by Saionji and Makino to respect the army and the *kokuryūkai*, so that when he succeeded his father, some four years later, he was to be a *dōgu* in the hands of the oligarchy. If this was so, he had lost the game before it even started.

The one bright prospect for the following year, 1923, should have been the wedding of the Prince Regent with the Princess Nagako, after an engagement which had already lasted five years. This was not to be. Nemesis once more intervened in the form of the Great Kanto Earthquake on 1 September 1923. In the sprawling working-class districts of Tokyo and Yokohama the flimsy wooden houses collapsed and caught fire, while tidal waves engulfed the towns along the coast. Destruction was on a scale hardly equalled by the American fire-bomb raids during the last year of the Pacific War.

The emperor was at that time resting in his estate in Nikko, in the mountains north of Tokyo, but the Prince Regent was in town, lunching at the Akasaka Palace. He and his guests, knowing where safety lay, calmly went outside into the palace grounds, where they survived the earthquake quite unharmed. The palace, also, was little damaged, and the same was true of the whole Imperial Precinct, and the moat and ramparts surrounding it, a mile or two away from Akasaka.

The government's reaction to the disaster was appalling. On the night which followed it, the thousands of homeless refugees who had congregated in the great Tokyo parks of Hibiya and Ueno were still mainly concerned about the danger of fire, but on the following night they became prey to a scare about raiders and looters. In their misery they found in the despised Korean population a scapegoat, and in the following days vigilante groups murdered hundreds of Koreans. The police did nothing to restore order: instead they used the occasion to arrest over a thousand socialists and labour leaders, some of whom were summarily executed.

At the same time the Prince Regent was kept confined to the Akasaka Palace, and when finally he was allowed to visit the devastated areas of Tokyo, the reception of the crowds was even more enthusiastic than it had been on his return from the European tour. Once more the popular image was gaining ground, but then nemesis was to play another card. Three months later, just before the end of the year, the Prince Regent drove in his State carriage to open a special session of the Diet. On the way, a young man, who was to give his name as Daisuke Namba, dashed out of the crowd and fired a revolver at the carriage. He missed, and was immediately carried away by the police. Although Namba was never to say a single word about his motives or any associates, the official line was that he represented a left-wing organization. Once more the policy of separating the court from the people was justified by events.

Within a month, on 26 January 1924, the wedding of the Prince Regent with the Princess Nagako at last took place, after nearly six years of waiting. To everyone's relief the Taisho Emperor was unable to attend. No foreign guests were invited to the ceremony, which was purely Japanese. Almost all the 700 guests, if not related by blood to the imperial house, came from Chōshū and Satsuma. According to the report in *The Times* of London:

Prince Kujo, Master of the Rites, performed the main ceremony, which lasted 45 minutes, concluding with the exchange of the sacred wine cup. At a quarter of 11 the first salute of 101 guns from the battery at Miyake Hill announced the completion of the ritual; it was taken up simultaneously by the warships in Shinagawa Bay and other warships and forts throughout the country. The whole nation is making holiday in the brilliant sunshine. Public entertainments are being held everywhere, while here in the capital quaint costumed processions are being carried through in a spirit of merrymaking which is entirely lifting the pall of depression and apprehension which has been a marked feature of life in Tokyo for the last four months.

The Princess Nagako wore a wonderful four-fold silk marriage kimono, her hair done in old-time looped style. The Regent, dressed in full ceremonial marriage costume, emerged carrying a sceptre and joined the Princess, who carried a Hinoki Court fan. The massive doors of the outer shrine swung back, and as the imposing gathering stood facing the approach to the inner shrine, Prince Kujo recited in a monotone the Shinto scripture messages. Then the inner shrine was opened and the bridegroom approached and paid homage to the altar, afterwards reading a report to his ancestral shades. Then the couple retired to the outer shrine, where Prince Kujo filled and handed the cup of sacred wine first to the Regent, and after he had drunk, to the bride.

The Taisho era was almost at an end. The imperial wedding was a bright period in an uncertain time. With the extended franchise introduced in 1925 the future of democracy in Japan was not unpromising. The House of Representatives, however much its members represented the different interests of the people at large, still lacked the power to enforce any policies of its own. The descendants of the old Meiji oligarchy, well represented in the House of Peers, were much more powerful, as can be seen from the members of every cabinet from this time. This power, in turn, was circumscribed by that of the armed services, who were already restless for action abroad. The government did too little to improve the structure of the economy, so that a depressed and poorly developed traditional agriculture still had to carry the burden of taxation required by excessive expenditure on armaments. In the combination of these factors, the seeds of future disaster had already been sown, and in the coming twenty years and more, not only the Showa Emperor but all his people would be reaping the harvest.

6

The making of an emperor

WHEN the Taisho Emperor died on 25 December 1926, his son, the Showa Emperor, like every *tennō* before him, faced a long and complicated ritual process before the final consummation of the succession. The process was directed to two different, but complementary, goals. The first was to establish the temporal powers of the new emperor. The second was to bestow upon him the supernatural powers of an *arahitogami*, that is the living god upon whom the welfare of the whole country ultimately depends. This, the final consummation, is the purpose of the *daijōsai*, a pure Shinto rite of great antiquity. For the Showa Emperor it is this rite which is, historically, so significant, because on New Year's Day, 1946, he disclaimed the status of *arahitogami* (in circumstances described in Chapter 9), and by doing so cast doubt upon the validity of the whole ceremony. The result, some forty-two years later, was that the Showa Emperor was to bequeath to his successor, the present Emperor Akihito, a problem of status (to which I return in Chapter 12), quite unprecedented in the history of Japan. As it relates to the *tennō*, the *daijōsai* is a rite of *transfiguration*, in which the status of the *tennō* (in its literal meaning of 'prince of heaven'), *above the clouds*, is revealed to but two or three privileged onlookers. The *daijōsai*, being the climax to the ritual process of inauguration, is described in detail at the end of this chapter, where I also suggest a number of possible interpretations. It cannot take place, however, until the rites of temporal succession have been completed, and these I describe first. In relation to all the rites, both temporal and spiritual, three interrelated points constantly recur, making the whole process seem strange and alien to any Western cultural tradition.

The first point is that almost all the rites take place in temporary purpose-built structures. To take the most striking instance, the three buildings constructed for the *daijōsai* are put together the day before the event, and dismantled the day after.

The second point (which is critically important for the *daijōsai*) is that for much of the time the new emperor, or *tennō* to be, is acting in private, sometimes completely alone, and sometimes supported by one or two ritual officials. In the language of Chapter 3, the succession of ritual events is essentially *uchi*, not *soto*. As such it reflects the whole tradition of the imperial institution as it was established in the *kindairi* in Kyoto, during the Edo period. True the ceremonies also involve considerable pageantry, which provides a magnificent public spectacle, but this is only the packaging: the contents are not essentially in the public domain.

The third point is that the *tennō* is not only the chief performer, but also the object of the main rites. To draw a parallel from early European history, Charlemagne became the first of the Holy Roman Emperors when he was crowned by Pope Leo III in the cathedral at Aachen on Christmas Day in the year 800. From this time onwards the office of emperor, as well as that of the Pope, had its own rules of succession: the temporal domain was the emperor's, the spiritual domain, the Pope's. Suppose now that the two separate offices, the two separate office-holders and the two separate domains were all to be conflated so that, at least formally, no distinction could be made between the imperial throne and the Holy See, emperor and Pope, State and Church. Then, on that historic Christmas Day, the Pope would have crowned himself Emperor, to establish a precedent of indefinite duration, and with imponderable consequences.

In much of medieval European history, the one side did encroach on the other, leading to all kinds of problems, some of which have dragged on, in limited local situations, until the present day. None the less Europe has long accepted the dichotomy, and no one questions the principle behind it. In Japan the case is quite different: every new *tennō* must accept the spiritualities as well as the temporalities of the realm. Having done so, the question he must resolve (at least if he is allowed any free choice in the matter) is what his status then is, both religious and political. In so far as the rites of initiation described in this chapter define the *tennō*'s religious status, the question is largely one of exegesis in Shinto theology, upon which the court will have its own expert advisers. In practice the political status of the emperor is determined by historical factors over which he has little control: this point, in relation to the Meiji Emperor, provided the subject matter of Chapter 4; in relation to the Showa Emperor, it provides that of Chapter 7. (Part of the problem here is that in modern times the political and religious issues have been confused by the contradictory terms of the two constitutions, of 1889 and 1947, as much as by the Showa Emperor's disclaimer of 1 January 1946: there was no real problem, however, at the time of the initiation of the Showa Emperor in the period 1926–28. The present emperor, Akihito, will be the first to be confronted by this issue: the possible consequences are considered in Chapter 12.)

The initiation of a new *tennō* takes place in three stages, known in Japanese as *sensō*, *sokui-rei* and *daijōsai*. These terms may be translated as 'accession', 'ascending the throne' and 'the great thanksgiving'. The *sensō* rites take place within the precinct of the Imperial Palace immediately after the death of the previous emperor, so that they are inevitably interlaced with the opening phases of the protracted mortuary ceremonies. They consist first of announcing the new succession before the portable shrine of the *kashikodokoro* (where the copy of the sacred mirror is kept), and then doing the same before the shrines of *kōreiden* (hall of the imperial ancestor spirits) and *shinden* (hall of the *kami*). This is followed by the ceremony of *kenjitō-shōkei no gi*, which takes place in the palace itself (and was televised on the accession of the present emperor). In the first, and ancient, part of this ceremony, the new emperor receives the sacred sword and jewel: in the second and modern part he receives the *kokuji* (State seal) and *gyoji* (imperial seal), to be used in the performance of acts of State stipulated in the constitution. The series of ceremonies comprising the *sensō* is concluded with the *sokui-chōken no gi*, the new emperor's first official audience.

Originally the *sensō* and the *sokui* were a single ceremony, but with the accession of the Emperor Tenchi (661 – 71), the steadily increasing influence of Chinese culture ensured that the two were separated. The *sokui-rei* now directly precedes the *daijōsai*, and because preparations for the latter cannot begin until the mortuary rites are completed, a period which can never be much less than two years must elapse between the *sensō* and the completion of the *sokui-rei*. The precise reason for this will become clear when the *daijōsai* is looked at in detail. For the time being it is sufficient to note that the *sokui-rei* and the *daijōsai*, if close to each other in point of time, are quite different in both form and function. Both are extremely protracted, with the different stages running parallel over a period lasting nearly a whole year. The *sokui-rei*, whose present form shows considerable Chinese influence, is focused on the *tennō*'s earthly status, whereas the *daijōsai*, which is authentically Japanese, is focused on his heavenly status, conceived of, *a fortiori*, according to the canons of Shinto.

The whole process leading up to and including the final ceremony of the *sokui*, and consisting largely of official (though not always public) announcements, processions and ritual offerings, is extended over a period of nearly a year. In the case of the Showa Emperor it began on 17 January 1928, when the emperor himself announced the dates of the whole programme before the three shrines in the Imperial Precinct in Tokyo, and sent messagers to make the same announcement before the inner shrine at Ise (the home of the sun-goddess) and the *sanryō* (or mausolea) of his four immediate predecessors, together with that of the founder of the line, the Emperor Jimmu. This was followed two days later by offerings of cloth sent to Ise and the *sanryō*.

The *sokui* (but not the *daijōsai*) required no further action until 6 November 1928, a day marking the beginning of a very crowded two-week programme, which must have left the emperor and his court quite exhausted. On this day began the imperial procession from Tokyo to Kyoto, where it was to arrive the following day. The ritual purpose of the procession was to bring back to its proper home in Kyoto the *shunkōden*, the portable shrine, or *kashikodokoro*, containing the copy of the sacred *yata* mirror (of which the original remains always in the *naigū* at Ise). This is essential for the next stage of the *sokui-rei*, which the Showa Emperor performed on 10 November 1928.

The *shunkōden*, a building made of *hinoki*, the wood of the Japanese cypress, is connected with the *gosho*, that is the old imperial palace in Kyoto. It contains three divisions: the first is the inner room which houses the *kashikodokoro*, and *a fortiori* the *yata* mirror. The second is a room for the emperor and empress, and the third, an outer space for all the dignitaries taking part. The object of the ceremony before the *kashikodokoro*, at 10 a.m., is to enable the new emperor to announce his succession to the sun-goddess, in the presence of all three sacred objects: it is achieved in the following way. The emperor, the empress, the imperial family and all the other participants assemble in the *giyōden*, a hall adjacent to the *shunkōden*, where they put on ceremonial robes; the hands of the emperor and empress are cleansed with consecrated water, and the emperor is given a *shaku*, the baton which symbolizes the office of a Shinto priest.

The actual ceremony is opened by drums and gongs being sounded three times: this is the signal for opening the screens before the *kashikodokoro*, with food offerings being placed on the altar (which is in the middle room), while the master of ceremonies reads a *norito*, or Shinto prayer – the whole being accompanied by ancient music. The party assembled in the *giyōden* then proceed to their appropriate places within the *shunkōden*, passing across the forecourt between the ranks of officials, in traditional costume and bearing various ancient weapons.

When the emperor has taken his place in the middle room of the *shunkōden*, a court chamberlain places the sacred sword and jewel on stands next to him. This is the signal for the emperor to proceed to worship at the altar and read a proclamation to the spirit of the sun-goddess, which is the formal announcement of the accession. (At the same time the accession is announced before the *kōreiden* and the *shinden*, the two fixed shrines in the Imperial Precinct in Tokyo.) This is also the only occasion when all three of the sacred regalia, or *sanshū no shinki*, are present at the same time, for whereas the sword and the jewel, being in the personal custody of the emperor, have to be transferred as part of the succession ritual, the mirror is permanently enshrined in the *kashikodokoro*.

The emperor, having worshipped before the *kashikodokoro*, is followed by the empress, the imperial family, and all the other official participants. When they have all passed by, the offerings are removed, the inner doors of the shrine are closed, and once more the gongs and drums sound three times, giving the signal for all to retire.

If the morning ceremony in the *shunkōden* announces the accession to the sun-goddess, the ceremony in the afternoon of the same day – which is the *sokui* proper – announces it to the people of Japan. This takes place in a hall, known as the *shishinden*, and built for the purpose of the ceremony from *hinoki* wood. The connotations of the name *shishinden* belong more to the old Chinese emperors than to any autochthonous Japanese tradition, although legislation from the beginning of the Meiji era tried to correct the Chinese bias of the *sokui-rei*. The *shishin*, in the Chinese tradition, were the pole-star and the stars around it, which were taken to symbolize the authority of the emperor.

The *shishinden*, therefore, is on the northern side of a court, and is entered by the emperor from the north, so that he faces south when he mounts his throne to address his people and receive their congratulations. The building is in the form of a vast pavilion, open on all sides except the north, surrounded by a balcony, and with a massive roof supported by symmetrical rows of wooden columns. The throne, or *takamikura*, also of *hinoki*, rests on three rugs and is surmounted by an octagonal canopy: this also provides the means for hanging curtains, which in the normal state hide the throne from view. To the right and left of the throne are stands for the sacred sword and jewels. Just to the east of it is the 'curtained throne', or *michōdai*, for the empress.

The *nanten* (literally 'southern court') is the area in front of the *shishinden* where the various participants in the ceremony take their place. On both the east and the west side is a covered, earthen-floored corridor, called *konrō*, which is where the invited guests take their stand under temporary awnings. Directly in front of the *shishinden* are two trees – a cherry tree (*sakura*) to the east, and an orange tree (*tachibana*) to the west of the main stairway. The former symbolizes the loyalty of the Japanese people, the latter, the home and birthplace of the traditional *ie*. A line of twelve banners extends southwards from each tree, the number being that of the months in the year. On the right side, the banner closest to the cherry tree symbolizes the sun, whereas on the left side that closest to the orange tree symbolizes the moon. The next banners on either side represent, respectively, the *yata* crow and the *reishi* kite, both sacred birds in the imperial mythology, representing, if in different contexts, the support which the emperor receives from the sun-goddess in overcoming his enemies. The last ten banners on each side represent twice over the five sacred colours, green, yellow, red, white and purple, with the set of five banners furthest from the *shishinden* being slightly smaller in size.

The most conspicuous banners in the *nanten* are the *banzai no hata*, literally 'banners of 10,000 years'. On a ground of red brocade, the Chinese characters 万歳 for 10,000 years are embroidered in gold. '*Banzai*' is the traditional Japanese exclamation for wishing success or prosperity which, in the case of the emperor, means that he, and his successors, must reign forever.

Finally, on each side of the *nanten*, in front of and parellel to the five smaller coloured banners, is a row of percussion instruments, consisting of three drums and three gongs, interspersed with five spear standards – so that in all there are twelve instruments and ten standards. (In the context of Japan, the coincidence with the ten *kan* and the twelve *shi* described in Chapter 1 can be no accident.)

When the ceremony is due to begin, all those taking part, whether as officials or mere spectators, assemble outside the Nikka gate on the east side or the Gekka gate on the west side of the courtyard overlooked by the *shishinden*. The officials, of whom there are seventy-four, wear ancient ceremonial robes, with the men carrying swords: they are the first to enter the courtyard, and when they do so, each, according to his own function, takes up a position in one of two parallel rows in front of the banners, gongs and drums.

The gongs and drums are then sounded three times. This provides the signal for the *taireishi kōtōkan*, twenty officials of high rank, to guide the guests to their places. Within the *shishinden*, the princes of the blood have places just before the throne, while the Prime Minister, the Minister of the Kunaishō (the imperial household) and the other senior officials also have places near the throne. The master of ceremonies, the vice-master and the court ritualists have their own places in the south-western part of the hall. The remaining guests, who are no more than spectators, are shown to places reserved for them in the *konrō*.

When everyone is settled a cry announces the arrival of the emperor, who ascends his throne by the northern stairs. The Minister of the Kunaishō then stands as guard of honour on the first dais, outside the curtains just to the north-west of the throne. Other officials mount guard on the floor behind the throne. The empress then follows with her own retinue, with a guard of honour behind her throne. Two chamberlains, one approaching from the east side and the other from the west, mount the emperor's dais, and draw the curtains. Two ladies of the court do the same for the empress. The emperor and the empress, seated on their thrones, are in this way revealed to the whole assembly.

The ceremony which then takes place is short and simple. The emperor stands with his *shaku* upright in his hand, while the empress follows, holding the *hiōgi*, a ceremonial fan. The Prime Minister then leaves his place within the *shishinden* to take up a position in the *nanten* between the two rows of banners. The emperor reads a rescript announcing his succession, and the Prime Minister then mounts the steps leading to the throne to read a loyal address of felicitation on behalf of the whole people of Japan.

Having done this, the Prime Minister withdraws to a position in the *nanten* between the two *banzai* banners, and in the presence of all the princes, nobility, priests, officials and foreign representatives, leads the whole company in three shouts of *Banzai* for the emperor. At precisely the same moment, throughout the country, people assembled together to welcome the new reign take up the same cheer.

The Prime Minister returns to his place in the *shishinden*, the curtains are drawn once again in front of the two thrones, and following a warning cry from the masters of ceremony, the emperor and the empress withdraw by the same route as they followed on arrival. The gongs and drums once more sound three times, to signal the end of the ceremony, which the same day will be announced by messengers before the *shinden* and the *kōreiden*, the shrines within the Imperial Precinct in Tokyo. The following day, to celebrate the completion of the *sokui*, sacred dances (*kagura*), attended by the emperor and empress, take place before the *kashikodokoro*. For the Showa Emperor this happened on 11 November 1928.

It would be reasonable to think that once the *sokui-rei* had been performed, nothing more was needed to complete the process of initiation. After all, the sun-goddess, the imperial ancestors, the court, the government and people of Japan, and, in the twentieth century, representatives of the rest of the world, are none of them left out of account. At the same time the *sanshū no shinki* – the mirror, sword and jewel – all play their appropriate symbolic role. None the less, it is the *daijōsai* (already introduced at the beginning of this chapter) – the rite which then follows – that really counts. This is one of the most curious of all known ritual procedures, not only in Japan but anywhere, and I devote the remaining part of this chapter to describing and interpreting it.

Daijōsai means literally the 'great new food festival': it is strictly speaking but a variant of the first fruits festival, or *niiname matsuri*, by which, every year on 23 November, the Japanese celebrate the rice harvest. In a normal year the emperor himself offers to the *kami* the first fruits of the harvest, and partakes of the new rice, in a special ceremony in the imperial palace. Once, however, in every reign, the *daijōsai* must be celebrated in Kyoto, in place of the *niiname matsuri*. Ideally the celebration should take place earlier rather than later in the reign of the emperor, but there have also been long periods of Japanese history during which the rite fell into abeyance. For the present emperor, Akihito, the *daijōsai* was timed to take place ten days after the *sokui-rei*, so that, clearly, on the official view, no reign is complete without it.

The *daijōsai* is essentially a first fruits ceremony, performed twice in the course of a single night in November, first in a building called the *yukiden*, and then in an adjacent and identical building called the *sukiden*. Since the preparations comprise the whole cultivation cycle for the rice used in the ceremony, they are long drawn out. They begin with the New Year in a temporary thatched structure constructed in front of the *shinden* in the Imperial Precinct. In this divination shelter, on an auspicious day or *kichijitsu* (which for the Showa Emperor was 5 February 1928, the first day after *setsubun*, the festival celebrating the end of winter), an oracle is consulted. The shelter contains a structure known as *himorogi*, which probably represents the most primitive Shinto shrine. This consists of a *sakaki*, or sacred tree hung with strips of hemp and white paper (such as one can see in almost any Shinto shrine), placed upon a special eight-legged stand.

The actual rites of divination open by summoning two ancient *kami* named Ame-no-koyane-no-mikoto and Futotama-no-mikoto to come down into the *himorogi*. Then the officiating priest (who has undergone three days of special purification rites) kindles a wood fire by rubbing together two pieces of *hinoki*. A shell, cut roughly in the form of a tortoise, is held above the flames until it cracks, and the markings on the shell (which reveal the meaning of the two *kami*) are read according to a traditional secret formula, and the interpretation written down on a piece of paper. This is placed on a box in front of the *himorogi*, which is later handed over to the chairman of the enthronement commission. He in turn informs the Prime Minister, who reports the advice of the oracle to the emperor.

What then does the information consist of? The answer is simply the names of the two prefectures where the rice is to be grown for the *daijōsai*. The principle is that the north-south axis separating the *sukiden* and the *yukiden* also divides Japan into two more or less equal halves, so that the eastern half must provide the rice for the *yukiden*, and the western half, that for the *sukiden*. The *himorogi* oracle identifies only the prefectures where the rice is to come from: the actual location of the *saiden*, or sacred rice field, within each prefecture is determined by a more rational process according to guide-lines issued by the Department of Agriculture and Forestry. In 1928 this led to the *yuki*-field being located in the village of Mikami in the Shiga prefecture, with the *suki*-field in the village of Wakiyama in the Fukuoka prefecture.

Choosing the two *saiden* is but the beginning of a long and complicated ritual process governing every stage in the cultivation, starting in April with purification of the *saiden*, and continuing through the ceremonies of breaking the ground, planting the rice in the seed-beds, then in May purifying the flow of water used for irrigation, in June transplanting the young plants to the *saiden*, in August consecrating the site of the buildings to be used for gathering the grain, in September plucking the heads of grain – or *nukiho* – until finally, in October, the new grain is presented in Kyoto. Not only is every stage in the process accompanied by purification rituals, but the marking and maintenance of boundaries is equally important.

The complex September ceremony of *nukiho* is the most important stage in the process. It is performed in specially constructed buildings on the *saijō*, a consecrated area on the west side of the *saiden*. The first of these, the *hasshinden*, or 'hall of the eight gods', faces east. Just to the north is the second building, the *inanominoya* or 'rice-fruit-house', which is a shrine without the inner sanctum containing the normal 'god-seat' or *shinza* where the enshrined *kami* is believed to reside. The reason is that it is the rice-spirit, represented by the new grain, which is the *kami* of the *inanominoya*.

In the ancient form of the ceremony of *nukiho* the first stalks were gathered by young virgins, known as *sakatsuko*, that is 'sake-child', but for the *daijōsai* of the Showa Emperor the rice was simply gathered by peasants wearing the garb of ancient times, led by the *otanushi*, or owner of the field. The actual harvest was preceded by the worship by Shinto priests of the eight gods of food in the *hasshinden*, with all the local officials, led by the imperial commissioner and the governor of the prefecture, taking part. Then, after the harvest was completed, the first fruits were placed by the *otanushi* in the *inanominoya*.

Finally, after an elaborate process of cleaning, hulling, sorting and polishing, the rice, in sacks of double white linen, is transported to Kyoto in special, six-legged, ceremonial boxes known as *karabitsu*. Once in Kyoto the *karabitsu*, after being carried by young men through the purified streets of the city, are placed in the *saiko*, a sacred storehouse within the palace precinct, where the southern section is used for rice for the *yukiden*, and the northern section for that for the *sukiden*.

In Kyoto ritual purification is an almost obsessional feature of all the preparatory ceremonies. In August the sites of the *yukiden* and *sukiden* are guarded against earthquakes by the *jichinsai*, or 'land tranquillization ceremony', and then just before the *daijōsai* proper the emperor undergoes the body-cleansing rite of *misogi*. (In medieval times he was carried by palanquin to the Kamo river, accompanied by a vast and magnificent retinue.) This is followed by the ritual purifi-cation of the imperial family, and all others participating in the *daijōsai*, which is carried out by a priest waving the *onusa*, a branch of *sakaki* hung with cut paper and linen fibre. (This closely resembles the wand constantly seen in ordinary Shinto ceremonies.) Originally special messengers went throughout Japan to extend this ritual to the entire population, but this practice was not followed in 1928.

Finally, on the day before the *daijōsai* proper, the rites of purification and consecration are directed not only to the *daijōgū*, the shrine comprising the *yukiden* and *sukiden* and all the other buildings involved in the ceremony, but also to the gates in the brush-wood fence surrounding the enclosure. The building ceremony is known as *densai*, the gate ceremony as *monsai*.

All this is merely the preparation for the *chinkonsai*, a most remark-able ceremony which takes place the night immediately before the *daijōsai*. The ceremony also precedes the *niiname* in an ordinary year, in which case it takes place in the *ryōkiden*, a special shrine in the Imperial Precinct in Tokyo. Its object, in any case, is to ensure that all the different 'spirits' of the emperor remain within his body during the whole of the *daijōsai*. For this purpose two *himorogi* are set up in the *kairyūden*, one as the dwelling place of the eight *kami* enshrined in the *shinden* in Tokyo, and the other for a *kami* known as *onaobinokami*, whose name, in Japanese, defines his role of correcting all wrongs. After these nine *kami* have been summoned to take up residence, eight treasures, making up a heterogeneous collection of ancient weapons, bells and bales of cloth, are placed in front of the *himorogi*: to these are added offerings of sake, rice cakes known as *mochi*, fish, seaweed and vegetables.

The next step is to place two willow wood boxes on tables set before the *himorogi*. One of these contains clothes for the emperor, while the other contains the *mitamanowo*, a sacred rope of white silk representing the life of the emperor. The chief priest then claps his hands thirty-two times, in four bursts of eight. A priestess, holding bells in one hand and a vine-draped spear in the other, then performs a dance on an object resembling an up-turned coracle. (This object is the *ukefune*, and *fune* is the Japanese for boat.) As she dances she strikes the *ukefune* with her spear ten times, counting up to ten as she does so, and as each number is spoken the chief priest ties a knot in the *mitamanowo*. He then takes the box containing the emperor's clothes, and shakes it ten times before the *himorogi*. The two boxes are then carried out, to be replaced by two similar boxes, so that the whole process can be repeated for the empress.

This ritual goes back to the mythical origins of Japan. The dance on the *ukefune* is that performed for the sun-goddess, Amaterasu Omikami, when she had locked herself up in the cave in Takachiho, so depriving the world of light. The knots in the rope ensure that no part of the emperor's spirit can wander away from his body; signifi- cantly, a similar rope is now tied across the entrance to the sun- goddess's cave, to prevent her ever returning there. The treasures are primitive devices for protecting and restoring life, for it is the renewal of life, with the first fruits of the new harvest, that provides the whole rationale of the *daijōsai*, or, in a normal year, of the *niiname*.

According to tradition, the *daijōsai* takes place within the confines of the *nanten* – where, by this time, all the structures needed for the *sokui-rei* will have been dismantled. In terms of drama, the final act of the initiation ceremonies takes place on the same stage, but with quite different scenery. For the *daijōsai* this consists of two identical small buildings, the *yukiden* and *sukiden*, reproducing in form and size the most primitive Japanese dwelling, and providing – in an inner room – the actual site for the essential ritual. These two buildings are in a small enclosure, surrounded by a brush-wood fence: a third building, the *kairyūden*, where the emperor makes his ritual preparations, is outside and immediately to the north of the enclosure. In general orientation, therefore, the *sukiden* and *yukiden* correspond to the *konrō*, and the *kairyūden* to the *shishinden*, at the time of the *sokui-rei*. The structures, however, are not only quite unlike in appearance, but have quite different functions. The whole complex, known as the *daijōgū*, is built immediately before the *daijōsai*, and dismantled immediately afterwards.

The ceremonies open at 6 p.m. when the guards of honour, in ceremonial costume, take their places at the four gates of the inner enclosure, one on each side. The official guests are then shown to their places in special buildings outside and just to the south of the enclosure, from which vantage point they will be able to see next to nothing of ceremonies which will continue until shortly before day-break. Following this the *shinza*, or 'god-seats', are placed within the *yukiden* and *sukiden*. The lights are lit, as are the watch-fires at the four gates to the enclosure. The stage is now set for the arrival of the emperor.

The emperor begins by purifying himself in the *miyu no fune*, or 'hot-bath-boat', which he enters wearing the *ama no hagoromo*, or 'heavenly feather robe' – in fact a simple hemp garment. He then puts on the ceremonial robes of pure white silk, and after a final hand-cleansing rite, he receives his royal baton and is ready, as high-priest of the nation, to enter into communion with the great *kami* of the food ritual. The empress then arrives, and after somewhat simpler rites of purification she is given a *hiōgi*, or fan. These ceremonies take place in the *kairyūden*.

The next stage is the rice-pounding, or *inatsuki*, ceremony, which is now purely symbolic, since the rice is actually prepared at the site of the harvest. Maidens still re-enact the old ceremony in mime, and it is accompanied by the traditional song, the *inatsuki uta*. In the modern era food offerings from every prefecture are placed within special shelters just to the south of the *yukiden*.

The chief priest, accompanied by two torch-bearers, then enters the outer room of the *yukiden*, and reads a *norito* or Shinto prayer. This is the signal for the procession of the emperor from the *kairyūden* to the *yukiden* to begin. The procession is led by the Minister of the Kunaishō and the master of ceremonies, walking on either side of the central corridor, between the *yukiden* and the *sukiden*; the corridor is reserved exclusively for the emperor, who walks 'between heaven and earth'. He is barefooted, and as he proceeds a rush-mat is unrolled before, and rolled up after him. Over his head is a great umbrella, called the *kangai*. In this way neither the ground below, nor the air above is exposed to the sacred person of the emperor, for otherwise his sacred virtue would be drained off.

The procession, in which the emperor is followed by the princes, the Prime Minister and other dignitaries, moves southwards from the *kairyūden*, then turns to the east, and then north, to face the southern steps of the *yukiden*, where the chief priest and his attendants wait with torches. The sword and jewel of the imperial regalia are carried into the outer room to be placed on special tables. The emperor and his retinue then follow. The procession is repeated by the empress and her retinue, but their destination is not the *yukiden*, but the *chōden*, a small waiting-room just outside it. A group of court musicians sings the *kuzu* song, which is supposed to date from the time of the first emperor, Jimmu, to be followed by another group singing songs of the *yuki* district (which in the case of the Showa Emperor was the Shiga village of Mikami). Once the music is over, the empress and her retinue return to the *kairyūden*, and the princes withdraw to the veranda of the *yukiden*.

The scene is now set for the procession of the sacred food offerings. This is made up of a varied group of ritual players, both male and female, carrying torches and ceremonial wands, washing and eating utensils, boxes of food, tables for soup, sake, boiled rice and millet, and finally a special table for the emperor's own food, or *onaorai*. When the procession arrives in front of the *yukiden*, the priest bearing the *kezuriki*, a three-foot long *hinoki* wand used in ancient times for casting out evil, gives a cry of warning. Then, to the accompaniment of sacred music, the emperor passes into the inner, northern room, and the princes, the grand chamberlain and the chief priest into the outer, southern room of the *yukiden*.

In the inner room the emperor passes to the west and north of the *shinza*, and seats himself on a mat on the east side, facing south-east in the direction of Ise, the home of the sun-goddess. Maid-servants, or *haizen*, then perform the hand-cleansing rites for the emperor, which are the final purification in the ritual sequence. The washing utensils are removed, and the emperor is then ready for the ritual food oblation and sacramental communion with the *kami*, who is enshrined in the rice presented from the *yuki*-field.

For this the food mats of both the emperor and the *kami* are brought in, followed by the boxes containing food for the emperor: these are then arranged by a *haizen* near the emperor's mat, so that they also are oriented towards Ise. Following this the *miki*, or sacred black and white sake, is presented to the emperor: two portions of white sake, followed by two of black are then offered up on the *kami* mat. This is followed by the offering of the *okayu*, or boiled rice and millet. At the end of all the offerings, the emperor claps his hands three times, and pronounces a prayer, or *gokōmon*, to the *kami*.

The ceremony ends with the emperor's communion meal. For this he partakes three times of the boiled rice, and three times of the millet, then receives from the *haizen* the sacred sake. He drinks four times of the white and four times of the black sake. All the remaining utensils and offerings are then removed, and the emperor withdraws to the *kairyūden*, reversing, for the recessional, the order of the procession in which he arrived. The time is nearly midnight, and the ritual of the *yukiden* has lasted for nearly four hours. In the whole time the ritual action takes place in the presence only of the occasional serving maid, or priest, who, one may be assured, keep their eyes fixed firmly on the ground. There are no other witnesses.

At midnight, after a respite of some two hours spent in the *kairyūden*, the emperor, and all the other persons involved, repeat the whole process in the *sukiden*.

What does it all mean? In the first place the *daijōsai*, and the rites preparatory to it, are directed to safeguarding the growth and fertility of crops. This explains the obsession with purification, which is designed to produce a harvest free of ceremonial defilement. The rice-spirit must be handed on not only through every stage of the cycle of cultivation, but from one cycle to the next. The first fruits are the key element in this process, for they are either offered to the *kami*, or used as seeds for new planting. In the *daijōsai*, however, they are both presented to the *kami* and eaten by the emperor: both the food and its consumer have been ritually purified. In bringing the two together the emperor becomes the repository of the rice-*kami*. He is no longer an ordinary man, but a supernatural being, whose person embraces the entire welfare of the people, and has the power to represent them before all the *kami*. The transfer of the rice-*kami* to the person of the emperor is essentially the climax to a ritual process intended to promote fertility, in which the emperor symbolically becomes one with his mythical ancestress, the sun-goddess, Amaterasu Omikami.

The fascination inherent in the *daijōsai* follows from the fact that it goes back to the time when the heavenly *kami* had yet to recognize the existence of the land which was to become Japan. The sun-goddess, Amaterasu Omikami, was herself celebrating the *daijōsai* when her brother, the god of thunder, so rudely interrupted her that she shut herself up in the cave in Takachiho to deprive the world of sunlight. According to one ancient record, when she had been enticed out of the cave, the *kami* led her to a new palace, which they had specially constructed for her.

It is also significant that the *shinza* at the centre of the inner room of the *yukiden* and *sukiden* is actually in the form of a bed, complete with pillow and blanket. The *hagoromo*, or feather robe, which the emperor puts on immediately after his ritual bath in the *Kairyūden*, is in Japanese mythology the garment worn by the heavenly maidens who serve the moon-*kami*. The emperor, by taking this garment for himself, assumes his divine status, at the same time reducing the moon maidens to earth-bound mortals who then, in the form of the *haizen*, serve him throughout the ritual. The implications for procreation, and the renewal of life, are too obvious to need further elaboration. The case for the association of the *daijōsai* with the moon is supported by the fact that the day prescribed for it is the second day of the hare (which is one of the twelve *shi* of the Chinese zodiac described in Chapter 1) in the month of November, and the hare is traditionally associated with the moon.

Why then must the whole ritual process be carried out twice? Anthropologically, there are a number of possible answers to this question. If the argument for the place of the moon is accepted, then not only does this explain why the rituals take place at night, but it provides also, in the cycle of the phases of the moon, a reason for repeating the ceremony. In this context the pronounced black and white symbolism, to be found in the lights used in the ceremony, or in the sake offered on the *kami* mat, also makes sense. Another possible explanation is that the *sukiden* represents the old, and the *yukiden*, the new emperor. In the first stage of the *daijōsai*, the ritual closes the chapter of the old emperor; in the second it opens the chapter of the new emperor. The continuous emphasis on purification fits in well with a culture in which death is seen as highly polluting. This also explains why the *yukiden* and the *sukiden* are dismantled immediately after the ceremony, but why is this true also of almost all the other buildings involved in the mortuary and succession rituals of the Chrysanthemum Throne? (The destruction and rebuilding of the *naigū* at Ise on a twenty-year cycle shows that this practice is symbolically important in other contexts.)

With the *daijōsai* the initiation of a new emperor reaches its climax in a ceremony embracing different aspects of Shinto ritual, of which the most significant are recorded in the oldest known records. On the face of it, this ceremony is a convincing proof of the importance, if not of the emperor as a person, then at least of the symbolism of his office, for the people of Japan. Once the ceremony is over, the days following are devoted first to its celebration in three great banquets, held in Kyoto, and then to visits by the emperor to the mausolea of the first emperor, Jimmu, and of his four immediate predecessors. Only then may the emperor return to Tokyo, to restore the *kashikodokoro* to its proper home in the palace precinct, which is celebated by a ceremony of sacred dances. Finally, with short services before the *kōreiden* and the *shinden*, the whole series of initiation rites comes to an end.

For the Showa Emperor this happened on 30 November 1928. He was to reign, thereafter, for more than sixty years. Whether, and to what extent, the rites described in this chapter will be performed for his son and successor, Akihito, is an open question (which I return to in Chapter 12). In any case practically none of those involved in this question will have played any role at all in the initiation of the Showa Emperor. The only exception is his youngest brother, the Prince Mikasa, who is still alive and well, but it is doubtful whether he will have much say in the ceremonies to be performed for his nephew, the Emperor Akihito. The next five chapters of this book will be concerned with the events surrounding the life of the Showa Emperor in the period of sixty years ending with his death on 7 January 1989. The changes wrought by these events, both in and outside Japan, are so fundamental that they make it uncertain whether the rites to be performed for the accession of the new emperor, whatever they may be, can have the same meaning as those described in this chapter, and relating to the accession of the Showa Emperor in the last months of 1928.

7

The Showa restoration

THE Showa Emperor succeeded his father Taisho in December 1926: almost exactly fifteen years later, in December 1941, the Pacific War began with the Japanese attack on Pearl Harbor. These fifteen years were a period of mounting violence and bloodshed, provoked by various militant groups, with uncertain popular support. The government was more often the creature than the master of circumstance. Assassination was the order of the day. Hardly one of the succession of Prime Ministers had any effective control of policy, particularly as it related to the armed forces. Nothing prevented junior officers from taking the law into their own hands and, so doing, masterminding events designed to change the course of government policy. Every such change – and there were many – led only in one direction: war on an ever-increasing scale. The end was, as we all know, Armageddon.

Even today, popular thinking about the Second World War focuses upon the great national leaders: Roosevelt, Churchill, Stalin, Chiang Kai-shek, lined up against Hitler, Mussolini, and someone from Japan. But who? Who can remember, now, precisely when it was that Japan signed the tripartite pact with Germany and Italy, to become the third of the axis powers? It was actually on 27 September 1940, a moment when Britain and the Commonwealth stood alone in the fight against Nazi Germany and Fascist Italy. And who, today, remembers the name of Prince Konoye, who was then Prime Minister of Japan? His record, at least until that time, hardly makes him a very likely war criminal, although he would have been tried as such after the war if he had not committed suicide at the last moment. Indeed, in October 1941, Konoye, ostensibly because he was working too hard for peace, was pushed out of office by the Minister of War, General Tojo, who then became his successor, and launched the attack on Pearl Harbor two months later. Tojo was executed as a war criminal, but he was hardly to be compared, politically, with any of the other great war leaders, on either side. A colourless but diligent career officer, he did no more than take over the ship of state when it was already set upon a collision course. A year or two earlier, when Hitler or Stalin had already long dominated the world's headlines, one would have had to have searched very far indeed, outside Japan, to find any mention of Tojo. If anything Japanese politics, internationally, were dominated at that time by the Foreign Minister, Matsuoka.

Two apparently contradictory statements made by Tojo, standing trial in 1946 before the International Military Tribunal for the Far East, give a useful lead to understanding the role of the emperor. First, under cross-examination, Tojo, comparing the role of the emperor to that of the American President, said, 'I know that the Emperor of Japan is the highest authority in Japan.' Second, in telling how, on 2 November 1941, he had broken the news to the emperor of the government's decision to wage war against America and Britain, he said, 'I could see from the expression of His Majesty that he was suffering from a painful sense of distress arising from his peace-loving faith. When His Majesty had listened to what we had to submit, He was grave and thoughtful for some time and then with a serious air of concern He declared, "Is there no way left but to determine, against our wishes, to wage war against America and Britain in case our effort in American-Japanese talks should fail to break the deadlock?" Then He continued, "If the state of affairs is just as you have stated now, there will be no alternative but to proceed in the preparations, but I still do hope that you will further adopt every possible means to tide over the difficulties in the American-Japanese negotiations." I still remember quite vividly, even today, that we were awe-stricken with these words.'

In the end the International Military Tribunal set up by the allied powers in 1945 (which I look at more closely in Chapter 10) found, by a majority, that a 'conspiracy dating back to 1928 to initiate and wage aggressive war was by any standards clearly proven'. True the Indian judge, Radhabinod Pal, dissenting, had pointed out that the facts allowed any number of other interpretations (most of which present-day historians would prefer to the judgement of the court), but, if the judges in the majority were right, then the only person continually involved in government policy in the seventeen years from 1928 to 1945 was the emperor. The President of the Tribunal, Sir William Webb (Chief Justice of Australia), accepting the logic of this argument, named the emperor as 'Leader in Crime', and found it inappropriate to sentence lesser criminals to death while the ringleader was not even prosecuted. This argument still finds favour, as witness Edward Behr's TV programme, 'Hirohito: behind the myth', broadcast by the BBC on 24 January 1989, in the middle of the period of mourning for the Showa Emperor. The question is, what is the historical record?

This must be looked at from a number of different perspectives. To begin with one can consider the economic and political factors governing the domestic scene. As to the former, Japan's successful participation in the First World War had provided an enormous boost to its economy. In the period of Taisho Democracy, which can be taken to have lasted until about the end of the 1920s, Japan's uncertain position in the world economy made it next to impossible to consolidate the gains made as a result of the war, and in these years the Japanese economy lost rather than gained ground. The domestic market, in particular, was very poorly developed. Henry Ford's philosophy of every worker with his own car had no appeal whatever to those who directed the Japnese economy. On the contrary, Japanese industrialists were more than content to rely on a labour force working under conditions no better than those of the Lancashire cotton workers which Engels had noted in the nineteenth century.

If working conditions in industry were poor, those in agriculture were, if possible, even worse. The enormous costs of industrialization were met by taxing the multitude of near-destitute tenant farmers. The fact that heavy industry and armaments always had first claim on investment funds meant that the mass of taxpayers got little direct return for the revenue they were forced to contribute to meet government expenditure. The typical labour-intensive Japanese farm had no surplus available for investment in modern equipment. The most basic benefits of public welfare, such as old age pensions and unemployment pay, were unknown. It helped little that voting rights were extended, in 1925, to substantially the whole of the male working population.

If the life of man, in the words of Hobbes, was 'solitary, poor, nasty, brutish and short', that of the Japanese woman in this period was even more desperate. Female labour was constantly used in all kinds of farming activity, and some, such as the production of silk, depended almost entirely upon it. (However important the export of silk was for the Japanese balance of payments, there was no question of granting the vote, or any other political rights, to the millions of women involved in its production.) Moreover, whatever women contributed to the agricultural economy, they came in increasing measure to represent surplus labour, insufficiently productive to cover the costs of support by their families. Young women left the farming villages to work as sweated labour in textile mills in the great cities, far from home, and if they were not content with such work, prostitution was almost the only alternative.

Above the mass of the working classes, whether in industry (including transport and communications) or agriculture, there was a considerable and not inarticulate middle class. Of this a substantial part was employed by the government, in the bureaucracy and in education: the latter, in particular, was critical for ensuring mass literacy in a language with the unbelievably complex written form which I have described briefly in Chapter 3. Furthermore, mass education was the vehicle for mass indoctrination: the Imperial Rescript on Education was no more than the starting point for making clear to schoolchildren what their country (or, better, those who governed it) expected from them. The basis of the appeal was invariably loyalty to the emperor. Mass literacy, of course, is a two-edged weapon: this was also a period of mass-circulation newspapers, which, if generally subject to government influence, were far from being completely subservient.

The middle class also contained (as it still does today) hundreds of thousands of small businesses: small retailers and workshops proliferated, even in the smallest towns, often operating on the narrowest of margins. This sector, as much as agriculture, was labour intensive, and equally vulnerable to changes in the economic climate.

At the top of Japanese society was a comparatively small group of nobles and landowners, directors of the great industrial combines known as *zaibatsu*, top bureaucrats and the senior officers in the armed services. Many of these were noted for conspicuous consumption, and their interests in any case dominated government policy. In particular the armaments industry provided a link between the *zaibatsu* and service chiefs, which gave both sides a quite disproportionate influence inside government circles. Once again, whatever the formal power, political or economic, of the different categories mentioned in this paragraph, they never succeeded in combining to direct events according to their own interests. The most that can be said is that they succeeded in maintaining in power a succession of largely ineffective cabinets, which were only too ready to block trade union activity and left-wing politics (often with the help of the *kempeitai*, or secret police), at the same time doing little to control right-wing groups and recalcitrant factions in the army. This was not of itself a way of government which had to lead to Pearl Harbor: for this other forces, beneath the surface of events, were necessary.

Internationally the focus of Japanese politics was China, as it had been almost from the beginning of the Meiji era. At the end of 1926, when the Showa Emperor succeeded his father, the key to Japanese policy was Manchuria, the northern Chinese province bordering on Korea, and separated from the Soviet Union by the Amur river. Japan, as a result of its victory in 1905 in the war against Russia, had acquired a leased territory in the Kwantung peninsula (which controlled Manchuria's only access to the sea), together with the ownership of the South Manchurian Railway, which gave it access to the interior of the province. There were in addition nine treaty ports in Manchuria where Japan had special interests. In practice these spoils of victory were more than sufficient to make the whole of Manchuria a Japanese sphere of influence, and in 1926 there was no reason why Japan should not continue developing, for its own profit, the economic resources of the area. The presence of Japan's Kwantung army should have been more than sufficient to maintain law and order.

China, in the late 1920s, was far from united. The economic resources of the country had been open to foreign exploitation ever since the Opium War of 1842, and by the end of the First World War foreign powers had acquired, by *force majeure*, special privileges in some fifty treaty ports. In the course of the 1920s the Kuomintang, led first by Sun Yat-sen and then after his death by Chiang Kai-shek, began to establish itself, from the base of the southern capital of Nanking, as the effective government of China. The part of the country not controlled by the Kuomintang was divided up between a large number of warlords, each with his own army; one of the most powerful of these, Chang Tso-lin, was the *de facto* ruler of Manchuria.

The Japanese had worked with Chang since the time of the war with Russia (1904–5). By the middle of the 1920s Chang's continued

The building in the Imperial Precinct in Tokyo which houses the portable *kashikodokoro* shrine where the copy of the sacred *yata* mirror is kept: the original never leaves the *naigū* at Ise, the home of the sun-goddess Amaterasu Omikami.

The official portrait of the Meiji Emperor in a Western-style uniform, in the period, at the end of the nineteenth century, during which Japan became open to the outside world (see Chapter 4).

New Year poetry party at the Imperial Court, in the late nineteenth century: seated centre are the Emperor Meiji and the Empress Shōken.

The Showa Emperor and his consort, the Empress Nagako, in traditional dress for the *sokui-rei* in November 1928 (see Chapter 6).

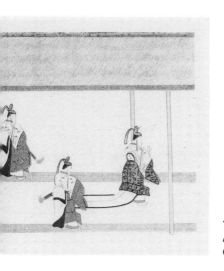

The procession of the Emperor in the *daijōsai* (described at the end of Chapter 6): from an old print.

One of the public appearances of the Showa Emperor, on his
white Lipizzaner Shirayuki (Snow White), during the Pacific
War.

The Japanese leaders accused of war crimes listening to the sentence of
the Military Tribunal on 11 December 1948 (see Chapter 9).

The only photograph of the meeting between General Douglas MacArthur and the Showa Emperor in September 1945 (see Chapter 10).

Formal portrait of the Showa Emperor in evening dress.

The informal, popular image of the Showa Emperor in the last years of his reign.

The funeral procession of the Showa Emperor in the Imperial Park of the Shinjuku Gyoen in Tokyo, as it approached the *sōjōden* for the Shinto rites described in Chapter 12.

The new Emperor, Akihito, with his wife, just after his succession in January 1989.

involvement in the struggle for power in the north of China had begun to embarrass the Japanese, and when, in the summer of 1928, he had to retire to his base in Manchuria in the face of the advancing armies of the Kuomintang, his armoured railway coach was blown up just outside the Manchurian capital, Mukden, and he lost his life. This event, which took place on 4 June 1928, was stage-managed by a certain Colonel Komoto Daisaku, serving in Japan's Kwantung army.

The way the Ministry of War handled this incident explains why the conspiracy to 'initiate and wage aggressive war', found proven by the International Military Tribunal in 1948, was taken to have originated in 1928. The first official reaction was to blame the explosion on Chinese guerillas, but so many reports came in, contradicting this version of events, that the opposition party in the Diet, the *minseitō*, was in a position to give the government party, the *seiyūkai*, a very rough ride indeed. It was at this stage that the Showa Emperor was to become involved in what was to prove to be one of the most important political actions of his entire reign.

First, however, a word must said about the background to Japanese politics in this period. The key to government was the nomination of the Prime Minister by the emperor, acting, in principle, upon the advice of his ministers – the normal position in a constitutional monarchy. In practice, because of the constant disarray in governing circles, such advice was often contradictory. This had led, in practice, to the emperor preferring the advice of the so-called *genrō*, senior statesmen and former Prime Ministers who had been prominent in the Meiji era. By the late 1920s there was only one *genrō* left, the Prince Saionji, who was born in 1849, three years before Commodore Perry's first visit to Japan and nearly twenty years before the Meiji restoration.

Saionji, who was to die in 1940 at the age of ninety-one, was, by any standards, the wisest of all Japanese statesmen in the period before the Pacific War. He was born into the family of one of the nine *seiga*, the rank in the *kuge* one below the five *go-sekke* described in Chapter 3. He was always the Showa Emperor's most trusted adviser (which is certainly a tribute to the emperor's sound judgement). His immediate (but private) reaction to the incident of 4 June 1928 was, 'I mustn't say this too loud but I suspect the army.' He was, needless to say, dead right.

Saionji did his best to persuade Tanaka, the Prime Minister and leader of the *seiyūkai* party, to bring to justice those responsible for the incident, and restore discipline in the Kwantung army, which was clearly becoming a law unto itself. Tanaka, taking advantage of the country's involvement in the preparatory rites for the *daijōsai* (described in Chapter 6), was able to temporize until the end of the year when, finally, he reported to the emperor that Colonel Komoto of the Kwantung army had planned the blowing-up of the train; Tanaka promised at the same time to take the necessary disciplinary action.

In the New Year a resolution in the Diet, calling for the disclosure of the results of an official inquiry into this incident, and proposed by the opposition *minseitō* party, was defeated by a vote of 220 to 198. This was sufficient for the Minister of War, Shirakawa, to close the books on the incident. Colonel Komoto and the general commanding the Kwantung army were removed from the active service list, and were reprimanded for failing to post the necessary railway guards on the night of the explosion.

Tanaka returned to the emperor with the army's official report on 26 June 1929, more than a year after the incident had taken place. The emperor, furious, exclaimed, 'What I have heard just now seems to be at variance with what you told me last time.' Tanaka, shocked by this reaction, could only say, 'Your Majesty will understand if I explain.' With the rejoinder, 'No need to explain,' the emperor ordered his Prime Minister to depart, leaving the report behind him. The cabinet resigned in imperial disgrace on 1 July 1929. Following the advice of Saionji, the emperor asked the *minseitō* leader, Kamaguchi, to form a government.

The Showa Emperor's confrontation with Tanaka is taken by many to be one of the very few instances, in a reign lasting more than sixty years, in which he actually took an independent political initiative. The last such instance was the decision to surrender in August 1945, which I describe in Chapter 8. Given the disastrous course of Japanese history in the seventeen-year period between these two instances, it is not surprising that many of the Showa Emperor's critics (not only outside Japan) have asked why he did not intervene more often. Certainly there were other occasions in the years leading up to the Pacific War in which the emperor (and others such as Saionji) well knew that government policy was leading the nation to disaster. Why then did the emperor so seldom take any action?

The answer to this question must be found in the *realpolitik* of pre-war Japan. The real lesson is that the Showa Emperor's intervention in June 1929 made no lasting difference, as he must soon, himself, have come to realize. True, the Tanaka government fell, but that cured nothing. As the rest of this chapter will show, junior officers went on plotting, leading to a succession of violent incidents, both at home and abroad; the service chiefs, far from having any will to curb their juniors, often secretly sympathized with them, so that in the end every such incident was accepted as a *fait accompli*, contributing in its own way to but a single line of policy, while a series of gutless cabinets in Tokyo quite failed to resist the tide of events imposed upon them by their recalcitrant, and essentially disloyal, subordinates in the armed forces.

Three factors are important in explaining the success of the belligerent policies of the armed forces. First, with a series of engagements which the Japanese invariably won, the services consistently won the public relations battle. As Japan entered the 1930s, with the unemployed being counted in millions, and the price of Japanese exports, such as silk, at little more than half the level reached in the 1920s, the chain of successes achieved by the army in China provided almost the only relief for much of the Japanese population. Second, the requirement that the two service ministers be senior serving officers gave the military the power to bring down any unacceptable government. Third, much of the real action was not in Japan at all, but in China.

The question is, were these factors alone decisive? The army continued to be popular even when the economy, in the course of the 1930s, steadily improved. The services' power to bring down the government by refusing to find officers to serve as ministers was only sparingly used, for it could well be counter-productive. And certainly when one looks at the record of such civilian politicians as Matsuoka and Konoye (which will be considered later in this chapter), one sees that the armed services were not alone in setting Japan on a course leading to war. None the less, these three factors are important in understanding not so much the true role of the emperor (whatever that may have been), but the roles which were projected upon him.

Having looked at the incident of 4 June 1928 in some detail (with particular attention to the part played by the emperor), it is still necessary to pass in review a number of comparable and equally violent incidents occurring in the following years. In November 1930, Hamaguchi, the Prime Minister nominated by the emperor to succeed the hapless Tanaka, was shot down in the main railway station of Tokyo by a member of one of the right-wing patriotic organizations: although he was to linger on for some months, he was in no state to lead the government, and was succeeded by another *minseitō* leader, Wakatsuki Reijiro.

Wakatsuki had to deal almost immediately with a *coup d'état* planned by young officers belonging to the *sakurakai* secret society to take place in March 1931, which even though foiled at the last moment, still brought down the government. Wakatsuki managed to form a second cabinet, but then in September of the same year, he had to deal with the much more serious 'Manchurian incident'.

Today this incident looks very much like a repeat of 4 June 1928. In Manchuria Chang Tso-lin had been succeeded by his son, Chang Hsueh-liang, who can hardly have been expected to like the Japanese after the way they had fixed his father. After a number of provocative acts from his side, the Japanese staged an explosion on the South Manchurian Railway north of Mukden. The explosion itself was so innocuous that a south-bound train came through only a few minutes after it had taken place.

The explosion provided the pretext for an immediate and violent reaction by the Japanese, to the point of massive overkill. The Chinese camp outside Mukden was shelled by two heavy guns, which the Japanese, conveniently, had secretly installed earlier in the month. Chang withdrew his forces, while the commander of the Kwantung army ordered all his troops into action 'in self defence': three days later, the Japanese commanding officer in Korea, without any authorization from Tokyo, sent troops to help him. Within a little over a month substantially the whole of Manchuria was under Japanese control. True to past practice, the Japanese government accepted the new state of affairs.

This was by no means the end of the matter. In November 1931, Colonel Itagaki, who had stage-managed the whole affair, went secretly to the northern Chinese treaty port of Tientsin, where Japan was one of the foreign powers allowed to maintain a garrison. At the same time Pu-yi, the last Chinese emperor, who had been forced to abdicate in 1912 when he was six years old, was living in seclusion in the Japanese quarter of the city. Soon after he arrived, Itagaki managed to throw the city into confusion by staging a gun battle between the Japanese garrison forces and the local Chinese. This made it possible to spirit

Pu-yi away by car, and the following day he arrived in Manchuria.

On 1 March 1932, Manchuria was proclaimed a republic with Pu-yi as regent. He rightly mistrusted the Kwantung army, but hoped none the less to be a true successor of his Manchu ancestors. Japan itself recognized the new state in September of the same year, and on 1 March 1934, Pu-yi was proclaimed emperor. The Japanese took care to allow him the trappings of power, and later, in May 1940, even arranged for a state visit to Tokyo, where the Showa Emperor gave him copies of the sacred sword and mirror, as symbols of imperial power. The reign of Pu-yi has become familiar to the Western world as a result of the recent film, *The Last Emperor*, which, historically, can hardly be faulted. As the film shows, the Chinese government of Manchuria under Pu-yi was completely subservient to the Japanese.

Outside Japan, no one believed the Japanese version of the Manchurian incident. The League of Nations sent out a commission of inquiry, led by Lord Lytton, a senior British statesman, which the Japanese, for diplomatic reasons, were forced to admit. The commission arrived in Tokyo on 29 February 1932, the day before the proclamation of the Manchurian Republic, which was clearly a pre-emptive move by the Japanese. The commission's report, presented on 1 October 1932, although moderate in its criticism of Japan, refused to recognize the military action taken in Mukden as self-defence, and insisted that Japan respect China's political and territorial integrity.

The League of Nations, after spending weeks in debate, finally moved to accept the substance of the Lytton commission's report, with only Japan voting against the motion. When the result of the voting was declared the Japanese delegation simply walked out. In this it was led by Yosuke Matsuoka, who was making his first appearance on the international stage: later, in the first months of 1941, Matsuoka, as Japanese Foreign Minister, would be the master-mind behind Japanese diplomacy directed to preparing the ground for the war against the allied powers.

Japan formally withdrew from the League of Nations on 27 March 1933, an example which Nazi Germany, led by Adolf Hitler, was to follow later in the year. From this point on, Japan was on its own, and it knew that it could no longer count on any support from abroad for its China policy. True, from 1940, it would have the nominal support of the two other axis powers, Germany and Italy, but then it was too late for help. By the end of 1933, the international goodwill which

Japan had gained as a result of the war with Russia nearly thirty years before had been forfeited.

In the three years following the settlement which Japan had imposed upon Manchuria two quite different incidents, both taking place in Tokyo, reveal the opposing forces then at the heart of Japanese politics, as they related to the emperor. The first incident followed the publication of a book, *Kempo Seigi*, which is best translated as 'The Correct Meaning of the Constitution'. Its author, Tatsukichi Minobe, an emeritus professor of Tokyo University, was also an independent member of the House of Peers in the Diet. Minobe contended that the emperor should be seen in terms of a theory known as '*Tennō kikansetsu*', which was little more than a Japanese version of the familiar Western idea of a constitutional monarchy. The term *kikan* is somewhat unfortunate in a Japanese context, since it connotes a mechanical system, such as that of a steam locomotive, but *kikansetsu*, far from being a neologism coined by Minobe, was a familiar and acceptable term in Japanese constitutional theory.

Minobe's book could well have appeared without attracting any hostile reaction beyond the normal critical comments of reviewers, but this was not to be. A right-wing patriot, also a member of the House of Peers, orchestrated a popular protest which effectively accused Minobe of sacrilege. The alternative doctrine propounded by the protesters was known as '*Tennō chūshinsetsu*': its appeal can be gauged by contrasting *chūshin*, meaning 'centre' or 'heart', with *kikan*. The conflict centred on a Japanese equivalent of 'the letter killeth, but the spirit giveth light', but the words of St Paul – if applied in this quite new context – could only mean that the emperor was to be regarded not as a constitutional monarch, but as a charismatic leader. This in turn identifies the imperial house with the ordinary *ie*, considered in Chapter 3, so that the whole of Japan can be seen as one big family, headed by the emperor.

The reasoned and entirely loyal defence of his book which Minobe presented in the House of Peers did not save him from the fate which his enemies wished upon him. Public opinion and patriotic fanaticism combined to ensure his downfall. Within a month of his speech, the lower house of the Diet adopted a resolution calling for the government to 'take immediate and decisive measures against those schools of thought that uphold antagonistic theory to the divine structure, matched by no other nations, of our country'. Professors who had agreed with Minobe were deprived of their chairs, sometimes as the result of patriotic student action. Minobe himself was called before the local district attorney, to be arraigned for *lèse-majesté*, and for having provoked psychological disorder in the public mind. He was forced to resign from the Diet and the sale of his books was banned.

The second incident took the ideal of *tennō chūshinsetsu* to an insane, if perhaps logical conclusion. It represented in extreme form the idea of *Showa ishin*, which provides the title of the present chapter. The spirit of unrest in the Japanese army, which had played so important a part in the succession of incidents on the Chinese mainland, in the end led a group of young officers, based in Tokyo, to attempt to overthrow the Japanese government by force. This event, which took place on 26 February 1936, was to be known as the *ni-ni-roku jiken*, that is, the '2-2-6 affair'. What lay behind it was the belief that a sort of conspiracy of elder statesmen, top bureaucrats, *zaibatsu* chiefs and senior officers was preventing the young Showa Emperor from ruling Japan in a manner which would defend it against its enemies. The manifesto which the young officers had forced upon the *Mainichi* newspaper office specifically denounced Minobe, and contained also the following words:

> Were we to remain inactive at this gravest turn of events, the godly nation of Japan would in its turn most surely be destroyed by the foreign aggressive powers, namely Russia, China, England and America.

Somehow the young officers believed that by eliminating the key conspirators they would break through to the emperor, to serve him directly and carry out his policies. *Tennō chūshinsetsu* would triumph over *tennō kikansetsu*, the *Showa ishin* would be achieved, and the emperor restored to his ancient position.

The practical realization of the plan was simple enough. Some 1,400 soldiers from the Tokyo garrisons, led by one Captain Teruzo Ando supported by other officers, marched into the centre of the city, occupied a number of strategic points, proceeding at the same time to the residences of the Prime Minister and a number of other ministers and senior officials. Of these, some were assassinated, and others left seriously wounded. According to the first reports the Prime Minister, Admiral Keisuke Okada, was among the victims, but in fact he was able to escape by means of a strategy devised by his brother-in-law, a retired colonel, who was in his house at the time: the colonel was assassinated in his place, and the following day, the Prime Minister was able to pass, undetected, through the rebel guards outside his residence. Others were less lucky: the Lord Keeper of the Privy Seal, Viscount Saito, and the Minister of Finance, Takahashi, were both killed: the Grand Chamberlain, Admiral Suzuki, although severely wounded and left for dead, recovered to become the Prime Minister who was to negotiate the surrender of Japan in 1945.

It was three days before the mutiny was finally suppressed, and its leaders placed under arrest. Needless to say they had completely misjudged the mind of the emperor, who lost no time in making clear that he regarded them as traitors and enemies of the nation – providing another important instance of independent action on his part. Captain Ando shot himself at his headquarters in the Sanno Hotel, Akasaka. The subordinate leaders were tried by a specially convened military tribunal, and death sentences were carried out on seventeen officers; each and every one of them, as he died before the firing squad, cried out, 'Long live the Emperor.'

After the execution of the sentence, the secretariat of the military tribunal released to the press a summary of the mutineers' manifesto. This made clear their devotion to the cause of *Showa ishin*, and their worship of the emperor as *arahitogami*, the living god. Furthermore, the mutineers believed that 'in coping with the critical problems, the government authorities lacked thoroughness, and domestic adminis-tration and diplomatic dealings both suffered from inactivity, the political parties, bent on pursuing partisan profit, were indifferent to the crisis of the state, the financial cliques ignored the sufferings of the nation but were devoted to swelling their own coffers . . . The [mutineers] were convinced that in order to confirm the true principle of the Empire, based on one Ruler and subjects, it was urgently necessary to put an end to this so-called privileged class and speedily reform the state.'

The mutiny, in spite of its apparent failure, had immediate reper-cussions at the top level of the Japanese government. Okada resigned as Prime Minister, to be succeeded by his Foreign Minister, Koki Hirota, who was later to be convicted and executed as a war criminal. The military leaders, belonging to an army faction known as *tōseiha*, had little difficulty in enforcing their will upon the new government.

It was for complying with their wishes that Hirota – it now seems unjustly – was tried by the Allied Military Tribunal after the end of the Pacific War. The answer which he then gave to the question as to why he had yielded to the military is illuminating:

The military are like an untamed horse left to run wild. If you try to stop it head on, you'll get kicked to death. The only hope is to jump on from the side and try to get it under control while still allowing it to have its head to a certain extent. Of course, it's a hard job to jump on without stirrups, and since you're riding bareback there's no telling when you'll get thrown off. But somebody has to do it. That's why I've jumped on.

At all events the Hirota government did not last long. In January 1937, the Minister of War, General Terauchi, resigned, after a member of the *seiyūkai* had attacked the army in the Diet for its usurpation of power. The Minister resigned when Hirota refused to dissolve the House of Representatives, and the cabinet, as was almost inevitable, fell with him. Saionji's final choice as Hirota's successor was a supposedly moderate officer, General Hayashi. His government was a failure, and in the general election held in April 1937, the two major parties in the Diet, the *seiyūkai* and *minseitō*, combined to defeat him. This was the final, feeble triumph of what had survived into the Showa era of Taisho Democracy.

The new Prime Minister, Prince Konoye, must be judged as one of the most disastrous figures in Japanese history, although when he took office he seemed to be full of promise. He was young, popular, and at the very head of the Japanese nobility. The Konoyes were the senior of the *go-sekke*, the five top *kuge* families described in Chapter 3. The Fujiwara family, of which they were a branch, had been at the centre of imperial history for nearly 1,000 years. There was every hope that Konoye would be a latter-day Saionji, but this was not to be, as Saionji himself had feared. In fact Konoye would three times form a government, and his third and final administration would last until only two months before the beginning of the Pacific War, by which time all the necessary preparations had been taken. When General Tojo finally replaced him, it was too late to turn back the tide.

Given Konoye's background it is not surprising that the emperor felt more at ease with him than he had with any of his predecessors.

When Konoye was appointed, the emperor was confident that Konoye would observe the constitution better than General Hayashi had done. Konoye betrayed this confidence from the very beginning of his period of office by trying to achieve a general amnesty for all those who had been involved not only in the *ni-ni-roku jiken*, but also in the earlier incidents of 1928, 1931 and 1933; he persisted in this policy against the opposition of Saionji, court officials and high-ranking army officers. A document submitted to the cabinet gives some idea both of Konoye's character and of the rhetoric appropriate to an issue in which the emperor himself was to be involved:

> . . . to take no effective measures risks not only another outbreak of deplorable incidents, but also the compromise of the Imperial Virtue. Our government is guided by the imperative to manifest His Majesty's Virtue to the world, and the duty of those who assist the imperial rule ultimately lies therein. The state of our nation is, furthermore, critical; it requires reform of government policy in a spirit of national unity and enhancement of national prestige overseas. It is, therefore, most urgent that we eradicate both the conflicts within the national military forces and any ideology that advocates national reconstruction through unlawful means . . . I have at last arrived at a final decision. It is no other than to ask the Emperor to proclaim a general amnesty to the offenders in rebellions and uprisings and release them completely from the responsibilities of their crimes, thus moving them deeply by the vast imperial benevolence, and letting them leave their resentment in the past. In this way we can eradicate the root of domestic conflicts.

Konoye, in advocating the amnesty, may well have judged the popular mood correctly, but the emperor was in any case unmoved. When Konoye, in spite of all the opposition, finally put his proposal before him, he rejected it.

At the height of the controversy over the amnesty, there occurred, on 7 July 1937, the most cataclysmic event in the history of Konoye's government, and that only three months after it had come to power. This was the Marco Polo Bridge incident, which happened just outside Peking, where the Japanese, along with the Western powers, had maintained a garrison ever since the time of the Boxer Rebellion in 1900. This incident, in which a Japanese unit on a night exercise became engaged in fire with Chinese soldiers, is generally reckoned to be the beginning of the long war with China, which would only come to an end with the allied defeat of Japan in August 1945.

It is not absolutely certain that a local conspiracy of Japanese officers lay behind the Marco Polo Bridge incident. What is certain is that the high command, dominated by the *tōseiha*, took it as a pretext for moving against Chiang Kai-shek in north China. Konoye, hearing that a large Chinese force was on its way, followed the army lead, and authorized the dispatch not only of military units stationed in Manchuria and Korea, but also of three divisions of the home army.

The war in China escalated very rapidly. In August the battle of Shanghai began first with an exchange of fire from the Japanese garrison; this was followed by a bombardment by the Chinese air force of offshore ships of the Japanese navy, to which the Japanese retaliated by bombing the city with aircraft based in Japan proper. After three months' bitter fighting, the city fell, and with it any hope that the Japanese might have of support from the Western world, in particular the United States.

The Japanese continued their advance, and in December they captured the capital of Nanking, which was followed by the most appalling atrocities committed by Japanese soldiers (and revealed to the emperor only at the end of the Pacific War). The Chinese, led by Chiang Kai-shek, retreated up the Yangtze river, to set up a temporary capital at Hankow (which later had to be abandoned for a city yet further inland, Chungking). As this was happening, the Japanese bombed the *Panay*, an American gunboat on the Yangtze, causing a number of casualties and a major international row. The Japanese only avoided a break in diplomatic relations by making an immediate apology coupled with an offer of full indemnity for the damage caused.

In spite of the quick succession of victories in 1937, which gave Japan almost the entire coast-line of China, together with many of the important cities and lines of communication, the war with China showed no signs of coming to an end. The Japanese, after the fall of Nanking, had approached Chiang Kai-shek with a view to a settlement, but the conditions were too hard to be acceptable. The Konoye government, although pressed to modify its terms by representatives of the General Staff Headquarters in China, moved in the opposite direction. On 16 January 1938, Konoye issued a proclamation which read:

Beginning today, the government of Japan will not recognize the Nationalist Chinese government. We anticipate that a new political power, willing to co-operate with Japan, will eventually be established in China, and when that happens, we will adjust diplomatic relations and work with them to build a new China.

The proclamation was soon to become something of a self-fulfilling prophecy, for the Japanese managed to persuade Wang Ching-wei, a key figure in the Kuomintang, to desert Chiang Kai-shek, and form a Nationalist government acceptable to Japan. This government, finally inaugurated on 30 March 1940, signed a treaty with Japan on 30 October, recognizing Manchukuo (as the Japanese had renamed Manchuria).

The summer of 1938 witnessed a serious border incident between Japan and the Soviet Union, which is significant not only for the light it sheds on the possibility of war between the two countries (which a number of army leaders would have welcomed), but also for the attitude of the emperor in the face of this possibility. The actual battle was fought for the possession of a hill known as Changkufeng, located at the point where Korea, Manchuria and the Soviet Union meet. Having heard the news of the battle the emperor in a joint audience for the Minister of War and the Chief of the General Staff declared that past actions carried out by the army had been 'abominable', and added, 'From now on you may not move one soldier without my command.' The words seem to have had little effect. Within a year hostilities with the Soviet Union had broken out again, on a much larger scale, in Nomonhan in Outer Mongolia, to say nothing of the escalation of the war against China.

In this same period Japan's approach to foreign and military policy changed radically as a result of Nazi Germany's spectacular victories in Europe. On 22 June 1940, the Army General Staff and the Ministry of War, in a joint meeting, discussed the possibility of taking over all the economic resources of South East Asia, when only a few months previously many of those present had been advocating withdrawal from China. A month later, Konoye (who had resigned as Prime Minister in the summer of 1939) formed his second administration. Within four days the new cabinet approved a policy (whose basic aim was claimed to be world peace) of bringing about a new order in Asia by uniting Japan, Manchukuo and China under Japanese leadership.

This was the beginning of the Daitōa Kyōeiken, awkwardly translated into English as 'the Greater East Asia Co-prosperity Sphere'. With the Pacific War this would be extended to cover all the territories conquered by the Japanese: the basis of the underlying policy was that the local inhabitants would gladly accept Japanese tutelage in place of the old colonial administration of the Western powers.

The success of Japanese imperialism (however short-lived it would prove to be) required, in its turn, a new conception of the role of the emperor. The problem was simple enough. Historically the whole mystique surrounding the emperor took for granted that his empire consisted simply of the Japanese islands. As I have shown in Chapter 4, the position could be maintained by coupling the principle of *sonnō* or reverence for the emperor, with that of *jōi*, keeping out the barbarians. True the whole experience of Japan, since the Meiji restoration, was that the barbarians could not be kept out completely, but their influence, within the country, was still closely controlled. The enhanced status of the Chrysanthemum Throne, carefully built up by means of the appropriate rhetoric (of which I have already quoted a number of examples), could be used to counteract foreign subversion. In the cultural politics of Japan this may be judged, in the light of history, to have been the most useful function of the emperor.

With the establishment of the Daitōa Kyōeiken, the status of its subordinate populations, in relation to the emperor, was a problem recognized by the Japanese, but one which they had never adequately solved. In Korea and Taiwan, where they had been established for thirty years or more, a veneer, at least, of Japanese culture had been imposed upon the local populations. The Japanese language was widely used, and no doubt, given time, the same result would have been achieved in all the territory falling into Japanese hands after the beginning of the war with China in 1937.

By 1940 this problem came to be dealt with, in increasing measure, by means of carefully orchestrated imperial rhetoric emphasizing the *peace* brought by Japan to the area within the Daitōa Kyōeiken. In particular the concept of *hakkō ichiu*, literally, 'the eight corners of the world under one roof', was used to represent a universal brotherhood under the beneficent tutelage of the Japanese Imperial House. The Showa Emperor, needless to say, looked at the statements made in his name with pronounced scepticism.

The cult of the emperor reached its culmination in November 1940, when the 2,600th anniversary of the founding of the imperial line was celebrated in Tokyo. This was a spectacular occasion, staged in the imperial plaza, a large public open space on the east side of the Imperial Precinct. An invited company of some 50,000 people would watch two days of ceremonies.

The first day was devoted to a Shinto ceremony specially devised for the occasion. It took place in the *shinkaden*, a large, purpose-built structure, which – one hardly need add – would be demolished immediately after the celebrations were over. In a hall lit by paper lanterns, the emperor, in heavy white robes and carrying a *shaku* to represent his priestly office, made an offering of new rice and wine to the *kami*, to the accompaniment of ancient music. After reciting a prayer of thanksgiving he returned to his seat, where he remained while other members of the imperial family, followed by members of the government and other notables, went up to worship at the altar.

The following day the celebrations were deliberately popular. The emperor and his party lunched from a *bentōbako*, a small box containing hardly more than a snack, such as millions of ordinary Japanese take with them to work. Ceremonial dances, band music and patriotic songs formed the prelude to the loyal speech made by the emperor's second youngest brother, the Prince Takamatsu, who also led the shouts of 'Banzai'.

The American ambassador, Joseph Grew, who was doyen of the diplomatic corps, was called upon to reply. A text agreed by the State Department in Washington emphasized the need for peace and mutual co-operation for the betterment of all nations, and the emperor, who had been almost expressionless throughout the whole proceedings, was seen to nod vigorously in approval as each point was made by Grew. This was of little significance: events were already following a course determined without any real regard for the wishes of the emperor. The anniversary celebrations were a masquerade.

Already in October 1940, Konoye, now in his second term of office as Prime Minister, had seen to it that the political parties in the Diet, which until then had preserved their separate identity, went, one after the other, into liquidation. They were replaced by a single new party, the Taisei Yokusan-kai (the Society for Assisting Imperial Rule). This event, welcomed by Konoye with his usual rhetoric, was presented as the 'performance of His Majesty's subjects of their duties in assisting the august rule': all the members present responded by shouting

'*Banzai*'. Japan had become a one-party state, as it was to remain until its defeat in the Pacific War. The last flickering ember of Taisho Democracy had been extinguished. The event, if in its way the apotheosis of the Showa restoration, was to be the prelude to disaster.

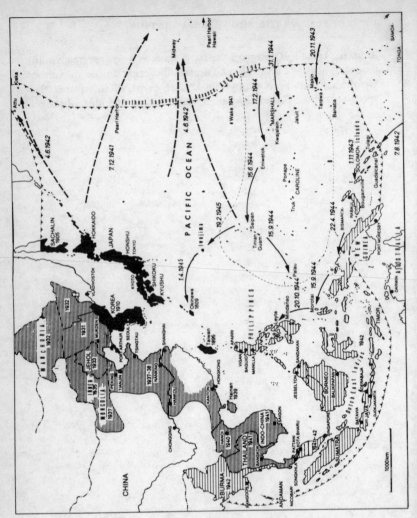

Map of Japanese military operations 1931–45

8

Inferno

THE chain of events which led Japan into the Pacific War can be taken to have started with Prince Konoye's second cabinet, which was formed on 22 July 1940. The most significant appointments were Yosuke Matsuoka as Foreign Minister and General Hideki Tojo as Minister of War. The machinations of these two quite different and mutually unsympathetic characters combined to turn Japan, at every critical moment, from the path which might have led to peace in the Far East.

The defeat of France and the Netherlands in the early summer of 1940 opened up an entirely new prospect for the Japanese, for it was clear that the defence of the French and Dutch colonies in the Far East could no longer rely on any sort of support, political, military or economic, from Europe. But there were also important differences between the French and Dutch positions. The French government had formally surrendered to the Germans, but had been allowed to continue in operation, in a new capital, Vichy, from which it would govern the so-called 'unoccupied' zone. It continued to maintain diplomatic relations abroad, which included an embassy in Tokyo, but the Japanese realized that the French were powerless to maintain any foreign policy which did not have strong German support. Holland, although occupied by the Germans after only four days of war, had not surrendered. The royal family, led by Queen Wilhelmina, and the government, led by the Prime Minister, Gerbrandy, had escaped to England, from where they would continue the war against Germany until its defeat in May 1945. Any rights in the Dutch colonies in the Far East could only be obtained by direct negotiation with the government in exile, which was certain to follow the policies adopted by Britain and the United States. At the same time, the Dutch armed forces in the Far East were far stronger than the French, and the Dutch colonies further away from Japan.

It is not surprising, therefore, that Japan moved first against the French colony of Indochina, comprising the present countries of Cambodia, Laos and Vietnam. Economically Indochina, with its rubber, tin, tungsten, coal and rice, was a valuable enough prize, but it was more important to Japan for its strategic value. Japanese control of Indochina would stop the flow of American and British war material to Chiang Kai-shek in Chungking, at the same time opening new lines of attack for the Japanese army, which had reached a stalemate in its war against China. Following a succession of diplomatic moves, the Vichy government had by September 1940 accepted that Japanese troops could be stationed in northern Indochina. In the words of one member of the Japanese government, Indochina was 'a treasure lying in the street waiting to be picked up'.

This was too much for the United States, which, in July 1940, placed an embargo on aviation fuel, which was followed by scrap iron in September and iron and steel in November. Although, by this time, relations between Japan and the United States had deteriorated to a very low level, the door to negotiation was not completely closed. The position became complicated because, in the early months of 1941, the Japanese government was trying to ride two horses at once: indeed, the question throughout the whole year was, which was going to win the race?

On the one side were the dealings with the United States, which were carried out with the help of a curious assortment of characters, including two American Catholic missionaries, who claimed to have good contacts with influential figures in Japan. Such informal negotiations had the support of Konoye, but they led to no satisfactory compromise between the United States and Japan, partly because Admiral Nomura, the inexperienced Japanese ambassador, failed to understand the policies of Cordell Hull, the American Secretary of State, and partly because Matsuoka, the Japanese Foreign Minister, consistently misrepresented American policy to his own government.

Yosuke Matsuoka, who consistently pushed Japan along the devious course which would lead to the Pacific War, was an egregious wheeler-dealer, hardly trusted by anyone he dealt with: Sir Robert Craigie, the

British ambassador to Japan, said of him, 'I have never known anyone talk so much to say so little,' while Hitler confided to Mussolini that 'one must conclude that he was combining the hypocrisy of an American Bible missionary with the craftiness of a Japanese Asiatic.' According to John Toland's book, *The Rising Sun*, 'Prince Konoye listened to practically everybody, Matsuoka to practically nobody.' A fellow-cabinet member, the Minister for the Navy, had remarked, 'The Foreign Minister is insane, isn't he?' President Roosevelt, after reading an intercept of coded instructions sent by Matsuoka to his Washington embassy, thought that they were 'the product of a mind which is deeply disturbed and unable to think quietly or logically'. Why then did such an intolerable man achieve such high office, and retain it for so long?

The answer must be that Matsuoka, through astute public relations, managed always to project an image of a born winner. Few troubled to note that he was consistently a judge in his own cause. Of course, if Japan had benefited from withdrawing from the League of Nations in 1933, Matsuoka was entitled to much of the credit: the same goes for the tripartite pact with Germany and Italy in September 1940.

In the early months of 1941 Matsuoka continued along the same course. The basis of his policy was that the United States would climb down, in its policy of sanctions, if Japan formed a really strong alliance with Germany, Italy and the Soviet Union. Considering that the Americans had broken the Japanese diplomatic code (as Matsuoka himself might have realized if he had listened better to his own advisers), Matsuoka's line of action was hardly likely to make the Americans trust him.

In March 1941 Matsuoka left Tokyo for Berlin, travelling across the Soviet Union by the trans-Siberian railway. In Berlin, Hitler tried to convince Matsuoka that the strong line taken by Japan would be yet more effective if Singapore were to be seized from the British. Matsuoka, knowing how frustrated Hitler was by his failure to bring Britain to terms, refused to be committed to a policy which was clearly more in the interests of Germany than of Japan. His real triumph, however, he achieved in Moscow, on the return journey to Japan. There he signed a neutrality pact with Stalin, which meant the end of any political or military threat to Japan's northern frontiers. (This was an important point, seeing that the Japanese had suffered quite serious casualties in clashes with the Soviet Union occurring as the result of their expansion into Manchuria and northern China in the 1930s: two of these incidents are mentioned in Chapter 7.)

Matsuoka, on his return to Japan, was scathing about the draft understanding reached with the United States while he was away, and himself took no immediate initiative to improve relations: on 14 May 1941, he greatly irritated the American ambassador to Tokyo, Joseph Grew (who for ten years had consistently given the Japanese government the benefit of every possible doubt), by urging that the United States 'declare war openly on Germany instead of engaging in acts of war under cover of neutrality'. With hindsight it seems as if Matsuoka, with his consistent lack of tact and insulting behaviour, was deliberately wrecking the negotiations with Washington.

Finally, on 21 June 1941, Cordell Hull, in answer to the latest Japanese proposal, answered that Japan would have to abandon the tripartite pact, and abandon its plan to maintain troops in northern China to help the Chinese combat the Communists. He added that recent public statements by Japanese officials were an insurmountable roadblock to further negotiations. Matsuoka was infuriated by the obvious reference to himself, and urged that the talks in Washington be broken off altogether.

The diplomatic position was eclipsed, the following day, by Hitler's invasion of the Soviet Union. Matsuoka's reaction was to ask for an immediate audience with the emperor. This was granted, but the emperor's closest adviser, the Marquis Koichi Kido, Lord Privy Seal, had warned him to accept nothing from Matsuoka which had not previously been approved by Konoye. Kido knew that this would not be the case, so the audience was soon over.

The policy advocated by Matsuoka, at this new turn of events, was to attack the Soviet Union: the logic was simple enough, for as Matsuoka himself put it, 'We can't simply share in the spoils of victory unless we've done something.' He believed his diplomacy would be sufficient to stall the United States for three or four months, so that 'If we hit the Soviets without delay, the United States won't enter the war.'

By the end of June the Japanese Supreme Command was clearly set on a course leading to war, and on 2 July, by a vote taken at a meeting presided over by the emperor, the decision was taken to go south, and not north, as Matsuoka had urged. Matsuoka by this time was himself ready to break off negotiations with the United States, but by the end of the month his machinations had become so intolerable, even to his colleagues, that General Tojo, the Minister of Defence, insisted that Konoye dismiss him. This result was achieved on 16 July by having the whole cabinet resign, allowing Konoye to begin his third and final administration with a cabinet in which Matsuoka was replaced by Admiral Toyoda as Foreign Minister.

Few men can ever so disastrously have influenced the course of history as Matsuoka. In the critical period before the Pacific War he was the only real demagogue in Japan. In his endless utterances one constantly notes the hysteria of the frustrated charismatic leader. Like any such leader he had the gift of appearing to share the feelings of ordinary people in a time of crisis. Oddly, though, he was not very Japanese, which explains, no doubt, the feelings of revulsion he aroused in such people as Konoye, Tojo and quite certainly the emperor. As a young man he had made his way through ten difficult years in the western United States, at a time of serious discrimination against Japanese immigrants. This period had given him a power to communicate with the Western world, which he never hesitated to use, without ever being concerned about his credibility. An essentially arrogant man, he saw himself as dealing with a bunch of suckers, who could always be fixed by some last-minute deal. It is impossible to gauge the real intentions of so confused a character: the only thing which is certain is that he was interested in power for its own sake. If, beyond that, Matsuoka was answerable to no one, this was not something which ever lost him a night's sleep.

If the first months of 1941 were dominated by Matsuoka, a quite different character, General Tojo, was the master-mind in the final months of the year. It may well be that when Matsuoka departed, Konoye, supported by Tojo and the rest of his cabinet, still hoped for peace. However, before the month was out, Japan had taken a step which made war in the Pacific much more certain. On 24 July the Japanese army occupied the whole of Indochina: true the Vichy government had agreed to this at the last moment, so that there was no actual fighting, but President Roosevelt, advised by Cordell Hull, was not inclined to make any allowances for this. On the contrary Roosevelt, at the express wish of Chiang Kai-shek, ordered all Japanese assets in the United States to be frozen: Britain and the Netherlands took similar steps, and on 1 August a complete oil embargo was imposed. For the materials needed for carrying on the war against

China, Japan could now trade only with Manchuria, Indochina and Thailand, none of which were able to supply the necessary oil.

History must judge this to be the point of no return. True, there were further negotiations with the United States, and there was at one time a plan for a direct meeting between Konoye and Roosevelt, but nothing came of it. The immediate reaction to the embargo was confusion among the Supreme Command. The naval Chief of Staff, Admiral Nagano, in an audience with the emperor, still hoped for peace, and in any case cleared the navy of any responsibility for the turn of events. But then, after reviewing Japan's uncertain military prospects in the light of the blockade, he added, 'Under such circumstances, we had better take the initiative. We will win.'

The emperor, remembering the defeat of the Russian fleet in 1905, then put what was to prove a very significant question: 'Will you win a great victory? Like the battle of Tsushima?'

'I am sorry but that will not be possible.'

'Then the war will be a desperate one.'

This was not to be the emperor's last word. At a conference held in the *kunaishō* (Imperial Household Ministry) on 3 September 1941, a deadline was agreed for an acceptable diplomatic solution: this, 10 October, was ratified by a meeting three days later presided over by the emperor. It was then that he recited the words of the poem written by his grandfather, the Emperor Meiji, which I have cited on page 56. At this meeting the two Chiefs of Staff again assured the emperor that they wished to accomplish their goals by diplomatic means, but, in spite of their denials, the emperor still suspected that the Supreme Command was bent on war, not diplomacy. Before the meeting, the Marquis Kido had tried to persuade the emperor to abandon all precedent, and simply order the Chiefs of Staff to co-operate with the government in making the diplomatic negotiations successful. The Showa restoration would then have become a political reality, but not in the way envisaged by the young rebellious officers of the *ni-ni-roku jiken*. But it was not to be. The emperor read his grandfather's poem, but his message did not get across.

No progress had been made by either side by the October deadline. At this stage the Army General Staff, represented by General Tojo, made it clear that there would be no concession requiring troops to be withdrawn from China, and inisted that the decision for war be made jointly by the government and by the Supreme Command. Tojo, in an impassioned speech in a cabinet meeting, declared that any concession would mean 'defeat of Japan by the United States – a stain on the history of the Japanese empire'. His eloquence won the day, and he had sufficient support to drive Konoye to resign. The question of Konoye's successor in the end allowed only one answer: Tojo. A man of character, with no political ambitions, always obedient to the emperor's wishes, he was the only person who could rely on complete loyalty from the military. Konoye hoped that the emperor would persuade Tojo to opt for peace, and carry the day.

Any optimism that Tojo might do better than Konoye was misplaced. By the time he became Prime Minister the plans for war had already been made, and he was not to reverse them. The mood of the public was on his side. A new deadline of 30 November was chosen for the decision to put the war plans into effect, and when the day came the order for war was given. Up to the very last moment there were some in Japan who hoped for some concession from the United States, but American public opinion was behind Cordell Hull's Japanese policy, and no concession came.

Needless to say, this was essentially a Chinese policy, as it had been throughout the late 1930s. During this whole period China was ruled by Chiang Kai-shek, whom the American General Stilwell had once described as 'the most astute politician of the twentieth century . . . he must be or he wouldn't be alive'. His wife, always known as Madame Chiang, was equally gifted in the field of American public relations, and between the two of them they had succeeded in projecting an image of China, under the Kuomintang government, as one of the great democracies. Although the historian Whitney Griswold had, in 1938, correctly identified China as a 'fascist dictatorship', the American correspondents active in China never reported it in such terms, partly for fear of losing their own right to remain there, and partly so as not to help the Japanese. Chiang Kai-shek was in fact always much more anxious about the Communists in his own back-yard than about the Japanese, whom the West in the end would take care of (and history was to prove him right on both points). Barbara Tuchman, in her study of Stilwell, *Sand against the Wind*, gets to the heart of American policy: 'The rise of international Fascism shaped America's view of China and the fervent syllogism at its core: democracy was threatened by the aggressor nations; China was under attack by an aggressor nation; therefore China was a democracy and her battle was the battle of world democracy,' but then, of course, '. . . Americans find it difficult to remember that Thomas Jefferson did not operate in Asia.'

In the end the position which had crystallized in the course of 1941 was simple: 'Japan could not consent to a settlement that did not recognize her colonial control of China; the United States would not consent to one that did. At bottom there was no area of bargaining.'

The Japanese began the Pacific War with a brilliant pre-emptive strike – the attack on Pearl Harbor on 7 December 1941. The news was announced in Tokyo in the early morning of 8 December. At first the popular reaction was tinged with anxiety, but by midday, when the full extent of the Japanese victory became clearer, any anxiety had given way to a great sense of satisfaction that Japan, in one single operation, had realized its manifest destiny. This was the sense of the radio announcement broadcast to the Japanese people which, with the familiar rhetoric deemed appropriate for such occasions, declared that in the name of the emperor, and of his illustrious ancestors, the war did but extend the Japanese policy of bringing stability to Asia and ensuring amity among the nations.

In the following months the Japanese armed forces achieved one success after another, so that by early in 1942 the Americans, the British, the French and, above all, the Dutch had been forced to surrender almost all of their possessions in the Far East. With one or two exceptions, such as the heroic American defence of Corregidor in the Philippines, the Japanese met no effective resistance, even though they often confronted forces numerically far stronger than their own.

The immediate results of the Japanese victories were favourable for both the armed forces and the Japanese people. The spoils of war not only provided the war industries and the services with essential raw materials, but also allowed some improvement in the standard of living of the ordinary people. At the same time, the fronts where the Japanese were engaged were thousands of miles from Japan itself, so that for those who manned the home front the war took on a surrealist aspect. Neither the newspaper reports nor the letters written home by servicemen could convey quite what the war involved for those actively engaged in it. Euphoria, restrained but none the less real, was the mood of the Japanese population in 1942, the first year of the Pacific War.

The emperor was more a distant figure-head than an active participant. He never visited any foreign front: indeed he seldom left Tokyo. His involvement in the lives of ordinary people, whether military or civilian, was far less than that of King George VI in Britain. The most familiar image from this period is of a Commander in Chief, in a resplendent uniform, mounted on a white horse: this was Shirayuki, his favourite Lipizzaner and his mount when he reviewed troops about to depart for the distant battlefields. Ordinary people still bowed down in his presence, even doing so as passengers in trams passing by outside the walls of the Imperial Precinct. The press reported the emperor receiving successful commanders, to congratulate them on their victories and award the appropriate decorations. More than anything, the flow of rhetoric, focused on the emperor, continued unabated and provided – at least in principle – the whole sacred rationale for the war. The emperor had never wanted the war, but was forced into it by the perversity of the United States and Great Britain. Once there was no turning back, then, in the words spoken in the name of the emperor immediately after Pearl Harbor, 'The revered spirits of our imperial ancestors protect us from on high, and we rely on the loyalty and courage of subjects, in the confident hope of continuing the task bequeathed by our forefathers, to eradicate the roots of evil, and re-establish in East Asia an everlasting peace, for the safeguard of the glory of our empire.' This set the tone for almost all future pronouncements, until it became clear that neither the protection of the imperial ancestors, nor the loyalty and courage of the people, could save Japan.

In fact the Japanese forces were to reach a position of stalemate within six months of Pearl Harbor, and before the end even of 1942 the tide had begun to turn. The battle of the Coral Sea, which took place almost six months to the day after Pearl Harbor, was to be the end of the Japanese march of conquest. At this point, if the Japanese were to continue to advance, they would have to deal with Australia. Substantially the whole of the eastern Pacific was in their hands: the only important foothold retained by the allied powers was the southern part of New Guinea, including Port Moresby, the largest town.

Japanese attempts to complete the conquest of New Guinea by land were defeated by the near-impenetrable jungle. Heavy aerial bombardment of Port Moresby failed to dislodge the heroic Australian defenders. The only solution left to the Japanese was to turn the eastern end of New Guinea with a substantial naval force. The force sent was engaged by the American fleet in the Coral Sea, in the first naval battle in history fought out between carrier-based aircraft. Both sides suffered heavy losses, which for the Americans included the *Lexington*, one of their few carriers (which being then at sea had escaped destruction at Pearl Harbor). The decisive point is that the Japanese had to turn back: they never conquered the whole of New Guinea, and having failed to do so, they had no prospects in Australia. This was in the long run to prove fatal, for it was from their bases in Australia that the allies, slowly but surely, were to retrieve the losses inflicted upon them in the first six months of the Pacific War.

A month after the battle of the Coral Sea, the battle of Midway, in the central Pacific, thousands of miles north of New Guinea, was an even more decisive set-back for the Japanese. The attack on the island of Midway, an outpost still retained by the Americans, was planned by Admiral Yamamoto, who had also planned the attack on Pearl Harbor. He had then wished to follow the aerial bombardment with an invasion by land-forces, but he had been unable to persuade the Supreme Command to agree to this plan. The attack on Midway was designed to redress the balance by following up a bombardment of the island by carrier-based aircraft with an actual invasion.

The Americans had broken the Japanese naval code, and so knew in advance of the impending attack: even though the Americans could only get a scratch force together, they were still able to repulse the attack, causing disproportionately heavy losses to the Japanese. There was no invasion, and the Japanese could only save the remnants of their task-force by seeking out the protection of bad weather to the north of the scene of action.

The Japanese Admiralty reported the battle as a great victory, and neither the emperor nor the Prime Minister, General Tojo, was allowed to know the truth. Tojo in fact discovered it by reading the monitored reports of American news broadcasts from Hawaii, but under pressure from Admiral Ito, the naval Chief of Staff responsible for the Japanese communiqués, did nothing to correct them. At the time, attention was diverted from Midway by publishing the news of the Japanese occupation of two small and quite undefended islands in the Aleutian chain, off the coast of Alaska, which was presented as a major loss to the United States.

In relation to the emperor's involvement in the conduct of military operations, the incident is important. No one doubts that a good deal of information about the state of the war was fed to the emperor, nor that he studied with great interest what was laid before him. So also, members of the General Staff in audience with the emperor were closely examined about the course of the war and, particularly after the tide had turned, they had to answer some very searching questions. The diaries of the Marquis Kido, Lord Privy Seal, now published in their Japanese original, provide abundant documentation of these confrontations. They provide, however, no proof that the emperor, before the final year, went beyond the normal concerns of a constitutional, but entirely nominal, head of a state at war. In the same period, King George VI was almost certainly much better informed about the course of the war (without there being any question of his being deliberately misled, say, by the British Admiralty), but would anyone suggest that he was completely impassive in the face of either defeat or victory? At the very beginning of the Pacific War, when the Japanese sank the *Repulse* and the *Prince of Wales*, two of the most modern battleships in the Royal Navy, was the King then unmoved? When, later in the war, British and Indian forces decisively defeated the Japanese in the battle for Imphal and Kohima in Burma, did not the King share in the British triumph? So much of the criticism of the Showa Emperor's behaviour at this time seems to disregard the fact that he was, after all, Japanese. Indeed, if there is any one thing which becomes clear from the record, it is that the emperor closely identified himself with the joys, and even more with the sorrows, of his own people.

Even more disastrous to the Japanese than Midway was the battle for the island of Guadalcanal, which began on 7 August 1942. This island, one of the Solomon group off the eastern end of New Guinea, was on the furthest perimeter of the Japanese advance. The greater part of it was mountainous, and covered with near-impenetrable jungle, but the Japanese had begun to construct a forward airbase on a flat area on the north side of the island. (Such bases were essential if the Japanese advance was to continue.) Here the battle for the island began with a surprise attack by an American marine division. The desperate Japanese defence of the island, which was hopeless almost from the start, lasted for just over six months. In the first three months it was accompanied by frequent naval engagements, in which Japanese and American losses were equally severe. The price for the Japanese was too high, in terms not only of the ships lost, but also of the consumption of oil. The losses suffered by the Japanese air and land forces were far heavier than those suffered by the Americans. With the American victory in Guadalcanal there was no longer any question even of stalemate: the tide had been turned. The allied forces had not only learnt that the price to be paid for final victory was one they could better afford than the Japanese, but had also discovered the strategy which would lead them to it.

Following the defeat in Guadalcanal, Admiral Yamamoto saw a decisive air battle as the only means of retrieving the situation. At his command post he received one report after another of enemy shipping sunk and aircraft shot down. These were sent on to the emperor who, delighted to receive some good news at last, commended Yamamoto for these successes. The reports, however, were as misleading as those sent out after the battle of Midway. Since Guadalcanal the Americans had been inflicting far heavier losses on the Japanese than they themselves had suffered.

Yamamoto, preparing for the planned counter-attack, made a tour of the advanced air-bases. His itinerary was known in advance to the Americans, who had been able to decode intercepted Japanese radio messages. Precisely on schedule, sixteen American fighters from Guadalcanal, at the limit of their range, attacked Yamamoto's airplane while it was on its way to the advanced airfield of Kahili. This event, which happened on 18 April 1943, was not announced until 21 May, more than a month later.

Two hundred thousand people attended Yamamoto's funeral in Tokyo. His death was seen as an ill omen. In 1941 he had consistently opposed the war against the United States, and he had conceived the plan for invading Hawaii, after the bombardment of Pearl Harbor, as providing the only possible chance of a victorious outcome. If the war came, then Japan would suffer its first defeat in battle even before the end of the first year of war – a prophecy which proved to be only too true. For Tojo, in particular, the death of Yamamoto was a painful reminder that he had much to answer for. The people of Japan had lost the last hope of victory.

The death of Yamamoto is a good point at which to take stock of the Japanese position at the turn of the tide. The armed forces had overrun and occupied a chain of territories within a perimeter whose length must be measured in thousands of miles. The heterogeneous populations under the Japanese yoke were numbered in hundreds of millions. Japan had not only to defend almost every point on the perimeter (which itself was an almost insoluble logistical problem), but in the vast expanse of the Pacific had to organize the defence of every one of the countless islands subject to it – all this against an enemy superior in manpower, material and, after the end of the first year, morale.

Seen from this perspective, the task of the allies was far simpler. Given that the ultimate objective was Japan itself, the question was simply which islands should be chosen as stepping stones along the way. Three, Saipan, Iwojima and Okinawa, were sufficient, although a fourth, Leyte (which was a part of the Philippines), was taken in along the way. Saipan, the furthest of the three islands from Japan, was attacked by three American divisions on 15 June 1944, barely a week after the allied invasion of Normandy. This island, once a German possession, had been allocated to Japan by the Treaty of Versailles, and was regarded by the Japanese as an overseas dominion. It fell to the American invaders after more than three weeks of bitter fighting, in which not only the soldiers defending it but also much of the Japanese civilian population were annihilated. The same pattern was followed with, if anything, more gruesome results in Iwojima and Okinawa at the beginning of 1945.

The loss of Saipan was decisive for the further course of the war, as many of the ruling obligarchy in Japan well realized. Konoye and Kido both foresaw that the war could only end in the defeat of Japan. Tojo, who by this time combined the offices of Prime Minister, Minister of War and Chief of the General Staff, tried to control the course of events as a sort of latter-day Shogun. He had not lost his nerve, and was not ready to surrender his power. Kido, however, succeeded in persuading him that he should reconstruct his cabinet so that he would no longer combine all three offices held by him. Tojo agreed, but on trying to form a new cabinet, he found that none of those asked to take office would do so, while his own Minister of Commerce, Nobusuke Kishi, refused to resign. This was an impasse from which Tojo could not escape, and so he resigned. When Kido asked him to suggest a successor, he gave the only possible answer: 'You threw me out, you should know better than I.'

The new Prime Minister, General Kuniaki Koiso, was an almost unknown political figure: he remained but eight months in office, giving up after American soldiers had landed on Okinawa on 1 April

1945. At the beginning of his term of office, he summed up in a few words his vision of the task before him: 'Japan is the country of the gods, but if the country does not achieve the impossible, we cannot count on their protection. The test to which they now submit us is the result of the nation being unable to understand the true and fundamental meaning of our national policy. If we can achieve the impossible, only then will the spirits of the gods give us their divine assistance.'

The gods withheld any help they could offer. The year which would follow would prove to be a nightmare, a descent into hell, without precedent in a long and often turbulent history. It was not so much that one military defeat followed another: there were even one or two local successes. The fact which counted above all others was that almost the whole population became totally involved in the war, so that in the end the level of casualties on the home front approached that of the armed forces overseas.

The capture of Saipan enabled the Americans, with their new Super-Fortresses, to reach the whole of Japan, and from November 1944, the American air raids reduced one city after another to dust and ashes. There was no effective defence, and no shelters were ever provided for the hapless inhabitants. In Tokyo the emperor was well protected by a substantial bunker in the palace precinct, where, as the raids progressed, he and his advisers spent more and more of their time.

By this time, Konoye, knowing that Japan must lose the war, became increasingly concerned about the future of the emperor. Since every major step in carrying on the war had been taken in the name of the emperor, Konoye could not believe that the allied powers would allow him to remain on the throne. If Konoye appreciated that the emperor's true position was summed up in the Japanese phrase, *yūmei mujitsu*, literally 'having a name [but] no substance', he realized that this point would be too subtle for the victorious allied powers. It is not surprising, then, that his main concern was to make certain that the emperor would not be arrested. The scenario planned by Konoye was that the Showa Emperor would abdicate (which as I have shown in Chapter 3 was the normal practice in the Edo period), to be succeeded by his eleven-year-old son, Akihito (the present emperor): then the emperor himself would become the *gomonzeki*, or abbot, of one of the Buddhist monasteries in Kyoto traditionally under imperial patronage.

Konoye had even found a suitable monastery, that of the Ninna temple, and persuaded the incumbent abbot, Okamoto, to agree to surrender his office to the emperor. He even went so far as to choose the new name which the emperor would take on entering into the religious life. The idea was supported by two other prominent figures in Japanese public life. Konoye himself would also enter the monastery.

On 26 January 1945, Konoye travelled to Kyoto to try to persuade Prince Takamatsu, the emperor's second brother, to support him. Takamatsu, however, refused to do so, and in this he was strongly supported by Kido, who saw that the allies would most probably regard the step proposed as a clear admission of responsibility for the war on the part of the emperor.

According to Japanese tradition, the plan was not unreasonable. There are any number of historical instances of national disasters being coupled with the name either of the emperor or of the current era of his reign. To the Japanese, the abdication of the emperor would have brought about the end of the ill-fated Showa era, without there being any question of any sort of moral responsibility on his part. As *tennō* he was above any morality. Nor would the Japanese have been troubled by the paradox that the emperor, who until his prospective abdication would be purely Shinto, could thereafter not only be a Buddhist, but an abbot. Kido was shrewd enough to realize that this too could be a stumbling block to the allied powers.

The American bombing continued, to reach an appalling climax on the night of 9 March. After a long and exceptionally severe winter, the first signs of spring were beginning to appear, but on this night there was a strong wind. Shortly before midnight countless American aircraft began to drop incendiary bombs, blanketing the extensive flat area to the north and east of Tokyo along both sides of the Sumida river. (The present-day traveller coming into Tokyo from the airport at Narita can see this whole area from the freeway.) This was the site not only of Tokyo's industry, but also of the working-class suburbs, where millions of families lived in small, densely packed, wooden houses.

In three hours the weight of bombs was ten times that dropped by the Germans on London in the whole of September 1940, at the height of the blitz. The resulting holocaust was appalling, even for a population which had already survived more than three months of heavy bombing. Nearly 200,000 people died as fire, blown by the wind, destroyed whole blocks at a time. Many, hoping to be saved by the intervention of the Kannon Buddha, the goddess of pity, gathered round the temple of Asakusa, but this too was completely destroyed. The devastation, and the number of casualties, both far exceeded the destruction wrought by the 1923 earthquake. The number of dead was to exceed even that of Hiroshima after its destruction by the first atomic bomb.

If the emperor's life was safe in his bunker, few of the buildings in the palace precinct survived the American bombing, and many members of the imperial family saw their homes completely destroyed. The emperor, having resisted the plan to send him off to a monastery in Kyoto, was equally adamant in rejecting an army plan to send him to a redoubt in the mountains, from where a last stand would be organized to resist an allied invasion. The emperor, if determined not to leave his capital city, hardly moved outside the palace in the first months of the aerial bombardment.

After the devastating raid on 9–10 March, he finally prevailed upon his advisers to allow him to visit the areas which had suffered the most. On 19 March, he made an extensive visit, and walked through the ruins, talking to the occasional survivor still to be encountered. If before this time he had still seen a chance of a successful outcome to the war, the destruction which he now witnessed destroyed any hope he might have had.

Before the end came, the Japanese were to use one final strategy which, according to their propaganda, could still change the course of the war. This was the use of *kamikaze* pilots, whose mission was simply to destroy allied targets – mostly ships of the American navy – by crashing airplanes, loaded with explosive. This form of warfare came into its own with the American attack on Okinawa in April 1945, where the *kamikaze* pilots sank sixteen ships and caused serious damage to nearly two hundred. The Americans, however disturbed they may have been by these losses, still continued their advance, and by the time Okinawa fell on 21 June 1945, the Japanese losses once again far exceeded the American.

The *kamikaze* operation was important to the hard-liners in the Japanese high command for the example the young pilots provided for the rest of the population. Not only they, but the 'hundred million' were being called to a 'national suicide' for the emperor. Appropriate ceremonial, with the usual imperial rhetoric, was a part of the preparation of every pilot for his one and only mission, and endless letters, written by 'pilot-gods' who had kept their appointment with destiny, were published in the press. These young men, often recruited as university students, would write to their fiancées in heart-rending terms, yet declaring that they were serene at the prospect of dying for the emperor.

At the time of the most bitter fighting in Okinawa, the Germans were finally defeated in Europe. The Japanese army by this time had accepted that the war would have to be fought out in Japan itself. Koiso, after the invasion of Okinawa, could no longer carry on as Prime Minister. His reluctant successor was the old Admiral Suzuki, who, after being critically wounded, had survived the attack on his life made in the course of *ni-ni-roku* uprising in 1936. Suzuki was Kido's choice, and Kido had hoped that Suzuki, with an emperor committed to peace, would be moved to follow in the same direction, notwithstanding the Japanese army's consistent hard-line policies.

Suzuki's Foreign Minister, Shigenori Togo, was also on Kido's side, but the army would certainly prevent him from opening any direct negotiations with the Americans. Instead he approached the Soviet Union, which for Japan was still a neutral country. The response was extremely cool, and it made no difference that Togo, with the full support of the emperor, wished to send Konoye to Moscow as a special envoy. The Japanese did not know that the Soviet Union, in the Yalta conference which had taken place in February 1945, had already agreed to enter the war against Japan in return for southern Sakhalin and the Kurile islands, which were part of metropolitan Japan.

On 17 July 1945, Truman (who had succeeded Roosevelt as the American President), Churchill and Stalin met at a conference in Potsdam, just outside Berlin, to agree the shape of the post-war world. Just over a week later, on 26 July, a declaration was published in the names of Truman, Churchill and Chiang Kai-shek, containing the terms upon which peace would be granted to Japan. The terms were harsh. Japanese territory would be restricted to the four main islands of metropolitan Japan, the country would be administered by a military government of the allied powers, there would be complete and permanent disarmament and war criminals would be punished. No concession was made to the imperial house. Togo wished to use the declaration as the basis for negotiations; Suzuki temporized by putting forward a compromise proposal; the army, supported by the press, was implacable in its opposition to any sort of acceptance of the Potsdam declaration. The allied powers could only conclude that it had been rejected out of hand.

Japan had no means of knowing that on 16 June Truman, while still at Potsdam, had been brought the news that the test of the atomic bomb had been successful. In the absence of any positive response by Japan to the Potsdam declaration, Truman gave the order for the operational use of the first atomic bomb: the target was the city of Hiroshima on the coast of the inland sea. At 8.15 a.m. on 6 August 1945 one bomb was sufficient to destroy a city with half a million inhabitants, causing the deaths of some 200,000. On 8 August the Soviet Union declared war, and on 9 August a second atomic bomb destroyed the city of Nagasaki.

No words adequately describe the horror of Hiroshima. Robert Guillain, a French journalist who had spent the whole war in Tokyo and had lived through the months of American fire-bomb raids, found the destruction in Hiroshima of a quite different kind. Even in the worst-hit areas of Tokyo some sign of life survived the raids: the city somehow retained its form, even though most of its buildings were in ruins, and many thousands of its citizens dead. The centre of Hiroshima was a complete wasteland. In the desolate landscape, a single bridge over one of the five rivers, and the skeleton dome of the old international exhibition hall, were the only signs of what had been a thriving city. All life was extinct, and it looked as if even the smallest plant would never grow again. If the dust and ashes were swept away, all that would be left was a vast, featureless expanse of grey earth, which could have been designed as a military parade ground on an absurdly large scale. The airplane in which Guillain himself arrived was able to land on a strip of ground prepared in just this way. One woman who survived could think only of the scenes of the Buddhist hell which her grandmother had described to her when she was a young girl. Of all the names still remembered from the Second World War, none – except perhaps Auschwitz – is equal to Hiroshima in the vision of pure horror which it recalls.

Suzuki, the Prime Minister, knew that Japan could no longer reject the terms of the Potsdam declaration. In the morning of 9 August 1945, the Supreme Council for the Conduct of the War was prevented by objections raised by the armed services from reaching any conclusion. In the afternoon of the same day, the cabinet could not reach a unanimous decision (such as precedent required), because of the opposition of the Minister of War, General Korechika Anami. Finally, at 10 p.m. (after the news of the second atomic bomb had been received from Nagasaki), Suzuki went to the palace to request an imperial conference at which the emperor would give his personal decision.

The conference began at midnight. It was held in the emperor's underground shelter, and took place in the appalling heat of Tokyo in midsummer. Everyone present was appalled by the condition of the emperor himself, sick with anxiety and exhausted from lack of sleep. The Potsdam declaration was read out to a company consisting of the emperor, Suzuki, the Prime Minister, Togo, the Foreign Minister, Kiichiro, the President of the Council, Anami, Minister of War, Umezu and Toyoda, the two Chiefs of Staff, and Yonai, the Minister for the Navy. With the emperor presiding, the Prime Minister abstained from voting, while the vote of the rest was split three-three, with Yonai and Kiichiro supporting Togo's proposal to accept the allied terms, provided that they required no change in the legal position of the emperor.

Suzuki's reaction to the split vote was to say, simply, 'We have spent a long time in debate but have finally failed to reach any conclusion. Therefore – without any precedent and with the utmost distress – I would respectfully submit that his Imperial Majesty give the final judgement.' Anami, still holding to the principle that no important matter of State policy could be determined without the agreement of the Minister of War, was unable to block this unprecedented move. After a short pause, the emperor responded:

To make things clear, I will tell you my reasons.

The army and navy reported just now that they could mount a decisive battle on the main islands and that they had confidence in their ability to do so, but here again I feel extremely worried. What the Chief of General Staff says is seriously at variance with the reports of my aides-de-camp. In fact, almost no defences are ready. According to what I hear, not all the troops have guns, even. What would happen if we embarked on a decisive battle in such a state of affairs? The Japanese people would be virtually wiped out. It is my duty to hand on to our descendants this land that we have inherited from our forebears. Now that things have reached this pass, the only hope, I feel, is to see that as many Japanese as possible survive so that they can rise again in the future and rebuild the nation. Nor would it be a good thing for the peoples of the world that the war should continue any further.

I understand very well that for the army and navy the idea of disarmament and occupation is intolerable. I, too, detest the idea that those who have served me loyally might be executed as war criminals. However I recall the distress of the Emperor Meiji at the time of the triple intervention, and believe that what has to be borne must be borne with patience. I have decided this war should be ended.

The formal reply by the allied powers to this declaration reached the Japanese government on the night of 12 August: the response to the Japanese request on behalf of the emperor was equivocal, and led to another cabinet meeting on the morning of 13 August, at which Anami once again blocked acceptance of the allied terms. A second imperial conference was called for the morning of 14 August, at which the emperor made clear that he had not changed his mind. He finished his speech with the following words:

At this point it does not matter what happens to me. I will do anything I can. I am sure that the people, unaware of the true state of affairs, will be greatly disturbed by this development, but I am ready to broadcast to them at any time if necessary. I am sure, too, that the war and navy ministers will have a hard time placating their officers and men, but I am willing to go anywhere to persuade them directly.

The imperial edict was signed by members of the cabinet in the evening of the same day, and Togo gave instructions for the formal acceptance of their terms to be communicated to the allied powers. At the very end of the day Anami came to the Prime Minister's official residence to apologize for his obstructive action. Suzuki accepted his apologies, saying:

I understand how you feel; it was all motivated by concern for your country. However the emperor's position will be preserved, I am sure – because His Majesty is so assiduous in paying his respects to his ancestors . . . I am convinced that His Majesty and the nation will join together in bringing about Japan's recovery.

The emperor's broadcast was scheduled for the following midday. In the late evening the Japan Broadcasting Corporation moved in the equipment for recording the emperor's words, and in the end two records were cut. Almost predictably, junior officers in the imperial guard, stationed just outside the palace, repeating the familiar pattern of *ni-ni-roku*, tried to intervene by force in the course of government. Throughout the night it seemed that they, and the troops they commanded, might yet prevent the broadcast being made, but they failed to find the two records, and in the morning General Tanaka, commander of the Eastern Army, succeeded in disbanding them. There would be no second chance, even though for a few days die-hard patriots made sporadic attempts to undo the government's decision for peace at any price.

The emperor's message was transmitted at noon. Everywhere in Japan people gathered to hear, for the first time in history, the voice of the crane – the bird, whose only song was an occasional note sounded from a great distance, being a traditional symbol for the emperor. The voice, once heard, was scarcely intelligible. Court Japanese, the only language in which the emperor was really at home, was far removed from that of his people. The position had been foreseen. The emperor's message was followed by the reading of a translation in everyday Japanese. In spite of its convoluted style and uncertain logic, the meaning was beyond doubt. The survival of Japan depended on accepting the allied terms for surrender. (Using rather simpler words the Showa Emperor gave a new twist to the same point in a letter written three weeks later to his elder son, Akihito, then eleven years old: '. . . if the war had continued, the three holy treasures [the mirror, sword and jewel of the imperial regalia] would have been lost. This would have meant the end of Japan.')

The address to the nation was the culmination of the most critical ten days not only in the life of the Showa Emperor, but in the history of his country. For a brief period of time the emperor did control his people's destiny and, almost alone, change the course of history. Not one of his predecessors had ever had such a moment on the world stage. Yet the apotheosis of the emperor meant also the total eclipse of his office: this lonely man was entering into a new stage in his life, in which he could recognize no sun-goddess who would illuminate his path. The emotion he had shown in accepting the inevitability of surrender, by 'enduring the unendurable and suffering what is insufferable' – to quote from his broadcast speech – was soon brought under control. He would come to terms with an uncertain future and, although nearly half his lifetime was still before him, he would remain emperor until the day he died.

9

The last Shogun

WITH the defeat of the Japanese in 1945, the status of the emperor became a live issue, open to public debate, in a way which it had never been before. For once there would be no government able to dictate its own policy, so that the emperor himself would be free of all the historical constraints which had denied him any real say in defining his own status. I describe in this chapter the radical reform of the emperor's status, largely brought about as a result of his own initiative, in circumstances which gave him unprecedented freedom of action.

After the Japanese had accepted the terms of the Potsdam agreement, the formal surrender took place on 2 September 1945. The scene was the deck of the American battleship, *Missouri*. The Japanese delegation was led by Mamoru Shigemitsu, Foreign Minister in the first post-war government which had been formed by Prince Higashikuni, a cousin of the emperor, on 15 August. The scene was dominated by one man, General Douglas MacArthur, who had been appointed Supreme Commander of the Allied Powers, almost invariably referred to under the acronym SCAP (which refers, according to context, to the *command* as well as to the *commander*).

The Japanese delegates were the first to sign the act of surrender. MacArthur then added his signature, to be followed by the American naval commander, Admiral Nimitz, and senior officers representing China, the United Kingdom, the Soviet Union, Australia, Canada, France, the Netherlands and New Zealand. Within a week MacArthur had taken up his position in Tokyo, where he would live at the American Embassy, but work from a sixth-floor office in the undamaged Dai-ichi building, almost immediately opposite the Imperial Precinct. He was to be there for six years, until his dismissal by President Truman in 1951. From the very beginning the occupation was run by Americans, both military and civilian, with but limited help from representatives of the other allied powers. So long as he remained in Japan, MacArthur's command was absolute, so that in Japanese eyes he had assumed the traditional power of the Shogun. According to his own interpretation, his office may be seen as comparable to that of the viceroy in British India, but he eschewed any sort of vice-regal pomp and splendour. In six years he never travelled outside Tokyo, and for most of that time he preferred to govern from an office to which access was very strictly controlled. In this period MacArthur attempted a radical transformation of Japanese politics and government, while at the same time the role of the emperor was fundamentally recast.

At his own request, the Showa Emperor visited MacArthur at the American Embassy on 27 September 1945, barely three weeks after the signing of the instrument of surrender. A single photograph is preserved of this historic occasion. It shows the emperor, in morning dress, standing, almost expressionless, next to MacArthur (who was almost a head taller) in shirt-sleeves. The meeting had a profound effect on both the emperor and the general, and set the tone for the whole of their future relationship.

The emperor, accepting his historical role as Head of State, was ready to accept, also, full responsibility for the Pacific War. To cite his own words, 'I come to you, General MacArthur, to offer myself to the judgement of the powers you represent as the one to bear sole responsibility for every political and military decision made and action taken by my people in the conduct of the war.'

MacArthur was deeply moved by the emperor's action. As he was later to report, 'He was an Emperor by inherent birth, but in that instant I knew I faced the First Gentleman of Japan in his own right.' MacArthur had already accepted the principle, required by the Japanese government as a condition for accepting the terms of the Potsdam declaration, that the position of the emperor should be preserved, but after the meeting of 27 September, there was for MacArthur no longer any question that only political expediency governed the relationship between them.

The Higashikuni cabinet, in contrast to the emperor, dragged its feet in collaborating with SCAP. The Japanese civil service, almost unavoidably, continued to be directed by officials who had built up their careers under the old regime. Their work was monitored by the different departments set up within the SCAP organization, and manned by military and civilian personnel recruited from the allied powers (which meant that the majority were American). At a very early stage it was realized within SCAP that the Japanese government would not, on its own initiative, carry out the reforms required by the Potsdam declaration. MacArthur, acting on such advice, issued a lengthly directive on 4 October 1945, ordering the Japanese government to abrogate and immediately suspend 'restrictions on freedom of thought, of religion, of assembly and of speech' and to encourage 'the unrestricted discussion of the Emperor, the Imperial Institution and the imperial Japanese government'. Quite specifically, the repeal was required of the Peace Preservation Law, under which unrestricted discussion of the emperor was a crime punishable by death.

The threat to the emperor's status was not well received by the Japanese establishment. Within two days of MacArthur's directive, Takagi Yasaka, a professor at the Tokyo Imperial University, expressed himself 'deeply anxious over the future of the Imperial Institution, especially since the issuance of the decree permitting free discussion of the Emperor and the Imperial Houshold'. A note sent to the American Secretary of State, in February 1946, noted the apprehension of the Japanese ruling classes, but pointed out that there was no sign of the political chaos predicted.

The *kunaichō* was more co-operative, and issued a typically cryptic directive of its own. 'New photographs of His Majesty the Emperor will be granted to replace those in the schools, local government offices and diplomatic and consular offices abroad. The new picture will show His Imperial Majesty in the imperial uniform recently instituted.' From this time on the emperor was always to be seen in civilian clothing.

The Showa Emperor himself consistently, and on his own initiative, followed a course of action in harmony with MacArthur's plans for the future of Japan. The next significant step was taken on New Year's Day, 1946, when he made a public statement disclaiming the status of *arahitogami*, which means 'the divine present emperor'. The statement was brief and to the point:

We stand by the people and we wish always to share with them in their moments of joy and sorrow. The ties between us and our people have always stood upon mutual trust and affection. They do not depend upon mere legends and myths. They are not predicated on the false conception that the Emperor is divine and that the Japanese people are superior to other races, and fated to rule the world.

MacArthur was delighted with this message, which he saw as guiding Japan in the direction of democracy. At the same time the Showa Emperor's life-style was radically revised. Until the end of the war he had never mixed with his subjects in the informal way of European royalty which he had observed during his world tour in 1921. His primary duty had been the performance of Shinto ceremonies in one or other of the three shrines within the palace precinct, already mentioned in Chapter 6. The most important were those at which he himself was the chief celebrant: in the course of the year the first of these, held on 3 January, celebrated the 'auspicious origins' of the imperial throne. The ceremonies which followed were largely focused on one or other of the imperial ancestors, so that both the accession of Jimmu, and his death, were commemorated. The most important exception is the *niiname matsuri*, celebrated on 23 November, the great harvest festival which, with the inauguration of every new emperor, is celebrated in the special form of the *daijōsai*. All these ceremonies were public in so far as appropriate guests, of generally aristocratic background, were invited to be present, often in quite considerable numbers.

In the post-war era the emperor still conducted, in private, some thirty ceremonies a year in the palace shrines, but at the same time he established himself as a figure known to the public. He travelled much more frequently outside the palace precinct, and it was no longer deemed necessary to ensure that none of his common subjects should see him. Under the MacArthur shogunate he visited many different parts of his devastated country, and made a point of meeting ordinary people. At first he was extremely shy, and became known for replying to any statement addressed to him with the words, '*Sō desu ka*', which are about equivalent to the English 'Really?' The image presented, steadily improving as the emperor's conversation became more relaxed, proved to be good public relations.

But can anyone, credited by tradition with divine status, simply disclaim it? If Shinto doctrine was true, could the emperor change it by means of such a disclaimer? A hypothetical parallel, in the context of Western Christianity, would be the following question: is there any formula, acceptable to Catholic doctrine, by which the Pope could disclaim the apostolic succession?

It cannot be said that the Japanese were ever completely convinced by the emperor's disclaimer. Politically, the circumstances in which it was made were quite exceptional. True, the Showa Emperor himself took the initiative, but he knew that it would be well received by MacArthur, who had been active in attempting to eliminate the ties between Shinto and the Japanese State. The Shinto Directive, had formally abolished any support, control or dissemination of Shinto by the government: this was followed a few days later by the Religious Corporations Ordinance, repealing the old Religious Organizations Law (under which the Japanese government had controlled religious observances), and guaranteeing religious freedom.

The opportunity to make the disclaimer was no doubt welcome to an emperor who, as a young man, had already expressed to Saionji his doubts about his divine status. Even then, the disclaimer never proved to be a complete break with Shinto. The Showa Emperor continued to carry out, if on a restricted scale and in private, Shinto rituals to the end of his life. His annual visits to Ise, the home of the sun-goddess, were certainly interpreted as an affirmation of belief in her divine powers. In a way which any Japanese would understand, the emperor never saw the question in simple black and white terms. What he did establish, by his disclaimer, was the principle that no political capital could be made out of his status in Shinto.

This principle, which represented a radical change from the position of the emperor up until the end of the war, was to be enshrined in the new constitution of 1947. By Article 1,

The Emperor shall be the symbol of the State and of the unity of the people, deriving his position from the will of the people with whom resides sovereign power.

At the same time, the position in relation to religion already established by the SCAP directives was strengthened by Articles 20 and 89. Article 20 guaranteed religious freedom to all, at the same time forbidding (a)

the exercise of political authority by religious organizations, and (b) the use of compulsion to bring about participation in 'any religious act, celebration, rite or practice'. Article 89 prohibited public money, or any other public property, from being 'expended or appropriated for the use, benefit or maintenance of any religious institution or association'. These articles in principle rule out any public support for imperial *rites de passage*, such as the accession rites described in Chapter 6 or the funeral rites described in Chapter 12.

Neither the imperial disclaimer of divine status, nor the provisions of Article 1 of the constitution, were sufficient to solve all problems relating to the emperor's status. On two matters, both dating from the Meiji era, SCAP had great difficulty in enforcing its policy on the Japanese government. The first of these was the question of *lèse-majesté*, which was a specific offence under Articles 74 and 76 of the Penal Code, which, on the interpretation urged by the Ministry of Justice, were still the law of the country. The issue was a sensitive one for MacArthur, for during the war a number of Japanese Christian leaders had been imprisoned for posing such questions as 'Who is superior, the emperor or God?', or 'Is not the emperor also a human being who will be judged for his sins?'

The matter was brought to a head in the very first year of the new constitution. In October 1946, a Communist newspaper, *Akahata*, published an article, 'The True Character of the Emperor'. The Tokyo District Prosecutor's decision not to indict the author, Tokuda Kyuichi, was immediately supported by MacArthur:

> As the Emperor becomes under this new constitution a symbol of the state, with neither inherent political power nor authority, the Japanese men and women are raised to a new status of political dignity, and, in fact, will become the rulers of Japan. In his new role, the Emperor will symbolize the repository of state authority – the citizen. The dignity of the state will become the dignity of the individual citizen, and the protection accorded him as the symbol of the state ought to be no more and no less than the protection accorded to the citizen.

This was not acceptable to the Prime Minister, Shigeru Yoshida (who was otherwise a strong supporter of MacArthur). Yoshida was concerned not so much with Articles 74 and 76 of the Penal Code (relating to *lèse-majesté*), but with Articles 73 and 75, which defined, as a specific criminal offence, all acts of violence against the person of the emperor, or of any member of his family. In a letter to MacArthur, Yoshida claimed that:

> . . . even under the new Constitution the Emperor's position as that of 'Symbol of the State and unity of the people' accords with the traditional faith which has been held firmly by the Japanese nation ever since the foundation of Japan. It is truly a high and lofty position. Moreover, it is undeniable that the Emperor is ethnically the centre of national veneration. That an act of violence against the person of the Emperor, occupying such a position, should be considered as of a character subversive to the State, and deserving of severe moral censure and a severer punishment than any act of violence against the person of an ordinary individual, is quite natural from the standpoint of Japanese national ethics. It is similar to the case of an act of violence against the person of one's parent or ancestor, which is considered as deserving of a severer punishment than an act of violence against the person of the ordinary individual.

If Yoshida were right, every effort made by SCAP to reform the Japanese imperial institution had been in vain. The reference to parents and ancestors is particularly significant in the light of history, for Article 897 of the Civil Code of 1947 (which would come into effect on 1 January 1948) specifically abolished the *ie* as a legal institution, and stripped the head of the *ie* of his powers. It did, however, make one exception: 'The ownership of genealogical records, of utensils of religious rites, and of tombs and burial grounds is succeeded to by the person who is, according to custom, to hold as a president the worship of the memory of the ancestors'.

MacArthur's reply to Yoshida's letter is too long to quote in full, but the following passages make its reasoning abundantly clear:

> As the symbol of the State and the unity of the people, the Emperor is entitled to no more and no less legal protection than that accorded to all other citizens of Japan who, in the aggregate, constitute the State itself. To hold otherwise would violate the fundamental concept, clearly and unequivocally expressed in the new Constitution, that all men are equal before the law, with the necessary

implication therefrom that no individual, whatever his position, shall be vouchsafed judicial safeguards denied the ordinary citizen, the ultimate repository of all State authority.

The respect and affection which the people of Japan have for the Emperor form a sufficient bulwark which need not be bolstered by special provisions of the criminal law implying suzerainty. The former concept of a peculiar Japanese national ethic distinctly differing from universally recognized ethical principles was repudiated by the Emperor himself in his Rescript of January 1st, 1946, eschewing the myths and legends from which this concept was created . . .

In view of the fact that the Japanese Penal Code provides the death penalty for murder and severe penalties for acts of violence against persons, the dignity of human life and the inviolability of the character and person of the individual are fully recognized. It follows that all articles of the Penal Code relating to crimes against the Imperial House are surplusage and should be eliminated by appropriate Ordinance.

In the end the Japanese did introduce a Revised Criminal Code, acceptable to MacArthur, but this was no guarantee that Yoshida's claim that the emperor was 'ethnically the centre of national veneration' was unfounded. Indeed a much more protracted struggle with SCAP, relating to the 1890 Imperial Rescript on Education, would show that the Japanese government was only too anxious to confirm that this claim was well-founded, and should be supported by government policy.

I have described the historical background to the Imperial Rescript on Education in Chapter 4, where I also give the full text. When, immediately after the surrender, a government was formed under Prince Higashikuni, the new Minister of Education, Tamon Maeda, lost no time in declaring that 'the foundation of Japanese education could not exist without the 1890 Rescript on Education.' This declaration was to be the beginning of a long struggle with SCAP, which in the end was to lead to the repeal of the 1890 Rescript. The simple question is, what was at issue in this struggle, and why did the Japanese government fight so hard to defend its position?

First a word must be said of the relationship between SCAP and the Japanese bureaucracy. SCAP, at the height of its power, could rely on a considerable expatriate (and largely American) staff, both civil and military, operating through a number of different departments. These corresponded roughly to the different ministries comprised in the Japanese government, which itself continued to operate without any interruption. According to President Truman's own instructions to MacArthur, ' . . . Control of Japan shall be exercised through the Japanese government to the extent that such an arrangement produces satisfactory results. This does not prejudice your right to act directly if required. You may enforce the orders issued by you by the employment of such measures as you deem necessary, including the use of power.'

There was no practical alternative to relying upon the Japanese bureaucracy. Few members of SCAP had any detailed knowledge of Japan, and even fewer had any useful command of the language. In a period of less than seven years SCAP had to concentrate on reforms which would give Japan an institutional structure in which the democratic ideals of the Western allies would be preserved. This explains, for instance, the measures taken by MacArthur to ensure that the emperor had no special status in the Criminal Code. The way was made easier (at least in principle) by an initial purge of some 186,000 Japanese government employees, as a result of MacArthur's Civil Liberties Directive of 4 October 1945. There was no question of the offices made vacant being taken over by SCAP officials: it was simply a matter of one bureaucrat being succeeded by another, without there being any guarantee that the new official would be any more willing and able to carry out SCAP policy. The historical evidence now available points in the opposite direction: the purges made no substantial difference to the direction taken by the Japanese government. What counted were the specific measures, in every field of public life, imposed by SCAP. Many of these were far-reaching, and required drastic legislation to become effective. In the end, it was the new constitution which would ensure that the democratic reforms required by SCAP would endure even after the end of the occupation period.

From the Japanese point of view – or at least that of the Japanese government – the first priority was to ensure the perpetuation of *kokutai*, the idealized conception of national polity established in the Meiji era. This was the reason for Maeda's insistence on the preservation of the Rescript on Education. In his own words, 'with dauntless bearing we should defend the national polity [*kokutai*] and international peace', and the emperor himself, in his broadcast surrender speech, had used the same word when he had asked the Japanese people to 'protect the national polity'. SCAP had failed to realize that the Japanese government, in its insistence that the position of the emperor should be unimpaired, had always intended that the immunity of the emperor would extend to all that was meant by *kokutai*. To SCAP, on the other hand, *kokutai* could only mean the governing principle behind the historical process which had led Japan to unleash a war of unparalleled destruction.

As in so many matters, SCAP and the Japanese government were talking at cross-purposes. The government reaction was to recast *kokutai* in a form which excluded any possibility of its being realized by military action (which in any case was ruled out by Article 9 of the new constitution). By the end of the period of occupation, when the United States' main concern was to reach a satisfactory conclusion to the Korean War, this position had become more or less acceptable, if only for the purely pragmatic reason that Japan, sooner or later, must be free to govern itself in its own way.

There is no evidence that the government policy, in its relation either to *kokutai* or more specifically to the Rescript on Education, had any popular support. If anything the Japanese people, after a war which had ended in a state of unprecedented devastation, had lost faith in their own government, and the liberal policies of SCAP were a welcome alternative. The fact that Maeda had seen this attitude as 'the root of our recent moral decay' goes a long way towards explaining his enthusiasm for the Rescript on Education. As he explained to the Diet, in January 1946, its spirit and letter had been unfortunately misinterpreted by self-righteous reactionaries and militarists, whereas with a correct interpretation ' . . . we shall regain the true understanding of the Emperor's wisdom and affection'.

The Japanese leaders overplayed their hand. Their constant harping on the virtues of the Rescript on Education led SCAP officials to look at it more closely, and what they saw did not please them at all. The matter came first before the Civil Education and Information Section of SCAP (which supervised the Japanese Ministry of Education), where W. K. Bunce, of the Religions Division, made the harshest comment:

The 1890 Imperial Rescript on Education is a Shinto-Confucianist document written for the purpose of keeping down 'radical' (i.e.

democratic) tendencies . . . the 'bible' of modern State Shinto . . . from it militarists and nationalists drew much of their ammunition . . . By the most liberal interpretation it is out of spirit with the new constitution . . . It should not be read in the public schools or included in textbooks, except perhaps at the college level where it might be included as an historical document.

The Japanese government remained blithely unaware of these criticisms. Kotaro Tanaka, who had succeeded Maeda as Minister of Education in May 1946, was to say within a month, in a speech to prefectural governors:

Recently the people's morals have greatly deteriorated; they even question the content of the Imperial Rescript on Education. Indeed, there are hardly any Japanese who now pay as much respect to His Majesty the Emperor as foreigners do to their own heads of state.

A month later Tanaka made the same point before the Diet, but added that other materials, such as the Bible and the Japanese classics, should be the basis of a new educational system. Since Tanaka's opinion was part of an address made to the Committee of the House of Representatives which was about to advise the acceptance of the new constitution, it could not go unnoticed by SCAP. There it was noted that the Rescript, being originally a personal proclamation of the Meiji Emperor, would 'not automatically go out with the new constitution'. This meant that it had to be formally banned by SCAP.

The conflict around the Rescript on Education showed how education had become the touchstone for judging the success of SCAP policy. MacArthur himself had ordered that the new education must teach and practise the sanctity and supremacy of the people and not of the State. The idea, implicit in this policy, that the emperor was just an ordinary individual, if a truly revolutionary concept for the Japanese people, was still one which MacArthur wished to put across.

MacArthur was, however, at one with the Japanese government in perceiving a moral vacuum in the Japanese soul, and recognizing the need for it to be filled with a specific theological doctrine. MacArthur saw Christianity as the means for leading the Japanese people 'from feudalistic slavery to human freedom, from the immaturity that comes from mythical teachings and legendary ritualism to the maturity of enlightened knowledge and truth, from the blind fatalism of war to the considered realism of peace'. With scant regard for what the Soviets and the Chinese might have thought, he declared that allied policy was based squarely on the Sermon on the Mount. Japan, according to MacArthur, was 'the world's great laboratory for an experiment [in which] a race long stunted by ancient concepts of mythological teaching [could be uplifted by] practical demonstrations of Christian ideals'.

In the ideological field MacArthur overplayed his hand as much as any of his Japanese rivals. When it came to the conversion of Japan, enthusiasm far outran discretion. MacArthur once told an American missionary, 'I could make the emperor and seventy million people Christian overnight, if I wanted to use the power I have.' One wonders why he did not do so. According to one report, he had even told Billy Graham that the emperor was sympathetic to this idea. Indeed he would have been nicely let off the hook on the matter of his divine status if MacArthur himself had assumed that burden. One Japanese had even gone so far as to say, 'We look to MacArthur as the second Jesus Christ' (although there was of course no precedent for a non-Japanese becoming an *arahitogami*).

By all reports, neither side ever tried to involve the emperor in this controversy, even though it was his status that was the real issue. This is not surprising. The Japanese government could hardly disregard the emperor's disclaimer of 1 January 1946, and it was SCAP's policy to keep the emperor out of politics at all costs. If the emperor had his own view, it was almost certainly that the Rescript on Education should be repealed. This in the end is what happened. For a time there were attempts to provide a new rescript, but none of the drafts were satisfactory. In October 1946, the Government Section of SCAP used its muscle to have the Diet pass a resolution terminating the use of the Rescript on Education. To complete the process of reform, the Fundamental Law on Education (whose drafting had been closely supervised by SCAP), effective from March 1947, established the responsibility of schools to inculcate the political knowledge necessary for democratic citizenship.

The reforms introduced in the occupation period not only brought about a radical change in the emperor's status, both political and religious, but also greatly reduced the power and scope of the imperial establishment. The *kunaishō*, from being the Imperial Household Ministry, with at its head a cabinet minister, became no more than the emperor's private administration, with a much smaller staff, to be known as the *kunaichō* or Imperial Household Agency.

The emperor's economic position was even more drastically cut down to size. In November 1945, SCAP ordered the assets of the imperial household to be seized: the Showa Emperor's personal wealth was then estimated at $100,000,000, but even this figure hardly reflects the extent of the imperial property. At the same time some 7,500 household retainers lost their jobs (and that at a time of high unemployment). After such reforms the expenses of the emperor and his household were to be met by sums voted annually by the Diet (which have proved to be more than sufficient to maintain an impressive imperial style). The Diet itself no longer requires the imperial seal for legislation, and it is the cabinet, and not the emperor, who is responsible for all State appointments. In practice the reverence shown by top officials for the principle of *kokutai* means that this is seen as a change more in form than in substance, and the suggestion made by a number of constitutional lawyers in the immediate post-war period, that Japan had become a republic in fact if not in name, is beside the point.

Politically, the reduction in the number of those officially recognized as members of the imperial family was a much more significant reform. At one stroke the number of those with imperial status was reduced from twenty-one to seven, so that only the empress, the dowager empress (mother of the Showa Emperor), his three brothers and two sons (of whom the older, Akihito, is now emperor) still counted. The position has changed over the course of the years, so that now, in 1989, the so-called Imperial Family of the Inner Court consists of the dowager empress, Nagako (widow of the Showa Emperor), the empress, Michiko, together with the three children (now all grown up) that she has borne to the emperor. Of these the oldest, Prince Hiro, is almost certain to be named as *kōtaishi*, or Crown Prince. The Imperial Family of the Outer Court consists of the emperor's younger brother, Prince Hitachi, and his wife, the Princess Hanako, together with the family of the emperor's uncle, Prince Mikasa, the only surviving brother of the Showa Emperor.

The reduction in the size of the imperial family meant that the Showa Emperor was no longer tied to members of his family, often of a senior generation, who had in the past proved to be unwelcome and embarrassing hostages to fortune. The point is simple enough. Before 1945, recognized members of the imperial family were often placed by the government in sensitive military commands, so that criticism of local actions could be suppressed on the principle of *lèse-majesté*. The most notorious case is probably that of the Showa Emperor's uncle, the Prince Yasuhiko Asaka, who at the end of 1937 arrived in Nanking to become deputy commander of the Japanese forces ten days before the appalling massacre of 140,000 Chinese prisoners of war and refugees. The actual commander, General Iwane Matsui, was one of the seven Japanese sentenced to death by the International Military Tribunal (whose work I describe in Chapter 10), but the prince was not even indicted. The case is made much more serious by the fact that at the actual time of the rape of Nanking General Matsui was absent on sick leave.

One political consequence of the reduction in scale, and in the scope of activity, of the imperial household and family is that in the period since 1945, the government has known that it could no longer find a compliant imperial prince as a cover for its activities. Indeed, in this period, the most articulate member of the much smaller imperial family, the Prince Mikasa – youngest of the Showa Emperor's three brothers – has proved to be something of a thorn in the flesh of those governing Japan.

The political influence of the imperial family was also reduced as a result of the abolition of the House of Peers by the constitution of 1948. True, the members of this House were not all related to the imperial family, but none the less it did provide the means for perpetuating the power of the Meiji oligarchy. The House of Peers, as originally constituted under the Meiji Emperor, was largely recruited from the Chōshū and Satsuma factions which had brought about the imperial restoration, supplemented by their allies from the old *kuge* families, such as the Princes Saionji and Konoye. In the pre-war period, the aristocracy represented by the House of Peers provided almost all the Prime Ministers who were not members of the armed forces. The most notable of these was Prince Konoye. The last word has yet to be pronounced on the merits of these members of the nobility, but certainly the House of Peers could never have been called a popular institution. The principal reason for the failure of Taisho Democracy in the Showa era may well be that all too often the main issues were fought out between the leaders of two hierarchies, civil and military. The former, defined by hereditary privilege, had its power base in the House of Peers: the latter, recruited largely on the basis of merit, had its power base in the two service ministries, always headed by senior serving officers. The contrast between the two was reflected in the year leading up to Pearl Harbor by that between Prince Konoye and General Tojo. The abolition, by the 1947 constitution, of both these alternative power bases was a reform of substance. There was no place for the House of Peers in the new constitution, and Article 9, by which war and arms were renounced for all time, rules out the resurgence of the power of the military on anything like the pre-war scale.

The reforms described in the previous paragraph left the emperor a much more isolated figure, and that not only in political terms. Just imagine what the life of the British royal family would be like if there were no peerage or armed services to support it. But then of course SCAP was essentially American, so few were troubled about the price the emperor would have to pay for its reforms. All the evidence is that the emperor gladly paid this price, since his position under the new constitution, with two elected Houses in the Diet, left him with much less responsibility. True he was deprived of much of the social support that the British court (which he saw as his model) takes for granted, but, then, at the same time, his public life was much more restricted. It may be that the constitutional positions of the two sovereigns are now comparable, but the British monarchy is still an essentially public institution in a way alien to any Japanese tradition. For what Japanese political and public life expect of the emperor, the present establishment is more than sufficient, and there has been no sign in the last forty-odd years that the imperial family have wished to increase it.

On the domestic scene, the Showa Emperor, early in 1946, took one particular initiative which caused great satisfaction both to MacArthur and to the American government. He decided to appoint an American woman as tutor to the Crown Prince Akihito, who was then twelve years old. The choice fell upon Elizabeth Gray Vining, whose book, *Windows for the Crown Prince*, gives a unique portrait of life in the imperial household in the MacArthur era. Whatever the weaknesses of this book as a work of historical scholarship or, for that matter, investigative journalism – and it was intended to be neither – the life it portrays is not, on any count, that of a family headed by a war criminal. The point is important, for Mrs Vining was present in Japan, carrying out her duties, while the International Military Tribunal was largely preoccupied by the question of her employer's responsibility for the crimes committed by the Japanese in, and before, the Pacific

War. Any number of reasons have been given for doubting the credibility or relevance of Mrs Vining's testimony, but it cannot be alleged that she was indifferent to the proceedings of the Tribunal, or to the involvement of the emperor in them. Indeed she took the trouble to discuss their meaning with the Dutch judge, Bernard Röling. Her book remains a historical document of great interest. Intelligence and integrity shine through on every page, and yet one sees, now, a portrait of a lost world, an ideal which in the end failed to be realized. One example is sufficient to make this point. According to Mrs Vining:

> What has changed the Japanese attitude to the Emperor more than the Imperial Rescript of 1946 [the disclaimer of any divine status] is the way he has come out among his people. Whereas formerly they were not allowed to look on his face, now they can press close to him in crowds as he goes about over Japan, visiting schools, factories, museums, hospitals, coal-mines, and a multitude of other institutions. He appears at department store exhibits in Tokyo and at baseball games. On New Year's Day the people go into the Palace by the thousands to sign their names as evidence of respect and affection, and the Emperor comes out on the roof of the Imperial Household Building to wave his hat at them. They have learned to love and respect him not for his divinity but for his own character.

I shall discuss in Chapter 11 the question as to why the emperor failed to maintain the popular style described by Mrs Vining in the years following the end of the allied occupation. Here it is sufficient to consider what permanent changes were brought about by MacArthur, not only in the place of the emperor in Japanese public life, but also in the organization of Japanese society. Chapter 11 will also show what SCAP failed to achieve.

In relation to the emperor, the allied occupation brought about two important changes. The first is that he was, as a man, cut down to size. On however restricted a scale, he was seen and heard by ordinary people. Theologically – if such a word can be used in the context of Shinto – the Showa Emperor's disclaimer of his divinity may add up to nothing, but the point is that the disclaimer is still accepted by the majority of the Japanese population, including the new emperor, Akihito. The presentation of Akihito, on his accession, particularly emphasized his human qualities.

The second change was to put the emperor not so much above as outside politics. Whatever mistakes have been made in governing Japan in the last forty years, it would be next to impossible to implicate the emperor in any way. There has been no incident remotely comparable to the fall of the Tanaka government in 1928, which I have described in Chapter 7.

As for the country at large, the elimination of the military as a political force must be counted as an enormous blessing, which the Japanese people have never failed to realize. Universal franchise has greatly improved the position of women. The emancipation of the millions of tenant farmers has transformed Japanese rural society. Free trade unions have greatly strengthened the position of labour. Free public education, enjoyed by almost all children up until the end of high school, has helped create a much more egalitarian society. Such advances may well have been consolidated by the unparalleled economic success of Japan, but their roots are still to be found in the MacArthur era.

And what of MacArthur himself? His career in Japan ended ignominiously, when he was dismissed by President Truman in April 1951, a year before the end of the allied occupation. By this time it was the American involvement in the Korean War which determined the part which MacArthur was to play, at least in the eyes of Washington. In Japan MacArthur *was* the occupation: SCAP was but an acronym for a latter-day Shogun. But MacArthur was a general in the United States Army, and as a soldier he all too readily disregarded the fact that he too had a commander-in-chief, the President of the United States. (Perhaps he had learnt from the Japanese generals who, in the years before 1941, had wilfully disregarded their government.)

If MacArthur saw President Truman as a 'vulgar little clown', it is not surprising that the latter had referred to him as 'Mr Prima Donna, Brass Hat, 5-Star MacArthur . . . play actor and bunco man'. The Secretary of State, Dean Acheson, in more moderate language, noted that MacArthur 'had many attributes of a foreign sovereign . . . and was quite as difficult as any'. At much the same time, Sir Alvary Gascoigne, the British representative in Japan, in a letter home, wrote, 'MacArthur really believes he is the one man who can save the world.' In Japan he succeeded largely because his style so well fitted the image he had himself built up. Twice every day in Tokyo, the traffic lights were set at green along the whole route between MacArthur's home in the American Embassy and his office in the Dai-ichi Building, as he travelled to and from his work. Otherwise he never appeared in public.

Although New York gave MacArthur a hero's welcome when he returned home in 1951, his reputation in the United States is that of a warmonger and a reactionary. This is the result of his aggressive stance against the Chinese in the Korean War (which was what ultimately led to his dismissal). In Japan he is remembered as a reformer and as a man of peace. Article 9 of the constitution, which ruled out the resort to arms, was largely his achievement. He is the man who once said, 'Could I have but a line a century hence crediting a contribution to the advance of peace, I would gladly yield every honor which has been accorded by war.'

MacArthur must finally be judged on the one policy from which he never wavered, which was that the emperor should continue to reign, immune from all process, after the defeat of Japan. The Showa Emperor, in turn, repaid the trust placed on him, and willingly accepted the provisions of MacArthur's constitution under which he would become a constitutional monarch, without any real power. The understanding reached between two such different men is altogether remarkable.

The joint act of Shogun and *tennō*, played out by MacArthur and the Showa Emperor over a period of nearly six years, is unique in Japanese history. No Shogun ever had so much power as MacArthur, no *tennō* so little as the Showa Emperor after the Japanese defeat in 1945. MacArthur, the man with the high profile, is forgotten; the Showa Emperor, with a profile sometimes so low that he was almost invisible, is on the way to being established as one of the most remarkable historical figures of the twentieth century. In this paradox is the key to understanding the history of twentieth-century Japan.

10

Judgement

NOT only in the West, but to a limited extent in Japan also, the months following the announcement of the Showa Emperor's final illness in September 1988 witnessed a strong revival of the accusation that he carried a major part of the responsibility for Japanese aggression in the years before 1945, and for the atrocities which accompanied it. In the United Kingdom, two popular newspapers, the *Sun* and the *Daily Star*, lost no time in publishing articles portraying the Showa Emperor, then on his death bed, as a major war criminal. Veterans' organizations throughout the English-speaking Commonwealth quickly recorded their agreement with this view. In Holland, the parliamentary leader of the Christian Democratic Alliance (the majority party in the ruling coalition) used all his political muscle to ensure that no member of the royal family would represent the country at the Showa Emperor's funeral. Within a few months of the emperor's death on 7 January 1989, two much-publicized books appeared, one in English and the other in German, whose main object was to prove his personal responsibility for war crimes for which twenty-eight Japanese leaders had stood trial more than forty years earlier.

In this chapter I deal with two questions. The first is, Was the emperor in any way guilty of the crimes alleged against him? The second question is, Why is it that even after more than forty years so many people are still obsessed by the need to establish such guilt?

Japanese responsibility for the wars in which it had been engaged in the period up to the surrender of August 1945 was the matter at issue before the International Military Tribunal for the Far East (IMTFE). This was first convened in May 1946, to pronounce its final verdict and sentence some two and a half years later, in November 1948. The twenty-eight accused were a somewhat heterogeneous collection of men who had been leading figures, both civil and military, during almost the whole period of the Showa Emperor's reign. Of these the best known was General Tojo, the Prime Minister who had given the final signal for the attack on Pearl Harbor, and who was thereafter to remain in office until the summer of 1944. At much the same time something under 6,000 other Japanese were tried by the allied powers for conventional war crimes, and of these nearly 1,000 were sentenced to death. (In contrast to Germany the Japanese government never took any initiative in trying its own citizens for such crimes.)

By the time the IMTFE began the trial, the decision had already long been taken by SCAP that the Showa Emperor was not to be among the accused. Before considering the political reasons for this decision, it is essential to look at the legal status of the IMTFE, particularly with regard to its constitution, and the basis of the law which it was to administer. In a normal case in the criminal law, these matters are taken for granted and even the most assiduous defence lawyer seldom questions them. The trial will be but one instance of a legal proceeding for which there will be any number of precedents, none of them involving the accused in any way. A legal historian may be able to find instances of laws being framed with a view to subjecting, retroactively, a particular class of persons to criminal process, where they would otherwise be immune, but such laws offend against the fundamental principle of *nullum crimen sine lege* – that is, no action is criminal, unless it is so defined by pre-existing law.

The Tokyo Charter, which constituted the IMTFE and defined the law which it was to administer, was an executive decree of General MacArthur, acting under orders of the United States Joint Chiefs of Staff. The precedent was the Nuremberg Charter under which war criminals from Nazi Germany had been tried. The Japanese government had accepted the principle of the trial by agreeing, in the instrument of surrender, to the terms of the Potsdam declaration. In contrast to Nuremberg, where each of the four great allied powers nominated one judge, plus an alternate judge, the Tokyo Charter provided for eleven judges and no alternates at all. The eleven judges were to be nominated, respectively, by the eleven member countries of the Far Eastern Commission; these in turn were the nine countries represented at the act of surrender, plus India and the Philippines. The same eleven countries would also each nominate a prosecuting counsel. In the event the president was to be an Australian, Sir William Webb, and the chief prosecuting counsel an American, Joseph B. Keenan (who at home had made his reputation prosecuting the Mafia).

The Tokyo Charter provided three main heads under which the accused could be tried. These were (a) Crimes against Peace, (b) Conventional War Crimes and (c) Crimes against Humanity. Heads (a) and (c) not only defined the offences in very wide terms, but extended responsibility to any participants 'in a common plan of conspiracy' to commit any of the offences so defined.

The indictment contained fifty-five specific counts, of which the first, after describing the 'criminal military clique' dominant within the Japanese government between 1 January 1928 and 2 September 1945, charged all the accused with a conspiracy whose '. . . main object . . . was to secure the domination and exploitation . . . of the rest of the world and to this end to commit, or encourage the commission of crimes against peace, war crimes and crimes against humanity', so that, to achieve the objects of the conspiracy, the accused 'intended to, and did plan, prepare, initiate or wage aggressive war . . .' Except for the fifth count, the following thirty-five counts related to specific instances of the first count. There were then seventeen counts relating to conventional war crimes, and two final counts relating to crimes against humanity. Of these the first charged the accused with 'ordering, authorizing or permitting atrocities', and the second with 'the disregard of duty to secure observance of and prevent breaches of the Laws of War'.

Conspiracy is, in the English-speaking world (or, in legal terms, that part of the world with a common law tradition), the most favoured instrument of prosecuting lawyers intent upon securing a conviction. It has no equivalent in the civil law jurisdictions of continental Europe (or, for that matter, Japan). The essence of the crime of conspiracy is that two or more persons share a joint intention to commit a wrongful act. The act need not even be criminal, so that if a single individual commits it, no prosecution is possible. Nor, in the case of a conspiracy, is it necessary that the act be carried out: conspirators who get cold feet at the last moment can still be convicted of the crime. What is more, in the climate of Anglo-Saxon jurisprudence (which dominated the Tokyo trial) conspiracy is regarded as a serious crime. Clarence Darrow, the well-known American defending counsel, put it this way: 'if a boy steals candy, he has committed a misdemeanor, if two boys plan to steal candy, *but don't do it*, they are guilty of conspiracy, a felony.'

Conspiracy is the political crime *par excellence*. This is clear both from its origins in English history, and from the way governments have chosen to use it: the Tolpuddle Martyrs, who made one of the earliest attempts to set up a trade union, were conspirators, sentenced by the court, in 1834, to seven years' transportation to Australia. Even earlier, in the United States, the prosecution had used, in the year 1806, a charge of conspiracy to secure a conviction in the famous Philadelphia Cordwainers case, which had much the same background in industrial relations.

In the Tokyo trial the use of conspiracy as the basis of the prosecution's case is all the more open to question, given that the drafting of the Charter, the framing of the indictment, the appointment of judges and prosecutors, and the choice of the accused were all part and parcel of one political operation carried out by the allied powers, which the Japanese, in the circumstances of the case, were powerless to resist. No wonder General Tojo at the end of the trial referred to it as 'victors' justice'.

Historically the Tokyo trial derived its legitimacy from Nuremberg. Of the Nazi leaders indicted at Nuremberg, eleven were sentenced to death and seven to terms of imprisonment, three were acquitted and one, Martin Bormann, was tried *in absentia*. If one looks just at the names of those sentenced to death, one recognizes, even today, figures such as Goering, von Ribbentrop, Keitel, Frick, Rosenberg, Streicher and Seyss-Inquart, who over a long period of time willingly and actively collaborated with Hitler in performing some of the most appalling atrocities ever recorded in history. Even today the holocaust casts its pall over the international political scene.

What is more, many of these Nazi leaders had been close to Hitler, and active in the party, for years before it came to power in 1933. Frick had first been associated with Hitler in 1919. From 1937, when Hitler more or less abandoned any form of cabinet government, these men remained close to him, and what is more, he was always in charge. Hermann Goering once told the British Ambassador, Sir Nevile Henderson, 'When a decision has to be taken, none of us count for more than the stones on which we are standing. It is the Führer alone who decides.' (This could conceivably have provided some sort of defence for all Hitler's subordinates, were not the defence of acting on superior orders specifically ruled out by the Nuremberg Charter.) In any case Hitler's policies are on record, whether they be declared in his book, *Mein Kampf*, or in his abundant speeches, and their direction was clearly that established by the Nuremberg trial. At this level, at least, those accused of following Hitler did so willingly. This being so, the Nuremberg verdicts (and *a fortiori* the sentences imposed) could have been reached, if much more laboriously, without the help of a conspiracy charge.

Let us now turn to the Tokyo trial, and begin by looking at the list of those convicted and sentenced to death: Doihara, Hirota, Itagaki, Kimura, Matsui, Muto, Tojo. Who knows today who these men were? Even after spending months researching the present book, I cannot recall having come across Kimura and Muto, although I could certainly track them down somewhere in my bibliography. Others I have hardly needed to mention. Only Tojo is remembered at all (other than by history specialists), and who now could say precisely who or, perhaps better, what he was?

Turning to Japanese politics in the period from 1928 to 1945, is there any sign of any identifiable clique, coalition or even conspiracy moving, with malice aforethought, to commit the appalling atrocities, such as the rape of Nanking or the Bataan death march, of which the Japanese were guilty? Look once again at the record (as I have tried to summarize it in Chapters 7 and 8). In the period of fifteen years leading up to Pearl Harbor, Japan had sixteen different governments, and only Wakatsuki and Konoye held the office of Prime Minister more than once. Although, as the rebel officers of *ni-ni-roku* alleged, all these administrations suffered from much the same political defects – such as favouring the interests of the *zaibatsu* and turning a blind eye to rampant corruption – the reason for the constant change was simply that no single combination of leaders, whether civil or military, ever succeeded in establishing a workable and coherent international policy.

Even when war was imminent, political order was beyond the reach of any Japanese government. The French journalist, Robert Guillain, who was in Tokyo at this time and was allowed to continue working throughout the war, finds only the vulgar French word *pagaille*, meaning an utterly degraded form of chaos or disorder, as apt to describe the political situation. Within the government there were always at least two parties, military or civilian, competing for power, and these parties in turn were far from being united. True, in the end Konoye took the desperate step of suppressing the separate political parties in the Diet, but this hardly added to his authority. Even the appointment of Tojo, to succeed Konoye two months before Pearl Harbor, was the result of a policy which faced in two directions. The emperor himself accepted Tojo's appointment for precisely the reason that only he could restrain the military if there was to be peace, or lead the country if there was to be war. In the words of a lapidary statement made by the emperor to Kido, 'Koketsu ni irazunba koji o ezu,' which means, 'You cannot get a tiger's cub, unless you enter the tiger's den.' Even then Tojo was no absolute ruler: his rivals remained not only free, but often retained influential posts. Cabinet government continued without a break right up to the present day.

The effective leaders in Japan were those such as Admiral Yamamoto who conceived of the plan to attack Pearl Harbor, and was then in command of the operation. Within his mandate he did have the power to realize his objective, and many other military and naval leaders were in the same position. Otherwise the extraordinary victories won by the Japanese in the first year of the Pacific War would have been impossible. On the other hand the idea that such a war could be won was pure folly: this was not the folly of a single megalomaniac like Hitler, but of a whole confused national polity (which the Japanese referred to as kokutai) with no identifiable individual at its head at any time. Tojo came closest to it, but he represented no more than a last-minute expedient to give some shape to Japanese policy at a time when it was already too late.

This is where the Showa Emperor comes in. For the victorious allies, the Tokyo tribunal was dominated by the Nuremberg mentality. Just as the Nuremberg trial took place in the shadow of Hitler (who had committed suicide on 30 April 1945), so also, for many of those involved in it, the Tokyo trial took place in the shadow of Hirohito (the alliteration, here, being an important psychological factor). The principal ambition of Sir William Webb, the presiding judge, was to include Hirohito among the accused (although Keenan, the chief prosecutor, had strict instructions from MacArthur not to implicate the emperor in any way). The emperor was at the head of the initial list of war criminals, and Australia, Britain, China, New Zealand and the Soviet Union all wished his name to remain there.

There is no doubt that the exclusion of the emperor was a political decision, urged by MacArthur, who, when the prosecution was being considered, had said:

> Realizing the tragic consequences that would follow from such an unjust action, I had stoutly resisted such efforts. When Washington seemed to be veering toward the British point of view, I had advised that I would need at least one million reinforcements should such action be taken. I believed that if the emperor was indicted, and perhaps hanged, as a war criminal, military government would have to be instituted throughout all Japan, and guerilla warfare would probably break out. The emperor's name had then been stricken from the list.

MacArthur's fears were no doubt exaggerated, although they were never put to the proof. The Japanese are an adaptable people, and it could well be that they would have adapted to a republican form of government. If it is difficult to judge history in the light of unfulfilled hypotheses, history can well provide a judgement on policies which are actually enforced.

The mere fact that it was a political decision which saved the emperor from prosecution does not necessarily mean that it was mistaken. The trial itself was from beginning to end political. The question is, was MacArthur right in describing the prosecution of the emperor as an 'unjust action', thereby deliberately implying that the emperor was not guilty on any of the counts listed in the indictment?

At one level MacArthur was clearly not correct in this view. The terms of the indictment (for reasons which I have already given) were almost certainly sufficient to secure the emperor's conviction. This was not only the view of Keenan, but also of Comyns Carr, the much more able British prosecutor (who, in a purely legal approach, based his argument on the extremely wide terms of the indictment in relation to the Anglo-Saxon law of conspiracy).

Keenan, a much less subtle man than Comyns Carr, gave his views in a radio interview in 1950. Asked whether the emperor should have been tried, he said, 'My answer to that, briefly, is no. From the evidence at the trial, it was clear that Hirohito himself did not want war . . . Strictly legally, Emperor Hirohito could have been tried and convicted, because under the Constitution of Japan, he did have the power to make war and stop it. We could have convicted him.'

Keenan's words introduce both a moral and a historical element into the debate about the emperor's guilt. Is it sufficient that he did not want war (a proposition which few now deny)? Did he in fact have the power to make war and stop it under the Meiji constitution? If so, why should he be freed from blame for failing to exercise this power?

On the face of it the Meiji constitution of 1889 gives the emperor almost unlimited powers in relation to the command and deployment of the armed forces, including, in Article XIII, the right to declare war. It is here that the contrast with the restrictive provisions of the 1947 constitution is the most remarkable. But like so many things in Japan, the Meiji constitution was never intended to be taken at its face value, as the Meiji Emperor himself well knew, and his grandson the Showa Emperor knew even better. The initiative behind the constitution was that of the Meiji oligarchy, of which two members, Inouye and Ito, were particularly active during the period of eight years of preparatory work. It was a part of the oligarchy's policy to establish Japan as an equal of the Western powers. It was Inouye, and Roessler, the German adviser to the oligarchy, who insisted on the principle of making the emperor the source of political power, with ministers of state responsible to him, and not to parliament. Roessler in fact wanted to go even further, and provide that the emperor should actually direct the cabinet, but Ito and Inouye rejected this advice, on the ostensible grounds that such provision was already implicit in the imperial system.

The history of the late Meiji era (which I have presented briefly in Chapter 4) is sufficient proof that the emperor provided the façade behind which others carried on the government of Japan. No one, not even the Meiji Emperor, had ever intended otherwise: the Meiji Emperor was more than content to leave politics to a succession of governments all of which contrived to enhance his status as the head of a modern industrial state which, at the same time, had become a force to be reckoned with on the world scene.

The Showa Emperor was always content to see the position in the same way as his grandfather had done: this was not only a matter of personal inclination (made clear by the emperor's taking the side of Minobe in 1935) but also of *realpolitik*. The real difference with the

Meiji era lay in the lack of any consistent direction in the succession of governments which sheltered behind the imperial façade. In contrast to their Meiji predecessors, these governments were quite unable to provide the emperor with any but the most fleeting and insubstantial moments of glory, such as the celebration of twenty-six centuries of imperial rule in 1940. Finally, in 1945, they had brought their country to a state where the emperor at its head was left not only to survey a scene of unparalleled devastation, but also to answer for it.

The remarkable thing is that the emperor was ready to accept such responsibility, as he made clear in the meeting with MacArthur in September 1945. If this could be disregarded as no more than a noble gesture by a man anxious to do his utmost for his devastated country, the position of the emperor threatened to become much more uncertain as the result of a statement made by Tojo in the course of the Tokyo trial, that 'no Japanese subject would go against the will of His Majesty'. Sir William Webb, who at the end of the trial was to name the emperor as the 'Leader in Crime' (in which case it would be inappropriate to hand down any death sentences upon those actually convicted), was only too eager to make use of this lapse. The way the prosecution was to go provided Tojo with the opportunity to make good the damage he had done to the emperor, so that in his final statement he was able to say, 'At the beginning of the trial, I was worried that the responsibility of the emperor might be questioned. I feel at rest now that the doubt has been cleared. From the beginning I was ready to take the entire responsibility for the war, but regrettably others have been brought into the trial . . . If you ask my opinion about the trial I can only say it is a victors' trial.'

Before turning to the question of the possible guilt of the Showa Emperor, arising out of specific incidents, such as the rape of Nanking in December 1937, it is worth while considering, once again, what the consequences would have been had he been one of the accused. Note first that he would never have been just one of the accused: the whole trial would have been focused upon him, and whatever might have been the decision of the court in relation to the remaining accused, no one would have been interested. This would have been so, even if the dire consequences feared by MacArthur had not been realized. Any sense of moral outrage felt by the Japanese at the behaviour of their war-time leaders would certainly have been completely neutralized. In any moral terms acceptable to the Japanese, the conviction of the emperor would have allowed all the remaining accused to shelter behind him, to be seen simply as the victims of retribution taken by those who had won the war. Even without the emperor as one of the accused, Tojo succeeded, in his final speech, in casting doubt upon the moral basis of the trial. Of course, the emperor might have been acquitted: but then, in the light of his willingness to accept responsibility (as communicated to General MacArthur on 27 September 1945), what justification would there have been for the conviction of any of the remaining accused?

Now this may add up to no more than a sort of tactical argument, providing additional support for the policy actually adopted by Mac-Arthur of not proceeding against the emperor. It could still be that the emperor was responsible, say, for the rape of Nanking. If so, then such responsibility must be found in the terms alleged by those latter-day prosecutors who still insist on the emperor's guilt. Whatever the merits of the case presented, its importance cannot be doubted, simply because of the very considerable support it still receives – some fifty years after the commission of the alleged crimes – in the Western world.

At this point it is worth noting that the self-appointed prosecutors are, in the first instance, almost all journalists, who base their case on the knowledge of events which they impute to the Showa Emperor, as much as on his failure to act upon them. The case, if looked at closely, is based essentially on a variant of the 'if I was a horse' argument, familiar to historians as well as anthropologists. In the present context, what is really being said is, 'If I had been the emperor, I would have known what was happening, and have taken the necessary action.' Now a journalist is trained to smell out news, and not only that, he has remarkable freedom in choosing his sources, and his field for investigation. This is coupled with exemplary freedom of movement, buttressed by special privileges such as 'press cards'. When Japanese soldiers massacred 100,000 Chinese civilians and prisoners of war, this appalling act was reported by any number of foreign correspondents, and their reports received full publicity in the press. There is no doubt that the world outside Japan knew, within days, about the rape of Nanking.

If the world knew, does this mean that the emperor should have known also, as for instance Edward Behr alleges in his book, *Hirohito*? The circumstances of his life confined the emperor to the palace, where all contact with the outside world was controlled by members of the court. The emperor's reading was confined to material written in Japanese, and the Japanese press published nothing about the rape of Nanking. True the news could not be prevented from reaching the government but when Hirota, the Foreign Minister, heard the news, he was, according to the report quoted by Behr, 'violently angry'. And if that was his reaction, what would have been that of the emperor? Is it not likely that Hirota's first concern would have been to ensure that the emperor did not hear the news? And then, if Prince Asaka, the emperor's uncle by marriage, and one of the army commanders largely responsible for the atrocities, played golf with the emperor some two months after the event, would he have chosen to break the news? Behr asks, rhetorically, 'What did they talk about, the weather?' Is it suggested then that the prince started the ball rolling by saying, 'I hope Your Majesty approves of the fact that troops under my command murdered 100,000 unarmed Chinese in Nanking last December'? By that time the prince would long have realized that the rape of Nanking was something which the government would rather forget; there would have been small hope of that if the emperor had been told about it. In the uncertain climate of the time, the prince could hardly not have known that discretion is the better part of valour. In any case, the virtue of discretion is something almost any Japanese, let alone an imperial prince, learns in the cradle.

The second question put at the beginning of this chapter is, Why is it that so many people are still obsessed with the need to establish the Showa Emperor's guilt as a war criminal? Before turning to this question, it is worth while to make one further point which distinguishes the Tokyo trial from Nuremberg, particularly as they were seen by the defeated populations. The Japanese, after Hiroshima, had the conviction that there was no further price to be paid for the war. Hiroshima (followed by Nagasaki) was the complete expiation of whatever wrongs had been committed by Japan. In so far as the Tokyo trial was acceptable to the Japanese, it was because it passed judgement on men whose policies had led large parts of their own country to be reduced to dust and ashes. The point was made in the dissenting judgement of the Indian judge, Radhabinod Pal: 'If any indiscriminate destruction of civilian life and property is still illegitimate in warfare, then, in the Pacific War, this decision to use the atomic bomb is the only near approach to the directives of . . . the Nazi leaders during the Second World War. Nothing like this could be traced to the credit of the present accused.' Now many saw Pal as a maverick, representing a country which survived the Pacific War unscathed (although any number of Indian soldiers fought against the Japanese), but then the same point was taken up, some twelve years later, by the Dutch judge, Bernard Röling, who represented a country whose losses in the Pacific War were never to be made good. In his judgement '. . . from the Second World War above all two things are remembered: the German gas chambers and the American atomic bombings'.

Röling was not entirely correct in his view. There are many, still today, whose memories of the Pacific War extend much further than Hiroshima. The trauma of the Bataan Death March and the Burma Railway has not been effaced for those involved, nor for the members of the families of those who failed to return. Less evocative but equally traumatic events still colour the lives of thousands of people who, in internment camps, had to start every day with a ceremony in which everyone bowed to the Emperor of Japan. Seeing that in the Dutch East Indies almost the entire European population (of well over 100,000), including women and children, was interned, it is not surprising that still today there are many in Holland who find it intolerable that the beloved House of Orange be represented at the funeral of the same man: even after more than forty years, some things cannot be forgotten, let alone forgiven. If Holland is the country which suffers the most from this trauma, it is still not entirely alone. In other countries, veterans' organizations (such as the British Burma Star Association) help keep memories alive, and find support among top politicians and the press.

One problem here is that the West has itself in the last forty years acquired too many hostages to fortune. Is Nixon's cover-up for Lieutenant Calley after the My-Lai massacre in Vietnam any different from Konoye's cover-up for the officers in the field who orchestrated the rape of Nanking? And what about Lt.-Col. Oliver North, who according to Reagan was a 'great American patriot'? This may be largely an American matter (which in part may explain why the Americans have so little animus against the Showa Emperor), but there are comparable instances to be found in, say, the war in which France was engaged in Algeria thirty years ago. It is because the Dutch are not frightened to look in their own back-yard that they are still ready to condemn the Showa Emperor, even though the real (though never admitted) charge laid against him is simply that he survived the defeat of his country, and that for a period of more than forty years.

This is not the real legacy of the years of the Showa era up to 1945. Time will cure the grief of the countless individuals who suffered, directly or indirectly, under Japanese occupation. The real charge, even if seldom made explicit, is that the Japanese destroyed a political, economic, social and cultural system in which the domination of the Western world was taken for granted. The point was made with brutal simplicity by J. R. Jayewardene, who represented Ceylon (where he was later to become President) at the San Francisco Peace Conference in 1951: 'Before the war, Japan alone was strong and free in Asia. The slogan of co-prosperity in Asia was attractive to its subject peoples. I still recall how certain leaders of Burma and Indonesia co-operated with Japan in the hope of liberating their countries.'

This was a quite explicit aim of Japanese policy-makers throughout the whole Showa era: Prince Konoye, as a young man, made this clear as early as 1918 when a piece he wrote with the title 'Reject the Anglo-American-Centred Peace' was published in *Nihon oyobi Nihon-jin*, a nationalist magazine. This contains the prophetic words, 'In actual fact, the present position of Japan in the world, like that of Germany before the war, demands the destruction of the status quo.' But this was not all that he said: he went on to add, 'In the coming peace conference [Versailles], should we decide to join the League of Nations, we should demand as the minimum *sine qua non* the eradication of economic imperialism and discriminatory treatment of Asian peoples by Caucasians . . . Should the peace conference fail to suppress this rampant economic imperialism, the Anglo-American powers will become the economic masters of the world, and in the name of preserving the status quo, dominate it through the League of Nations and arms reduction, thus serving their own selfish interests . . . Should their policy prevail, Japan, which is small, resource-poor, and unable to consume all its own industrial products, would have no resort but to destroy the status quo for the sake of self-preservation . . . That is why we must reject economic imperialism, not only for the sake of Japan, but to establish among all nations equally the right of existence based upon the principle of justice and humanity . . . It is also imperative that Japan insist on the eradication of racial discrimination . . . the peace conference will provide the opportunity to determine whether or not the human race is capable of reforming the world on those principles. Japan must not blindly submit to an Anglo-American-centred peace; it must struggle for the fulfilment of its own demands, which are grounded in justice and humanity.'

According to Konoye's biographer, Yoshitake Oka, '. . . the beliefs stated . . . by the 27-year-old Konoye remained basically unchanged. They are important, for they continued to influence his entire political career.' As early as the Peace Conference at Versailles in 1919 (which Konoye himself was to attend as a junior observer), the Australian Prime Minister, William Hughes, threatened to withdraw his delegation if Japan's proposal for a clause in the League of Nations Charter in favour of racial equality was adopted in any shape or form. Hughes, who feared defeat in the forthcoming Australian general election, got his way. Now, eighty years later, every objective stated by Konoye has been realized. Is it surprising then that Konoye, as the leading Japanese politician in the years 1937 to 1941 (in which he was to head three administrations), accepted – if often against his better judgement – a course of events which led to the Pacific War? Even after the end of the war, it looked as if Konoye would have a part to play in rebuilding Japan, but when on 6 December 1945 SCAP issued orders for his arrest to stand trial before the IMTFE, he took the law into his own hands. In the early morning of 16 December, he committed suicide by taking poison.

If the Pacific War is seen in any sense as a struggle centred on maintaining the status quo criticized by Konoye, in his 1918 essay, then its end was certainly a Pyrrhic victory for the allied powers. This is the real reason why, for so many people, the Showa Emperor remained on trial to the end of his life. Years of war against Japan had left Chiang Kai-shek too weak to turn back the tide of revolution with Mao Ze-dong at its head. In March 1945, in a desperate attempt to strengthen their position in Indochina, the Japanese abandoned the local French administration (which had looked after the civil government of the country following the agreement made between Japan and Vichy France in June 1941), unleashing, to take its place, a local cabal, called Vietminh, led by one Ho Chi-minh, whom the world was to get to know better in the years to come.

For one reason or another, the world, after years of anguish, has been able to accept these changes. At least no one blames them on Japan, let alone the Showa Emperor. (Neither President Bush of the United States nor President Mitterand of France had any difficulty about attending his funeral in February 1989.) It is the Dutch who have had the most difficulty in accepting the aftermath of the Pacific War. In Indonesia the Japanese, in March 1942, freed Achmed Sukarno, the leader of the independence movement, from the imprisonment imposed by the Dutch colonial government: after the Japanese defeat in 1945 he was to lead his country to independence, ending a colonial regime first established more than three centuries earlier. Even if this regime already contained the seeds of its own destruction (as the school led by the Dutch political scientist, W. F. Wertheim – himself interned by the Japanese as a young man – has always contended), its end still meant a traumatic loss of identity to the Dutch nation. The final reward for the hundreds of thousands of victims of Japanese aggression was the loss of almost everything for which they had suffered so much. This loss was shared by millions at home in Holland, who had been brought up as citizens of a power to be reckoned with on the world scene. In 1940, after the Germans had overrun Holland, the government, in exile in London, still ruled over a great empire, and indeed would have moved its capital to Batavia, on the island of Java, if the health of Queen Wilhelmina had allowed her to travel so far afield.

After four centuries in which the Dutch presence had been established in every part of the world, from the Bering straits to Tasmania (both named after Dutch navigators), Dutch culture and language were to count for little outside Europe, except in a few surviving enclaves. The other great colonial powers of modern European history, England, Spain, Portugal, even France, had left a permanent and substantial cultural legacy even in the post-colonial world: Holland, if economically more prosperous than any of these countries, has left no such legacy. It is precisely because the Showa Emperor survived the Pacific War to become the symbol of the Japanese State that he is denied by so many in Holland any right to rehabilitation. In the reversal of fortunes brought about by the Japanese in 1942, it is the humiliation which is so intolerable. At the same time as hundreds of thousands of Dutch citizens were imprisoned by the Japanese, the one man in the Indies who was bent upon destroying the whole Dutch heritage was released from prison, together with many of his most important followers – and he had history on his side.

The Pacific War brought about fundamental changes in attitudes to race, and that not only in the Western world. So long as the war continued, allied propaganda constantly portrayed the Japanese as members of a degraded race: cartoons encouraged allied soldiers to think of them as apes, and white soldiers often referred to them as such. At the same time black leaders, such as the American Roy Wilkins, were not slow to see that disaster at Pearl Harbor was due at least in part to the white habit of looking down on non-white nations.

With the allied victory, every appeal to racial prejudice had been forgotten, and the Tokyo trials, whatever their other failings, showed no sign of it. Yet the colonial world of South East Asia to which the Japanese had brought an end by their early victories in 1942 was a world familiar from the stories of Somerset Maugham, and no one who knew it would deny that its hallmark was the privileges assumed by whites, whether they were Dutch, English, French or whatever. This was the whole charm of the world lost to the Japanese, but in the years since 1945 the ethic of racial emancipation denies the losers the right to say so. In 1948, the National Party government in South Africa, elected on the policy of apartheid, succeeded in attaching a label not only to a policy, but to an attitude of mind which in the rest of the world was no longer to be respectable. What is more, this was a party in which many prominent members (some of whom had been detained during the war for security reasons) had openly sympathized with the racial policies of Nazi Germany. It is absurd to think that the South African National Party invented apartheid: their achievement was to crystallize the issue of race, and having done so adopt a policy directed to turning back the tide of history. At the same time the rest of the world had to face the issue of race, and take a stand: in the post-war climate the only possible stand was in favour of emancipation. This factor, more than any other, frustrated any policy intent on restoring the position of the pre-war colonial powers in what Japan had chosen to call the Daitōa Kyōeiken. Co-prosperity was not part of the pre-war colonial package, and no cosmetic operation would change that.

An old East India hand cannot come out in the open and blame anyone for the acceptance of the principle of racial emancipation (which has become embedded in the rhetoric of international politics): in the open he must accept it himself, but that does not prevent him from harbouring a grudge. The old culture has been forced underground, but its roots have spread more widely than people care to admit, and it is not only those who actually lived in the old colonial world of South East Asia who in their hearts still affirm it. Can it not be, then, that for such people the Showa Emperor, so long as he lived, was still the symbol of the forces which destroyed this world? For those, particularly in Holland, who wished to downgrade the emperor's funeral, at the beginning of 1989, this was the unforgivable crime. It was then easy to remember the hundreds of thousands in the Japanese internment camps who, every day of their lives, had been humiliated by being forced to bow down to the emperor.

Finally, a word for the emperor himself. In face of all the accusations made against him, he never said a word in his own defence. He was always content to let the record speak for itself. This was the mark of great wisdom, for the clearer the record becomes, the more certain it is that the Showa Emperor must be acquitted of any of the crimes alleged against him. General MacArthur's policy of granting immunity to the emperor was right on any terms. Moreover the emperor did pay a price not only for the defeat of his country, but for the judgements of the Tokyo trial. Men he had worked with for years were removed from his life. Whatever his own judgement was of Konoye, Tojo, Hirota, or even Matsuoka (who died before the trial began), these, and many others taken from the scene by the victorious allies, were the men he had known in the years before 1945. Some, such as Kido, served out a sentence of imprisonment to return to the life of the court, but even so the Showa Emperor, at the end of 1945, was left more lonely and isolated than ever, and this too was a judgement.

11

The Chrysanthemum Curtain

THE end of the allied occupation of Japan in 1952 followed the Peace Conference in San Francisco in September 1951. There fifty-two members of the United Nations agreed to readmit Japan to international society. The United States was represented by President Truman, who in his final speech rightly extolled the achievements of General MacArthur, and praised the Japanese people for their co-operation with him during the period of occupation. As Truman said, 'During these six years, Japan has become a new Japan.' Now, some thirty-eight years later, a Dutch journalist, Karel van Wolferen, has published a monumental book, *The Enigma of Japanese Power*, which maintains the thesis that in these six years nothing important changed in Japanese politics. My main object in this chapter is to consider whether, and to what extent, van Wolferen's judgement is right in its relation to the Chrysanthemum Throne (which he for the most part ignores).

In spite of unprecedented emancipation, both political and economic, of large sectors of the Japanese population (such as women and tenant farmers) during the time of the occupation, the period which then followed was to show that the Japanese still had not fully learnt to come to terms with the imperial family in any way which would make it more accessible to the general public. In contrast to the United Kingdom, where in the planning of any local event, the possibility of some member of the royal family being present is almost always on the agenda, in Japan, any such initiative is left to the court, and the courtiers are not particularly inclined to encourage such participation. This explains why the Prince Mikasa, youngest brother of the Showa

Emperor and something of a maverick in imperial circles, coined the term 'The Chrysanthemum Curtain', which I have chosen as the title of the present chapter.

In a broad historical perspective, the years after the end of the occupation, 1952–89, echo the years of the reign of the Meiji Emperor, 1889–1912, following the promulgation of the first Japanese constitution. In both cases, the emperor was allowed to take the credit for a period of enormously successful expansion, when in fact he had done very little to bring it about. The Showa Emperor's last important initiative was his disclaimer of divine status on New Year's Day, 1946. None the less, in the period after 1952, there were changes in the emperor's position which make it worth while to look at the historical record.

The most significant event at the beginning of this period took place on 10 November 1952, when, in a traditional State ceremony, the Showa Emperor's oldest son, the Prince Akihito, was recognized as the *kōtaishi*, or Crown Prince. This established his right of succession to the throne, even though he would have to wait thirty-seven years before he would actually become emperor. The new *kōtaishi* was then to follow in his father's footsteps, to represent Japan abroad, and make a grand tour, as the Prince Hirohito had in 1921. This enabled Akihito to be in London to represent Japan at the coronation of Queen Elizabeth II in June 1953.

The Crown Prince was to be at the centre of the next public occasion in which the emperor was to be involved. This was the engagement of the Crown Prince, which was announced on 27 November 1958, with the wedding following some four months later on 10 April 1959. The Crown Prince had had to clear many of the same hurdles as his father had faced in the early 1920s, for the future Princess Michiko was not a bride who satisfied the norms which the court would have liked to enforce. Akihito, like his father before him, had the support not only of his own parents, but of the Japanese press and public. The winter of 1958–59 provided one of the rare occasions for the Japanese people to show their interest and enthusiasm for the imperial house: every detail in the life of Michiko-sama was reported in the popular press. For a brief period of time the Chrysanthemum Curtain had been raised.

The actual wedding was true to type, and took place according to the best traditions of the Kyoto *kindairi* which I describe in

Chapter 3. The ceremony was performed in the *kashikodokoro*, the most important of the three Shinto shrines in the Imperial Precinct. Following custom, neither the emperor nor the empress attended, but there was one innovation: they were able to witness the ceremony on television from their house in the Imperial Precinct. Once it was over, the Chrysanthemum Curtain was lowered once more, and it was to be five years before the Showa Emperor was to make an important public appearance.

In 1955, four years before the imperial wedding, the Liberal Democratic Party – or in Japanese, simply the *jimintō* – was formed by the amalgamation of the two major conservative parties in the Diet. The *jimintō*, with the advantage of an electoral system which favours its candidates for the powerful lower house, has been in power ever since. Until 1955, the constellation of parties represented in the Diet recalled the situation in the era of the Taisho Democracy (with the important difference that the power of the military had been drastically reduced). Since 1955, Japan, according to van Wolferen, has maintained a 'socio-political "order", such as it has not experienced since the Tokugawa period'.

The actual system is not at all transparent. Providing interpretations and explanations of what goes on behind the scenes of government keeps any number of professional Japan-watchers in business. For the present it is sufficient to ask about the involvement of the emperor in the political process.

On the face of it, two points, one legal and the other historical, are sufficient to deal with this question. The first is the purely symbolic role of the emperor, as Head of State, provided for by the 1947 constitution. On any interpretation, the Showa Emperor, in the years since 1947, had no legal power to intervene in the government of Japan. The second point is that there has been nothing in Japanese history since 1947 comparable to the events in the years before 1945, in which the Showa Emperor did choose to enforce his own will. All these events, starting with the Mukden incident and fall of the Tanaka government, and ending with surrender, were the result of the policy of military expansion overseas which the succession of governments in this period chose, if sometimes unwillingly, to enforce.

The points made above do not however tell the whole story. Just as the *jimintō* has tried hard to restore the old pre-1945 power structure, and indeed improve upon it, so also has it tried to reinstate the emperor in his original image. This policy has been followed in spite of the obstacles which the reforms of the MacArthur shogunate put in its way. At first sight the operation is largely cosmetic, so that complaints about its results can be dismissed as exaggerated.

A number of instances taken from the history of the period after the end of the occupation illustrate this point. In 1953, the traditional reconstruction of the *naigū* at Ise took place for the first time since 1929. According to the twenty-year cycle, this meant a delay of four years, acceptable to even the more ardent Shinto traditionalists given the historical circumstances. Now at one level, what could be more innocuous than reviving a tradition established at the very dawn of Japanese history? What really counts is that the abandonment of the tradition would have reaffirmed the message contained in the Showa Emperor's disclaimer of January 1946. The old *naigū* would simply have remained as a monument to a past era, when the sun-goddess, whose home it was, still reigned through her divine descendant, the emperor for the time being. It is of course something of a paradox that a building dating only from 1929 would have become no more than an historical monument, whereas its actual replacement, built twenty-four years later, would represent a much older, but still *living* tradition.

The resumption of the twenty-year cycle paved the way for the revival, in 1955, of the Imperial Institute for the Study of the Ise Shrine, which had been suppressed by SCAP. The object of the revival was quite simply to provide a forum for investigating the possibility of reinstating Shinto as the official State religion. True, such an objective is subversive of the articles of the 1947 constitution (described in detail on page 158) prohibiting any involvement of the State in religion, but it was never the policy of the *jimintō* to take any counter-action. On the contrary, as time has gone on, it has become abundantly clear that the *jimintō* favours such initiatives. In 1960, Hayato Ikeda, the Prime Minister, answering a parliamentary question about the meaning of the *yata* mirror, said that Ise was important for the State because of the part it played in the Japanese identity. A Shinto official, Uzuhiko Ashitsu, in his history of Ise in the first fifteen years after the end of the Pacific War, gave a significant twist to the interpretation of this answer: 'The Ikeda cabinet confirmed, without any qualification, the principle of *kokutai* according to which the sacred mirror is transferred, by divine mediation, from father to son, in the imperial line. The mirror is tied inseparably to the fate of the emperor's throne. This recognition of the truth of this dogma removes all obstacles standing in the way of the further development of *kokutai*.' In spite of a number of *non sequiturs*, it is not difficult to see what Ashitsu was getting at.

The process, needless to say, continued unabated. 1966 saw the reinstatement, but with a different name, of *kigensetsu*, the public holiday which celebrates the foundation of the imperial line by the Emperor Jimmu. The Showa Emperor, it seemed, was intent not only on reinstating the *yata* mirror, but the jewel and sword as well. In 1972, a number of inhabitants of Ise petitioned for the reinstatement of another Shinto ceremony banned by SCAP, the *kenjinogodoza*, which is focused on the jewel and sword. The petitioners made their own view quite clear: 'The emperor remains in the end a divine being and the court ceremony of the *kenjinogodoza* bears unmistakable witness to the divinity of His Majesty.' The time was well chosen. The following year, 1973, would see the end of the twenty-year cycle which had begun in 1953, so that once more there would be a new *naigū* to be dedicated. This time the *kenjinogodoza* was one of the ceremonies performed.

In 1977, on the occasion of the press conference held in August of every year, the Showa Emperor appeared to give a new slant to the 1946 disclaimer. The new generation which had grown up in the intervening thirty years was to be told that 'It was urgently necessary to show that democracy was not something which had to be introduced into Japan. We made the proclamation because we wished our people not to forget their pride, by bringing to their attention the great ideas of Meiji.' The point to this somewhat cryptic interpretation is simply that the Showa Emperor, as he grew older, wished to see the historical continuity of the Chrysanthemum Throne re-established. This explains his unremitting devotion to his grandfather, the Meiji Emperor. It is easy enough to give a sinister interpretation to this, but an innocent one is equally convincing. The Japanese are masters of ambiguity, not only in what they say themselves, but in how they interpret what is said to them: any number of opinion polls in recent years have shown that there is no common meaning on questions of this kind. Their most striking and consistent result, however, is that something over three-quarters of the Japanese population wish to see no change in the role of the emperor. This may be less significant than the fact that those who control the system of government do wish to see such change.

The evidence for this is to be found in the tacit support given to the militant organizations belonging to the ultra-right, or *uyoku*. The actual number of active members of such organizations may be less than 200,000 and that in a population of 120,000,000, but these members maintain a conspicuously high profile. Small unofficial paramilitary groups, with armoured cars and loudspeaker vans, are to be seen in almost any Japanese city. In the course of the 1960s, when the *jimintō* was busy consolidating its own power, the *uyoku* formed a blanket organization called Zen Nippon Aikokusha Dantai Kaigi, which may be translated as the 'All Japan Council of Patriotic Organizations', and since this time the Zen Ai Kaigi (as it is known for short) has made no secret of the fact that its main objective is the complete political rehabilitation of the imperial tradition. Behind the Chrysanthemum Curtain Zen Ai Kaigi worked hard for a Showa restoration.

The fact that the Japanese government has made hardly any serious attempt to control the *uyoku* (whose political objectives, on a favourable view, can be seen as perfectly legitimate) still leaves open the question of its own policies in relation to the same objectives. And having answered this question, one must still ask how far the Showa Emperor was involved in these policies.

The centre of controversy may be taken to be the Yasukuni Jinja. This is a Shinto shrine, not particularly remarkable in form, in the Tokyo district of Kudan, close to the Imperial Precinct. It was, to quote the leaflet handed to visitors, 'founded by the Meiji Emperor in 1869 for the worship of the divine spirits of those who gave their lives in defence of the Empire of Japan'. As such it became the most important of the so-called *gokoku*, or 'defending the nation' shrines. The peculiarly Japanese character of the institution, as described in this leaflet, is so interesting as to justify further quotation.

The original name of the shrine, Shokonsha, 'means the shrine or place to which the divine spirits of those who have made the great sacrifice are invited, and is thus peculiar to Japan inasmuch as the unknown warriors of Europe have not been apotheosized.

'The term Yasukuni or Yasukuni Jinja, the new name being graciously bestowed by His Imperial Majesty the Emperor Meiji in Meiji 12 (1879), signifies "peaceful country" implying that, owing to the meritorious services of the spirits of the deities worshipped, the Empire enjoys peace and tranquillity.

'All the deities worshipped here at this shrine are those who, entertaining such sentiments as mentioned above, sacrificed themselves as the foundation stones for the making of modern Japan. In other words, during the period of about a hundred years, viz from the time before and after the Restoration of Meiji to that unforgettable year Showa 20 (1945) when World War II came to an end, there had been various engagements, outbreaks, rebellions, incidents and wars, internal and external, in which a great number of people including loyalists, warriors, soldiers, sailors and civilians employed by the military gave their invaluable lives for the cause of their sovereign and country. The number of spirits now worshipped amounts to some 2,500,000, and their names . . . are respectfully preserved at this shrine in the form of accurate records . . .

'Throughout the three periods of Meiji, Taisho and Showa (up to Showa 52) i.e. 1977 the Shrine has been honoured with 72 visits of Emperors, Empresses and Crown Princes. Visits from Princes of the Blood are too numerous to be chronicled, running into hundreds.

'Every year hundreds of thousands of the war bereaved including numerous fellow soldiers coming from various parts of the country are privileged to pay . . . homage to the Deities worshipped who were formerly their blood relations, close acquaintances or fellow country-men. In recent years the number of annual visitors to this shrine has increased rapidly and amounts to some 8 millions.

'From what has been stated above you may fully understand how highly the Deities worshipped here are revered by the people of Japan.'

The above passages plainly require some exegesis, but first some-thing must be said about the Yūshūkan, which is one of the buildings in the shrine complex. This is described as 'An exhibition of treasures in the possession of Yasukuni Jinja and items left by the war dead'. The Yūshūkan is in substance a museum of the Pacific War, as seen from a distinctively Japanese point of view. The perspective bears little relation to that which I have chosen for Chapter 8, and the whole presentation, to any foreign visitor, suggests a deliberate attempt to rewrite history.

This is largely a question of emphasis. A special display is devoted to 'Memorabilia of the late General Anami'. As I have related at the end of Chapter 8, it was Anami who, as Minister of War, opposed to the bitter end any acceptance by Japan of the terms of the Potsdam declaration. When, finally, he had to accept defeat, it was his influence which led to the inclusion in the emperor's rescript announcing the surrender of the words 'the war situation has developed not necessarily to Japan's advantage' – perhaps the most masterly understatement of the twentieth century. General Anami was to commit *seppuku* immediately after the surrender had been agreed, following the precedent of General Nogi on the death of the Meiji Emperor, and establishing his position as a cult figure in the same tradition.

To the cynical foreign observer Yasukuni is a shrine dedicated to the sort of Japanese doublethink immortalized by Anami. To many in Japan it is the focus of all attempts to re-establish historical continuity, and so to eliminate the period of the MacArthur shogunate from the Japanese consciousness. This in itself would not matter if Yasukuni were no more than a cult centre kept alive by a number of super-patriots. Once more one must look at the record to get to the truth of the matter.

Turning first to the publicity hand-out, there is no doubt that the revival of State Shinto is implicit in almost every line. The emphasis on peace and tranquillity in a memorial to more than two million war dead is characteristic of pre-1945 imperial rhetoric. The explicit recognition of these dead as *kami* unequivocally links Shinto with the Japanese military tradition of *bushidō*: the ghost of General Nogi would certainly approve. But what about the Japanese public, the Japanese government and last, but not least, the Showa Emperor?

As to the public, the open precinct of the Yasukuni Jinja, on an ordinary day, shows no sign of any particular interest in the cult to which the shrine is dedicated. In the concrete jungle of downtown Tokyo the shrine precinct, with its spacious tree-shaded avenues, is a pleasant and restful place to spend the lunch-hour. Many of the eight million annual visitors seem to be more interested in feeding the pigeons than worshipping any of the two million-odd deities.

There are of course many Japanese to whom Yasukuni means much more than this, and it is to these that the government looks for support for its own policy. This policy is simply to lose no chance to rehabilitate Yasukuni as a significant factor in Japanese public life. Considering that not only the ordinary war dead, but also General Tojo, the wartime Prime Minister who was executed as a war criminal, are commemorated at Yasukuni, it is not surprising that the reinstatement of Yasukuni has attracted criticism – and that not only from abroad. The process of rehabilitation may be taken to have started in 1975, when the Prime Minister Takeo Miki paid a private visit on 15 August, the day on which Japan commemorates the end of the Pacific War. This was a concession to the political influence of the Association of War Bereaved Families. Two of Miki's successors, Takeo Fukuda and Zenko Suzuki, followed in the same tradition, and the former, at least, signed the visitors' book as Prime Minister. It was Prime Minister Yasuhiro Nakasone ('Yasu' to his friend, Ron Reagan) who really forced the issue. On 15 August 1985, he not only prayed at the shrine and offered flowers (paid for by the government), but went straight to the inner room: the significance of such acts would not be lost on the Japanese. What is more Nakasone was accompanied by some 200 *jimintō* members of the Diet and most of his cabinet. In the two following years Nakasone stayed at home under diplomatic pressure from China (whose defeats by the Japanese, going back to 1895, are commemorated in the Yūshūkan). The *jimintō* representation, however, was as strong as in 1985.

What then was the Showa Emperor's position in relation to Yasukuni? Given his devotion to the memory of his grandfather, the Meiji Emperor, he could hardly have been expected to repudiate so important a monument of the Meiji era. Twice a year, on the occasion of the spring and autumn festivals celebrated at Yasukuni, an imperial messenger is present to read the *gosaimon*, the emperor's message to the deities. This, however, is about the extent of the imperial patronage in the period after 1952: there is no suggestion that the government's policy of reinstating Yasukuni was in any way a response to the will of the Showa Emperor. The emperor's position is none the less compromised by this policy for, given the history of Yasukuni, the emperor is inevitably involved in what happens at the shrine. His position under the 1947 constitution allowed him little scope for any negative reaction to what the government was doing, so that his failure to react can hardly be taken as a sign of approval. This does not mean that Yasukuni has played no significant part in a Showa restoration orchestrated by the *jimintō*. If anything the opposite is true: the best explanation of *jimintō* policy is that it was directed to precisely this end.

In the period of the Chrysanthemum Curtain the dramatic suicide of the writer Yukio Mishima was an event noted far outside Japan. Mishima was the self-appointed leader of his own patriotic movement, the *tate no kai*, or 'shield society'. Some idea of Mishima's gut response to the peaceful development of post-war Japan is to be found in the comment he made in 1968 about the *ni-ni-roku jiken*: 'The February 26 incident was not only the greatest political incident of the Showa era, but also the greatest clash between spirit and politics. In this clash politics won and the spirit lost.' The objective of the *tate no kai* was to revive the spirit of the *samurai*, and Mishima himself, in the *Hagakure Nyūmon*, had written an introduction to the *samurai* ethic of death. On 25 November 1970, Mishima, supported by four members of the *tate no kai*, overpowered the commander of the Tokyo regional headquarters of the Japanese Self-Defence Force (the closest approach to an army allowed by Article 9 of the 1947 constitution) and dressed in a military uniform of his own design (including a headband inscribed with a slogan from the *Hagakure*), addressed some 1,000-odd off-duty soldiers present on the parade ground, and urged them to follow his lead and demand the abolition of Article 9. This piece of theatre was but a pale shadow of *ni-ni-roku*. The soldiers were unmoved. After railing at them for ten minutes Mishima withdrew into the commander's office from the balcony where he had addressed the crowd, and with his short sword committed *seppuku* in the correct ritual fashion. The final stage in the drama did not go quite right: his lieutenant failed to decapitate him with his long sword, although he did then succeed in committing his own *seppuku*.

If Mishima was motivated by Oscar Wilde's principle that 'there is only one thing in the world worse than being talked about, and that is not being talked about', he certainly succeeded in his aim. As promotion for his book, his suicide was certainly good public relations. Otherwise his death was completely counter-productive. The soldiers had laughed at him, and the *jimintō* disowned him, Nakasone calling his gesture 'madness'. No reaction is reported from the Showa Emperor, but recalling his immediate and outspoken condemnation of the *ni-ni-roku jiken*, nearly thirty-five years earlier, he must have been appalled by what Mishima had done. The irony is that Mishima's suicide was the ultimate fulfilment of his loyalty to the emperor: it was in the tradition of General Nogi in 1912 and General Anami in 1945, and equally misconceived. Who was it who said, 'History repeats itself, the first time as tragedy, the second time as farce'?

Why then make so much fuss about Mishima if his final self-immolation set back rather than advanced the causes dear to his heart? The answer is to be found in his commentary upon 'a philosophy of love', the second of the three philosophies of the *Hagakure*:

The early modern European ideals of patriotism also may be said to have agape [spiritual love completely divorced from carnal desire] at their source. Without much exaggeration we can say, however, that in Japan there is no such thing as love for one's country. There is no such thing as love for a woman. In the basic spiritual make-up of the Japanese, eros and agape are melded. When love for a woman or a young man is pure and chaste, it is not different from loyalty and devotion to one's ruler. This concept of love, which makes no distinction between eros and agape, was called 'falling in love with the Imperial family' [*renketsu no jō*] at the end of the Tokugawa Period and laid the emotional groundwork for emperor worship.

The prewar emperor system has collapsed, but the concept of love in the spiritual make-up of the Japanese people has not necessarily collapsed along with it. This concept is based upon a firm belief that that which emanates from pure instinctive sincerity leads directly to an ideal to strive for, to die for if necessary. Jocho's [the original compiler (1659–1719) of the *Hagakure*] philosophy of love has its foundations here. Citing as an example the love of a man for another man, which in his day was regarded as a higher, more spiritual emotion than love for a woman, he maintains that the truest and most intense form of human love develops into loyalty and devotion to one's ruler.

Sincerity, connoted by the character 誠 which occurs in all the different words representing it, is seen by the Japanese as the supreme virtue. Mishima, in linking it to 'loyalty and devotion to one's ruler', was not saying anything new, but reviving a principle dear to many of his countrymen. If the self-styled patriots of *ni-ni-roku* were in the vanguard of the Showa restoration in its pre-1945 version, Mishima and the *tate no kai* had taken over the helm thirty-five years later. Whatever the present-day doom-watchers may say, it is significant (and indeed comforting) that in nearly twenty years the new patriots still have a long way to go before they realize their objective. This does not mean, however, that the prophetic role of Mishima has been effaced.

It is time to follow another tack, and look at another cultural phenomenon which has received much attention from the Japan-watchers.

This is *nihonjinron*, which, in the view of its proponents, is the art of being Japanese. It is summed up in the title of a recent book by Peter Dale, *The Myth of Japanese Uniqueness*, which follows Roy Miller's somewhat earlier book, *Japan's Modern Myth: the Language and Beyond*. Myth is the element common to both studies, and the main thesis of all the critics of *nihonjinron* is that it insists that the Japanese understand and interpret their own culture and society on a basis which is essentially mythical. Although the emperor is not even mentioned in the index of either Dale's or Miller's book, implicit in their argument is the proposition that since the emperor's denial, in the New Year's Day statement of 1946, of any mythical basis for the ties between him and his people, the Japanese have been looking for some other charter myth to take its place. This myth, once established, will then no doubt be conflated with some revised but still recognizable version of the original, discarded myth.

At first sight this is reading a lot into Dale and Miller, but then neither of these two scholars was directly concerned with the problem of the emperor. However Dale has discovered that Heisaku Kosawa, Japan's leading Freudian psychologist, has recast the Oedipus complex in a form which excludes the essential element of parricide. This transformation, based upon a dubious reading of a well-known Buddhist classic, represents an obvious political concession in a society such as Japan, where the supreme virtue of *chūkō* (which I discuss in Chapter 2) combines filial piety with loyalty to the emperor.

The spirit of *nihonjinron* also lies behind the significant reform of the calendar introduced by the government in 1979 (whose basis in Japanese tradition I explain in Chapter 1). This requires all official documents to be dated according to the *nengō*, that is the name of the current era followed by the number of years which have elapsed in the reign of the emperor. This system combines the worst of two worlds, the modern international world represented by the West in the context of *nihonjinron*, and the enclosed world of traditional Japan. This reform has the merit of reminding the Japanese that even time is measured by the lives of the emperors, but in doing so it denies the fact that the experience of time is shared by all mankind. The message is that Japanese time is different, and the way Japanese experience time not accessible to the general run of mankind. Once again the Japanese are unique.

The real focus of the myth is the Japanese language, as Roy Miller demonstrates almost to the point of overkill. It is particularly the written language, based on an extraordinarily involved use of Chinese characters, supplemented by two so-called syllabaries developed by the Japanese themselves more than 1,000 years ago, which is so distinctive. Four hundred years ago St Francis Xavier described this as an invention of the devil designed to prevent the spread of the gospel. Even the Japanese have immense problems with their written language. The need to learn some 1,000-odd *kanji*, or Chinese characters, dominates the primary school curriculum, and the same number must be mastered in the first three years of secondary school.

The question of the written language was a major concern of the MacArthur shogunate. Expatriate officials in the Civil Education and Information Section of SCAP seriously considered whether they should not enforce the complete abandonment of *kanji*, for anything in Japanese can be written in either *kana* syllabary, or indeed in the Latin alphabet (which the Japanese refer to as *rōmaji*). The top officials of the *mombushō*, the Japanese Ministry of Education, resisted such reform even more strongly than they resisted the repeal of the Imperial Rescript on Education. They did, however, find an expedient which was acceptable to SCAP as a compromise. This was the publication of an official list of 1,850 *tōyō* (or 'everyday') *kanji*, to be taught in schools and used by the press. This was only a small selection out of the tens of thousands of *kanji* to be found in written texts produced over the course of more than 1,200 years, but the *tōyō kanji* were more than sufficient to get on with for all normal purposes.

The *tōyō kanji*, promulgated in February 1946 to meet the demands of SCAP, proved to be the invention of an enduring tradition. On any common-sense view they are still in use, but this is not how the matter is seen by the *mombushō* (which may be seen as the cultural bastion of *nihonjinron*). The fact is that in 1982 the *tōyō kanji* were replaced by the *jōyō kanji*, a reform of truly oriental subtlety. In any Japanese-English dictionary, *tōyō* and *jōyō* are given the same meaning in English. What is more the actual *kanji* in the two lists are almost identical, so that the millions of Japanese who learnt the *tōyō kanji* at school now have no difficulty at all with the *jōyō kanji*. (Almost all Japanese have considerable difficulty with texts published before 1946 in which many of the most common *kanji* have a quite different form. This is an important psychological point in establishing the end of the Pacific War as a decisive break in Japanese cultural history: in the era of *arahitogami*, the divine present emperor, even the language was different.)

By any rational standards the *tōyō kanji* were an instant success. They established a degree of uniformity in the written language which had never been known beforehand. One might think then that the government, and more particularly the *jimintō*, would have been content to leave well alone. To think in this way shows little understanding of government mentality in Japan.

At a very early stage (in 1949) the regulation of the *tōyō kanji* was entrusted to an official body known as the *kokugo shingikai*, or 'National Language Council'. This was a self-perpetuating co-optive body, which recruited its members from education, publishing, broadcasting and so on, and there is no indication that it failed to do its job properly. In fact there was little to do: almost all the original *tōyō kanji* have stood the test of time.

In 1961, at the end of the fifth two-year session, four conservative members forming a minority of the *kokugo shingikai* tried to impose a new policy, based on two principles: the first, *kanji seigen hantai*, means simply 'opposition to the limitation of *kanji*', and the second, *kyūkana tsukai futtatsu*, 'restoration of old *kana* usage'. To an outside observer the whole affair would seem to be nothing but a storm in a teacup, but of course one must be on one's guard whenever a word such as *futtatsu*, or 'restoration', is part of the matter at issue. As it was, the *mombushō* intervened on the side of the minority, and from the sixth session onwards the minister himself has had the right to appoint the members of the council. In other words the *jimintō* usurped the power of what had been an independent body performing its tasks to the satisfaction of all concerned.

So what have they won? The victory is one of principle more than substance. The *tōyō kanji*, which represented a uniform level of proficiency in the written language within the reach of almost all Japanese, were downgraded. The new *jōyō kanji* are good enough for the masses, but they are no basis for the literate culture of the élite. (General Tojo, a good bridge-player, once remarked that having mastered 5,000 kanji, he had little difficulty remembering the fifty-two cards in a pack.)

The point to the whole operation is that the principle of hierarchy was re-established. The substance was less important. The Japanese are all equal but some are more equal than others. At the same time the protagonists succeeded in focusing attention on something which was uniquely Japanese, that is the written language. But where does the emperor come in?

There is no direct answer to this question. The art of calligraphy and the composition of the traditional thirty-one syllable poems know as *tanka* have a long tradition in the imperial court. The Meiji Emperor composed over 100,000 *tanka* in the course of his life, and his grandson, the Showa Emperor, if less prolific, was no less skilled in the art. This interest, which is shared by millions of Japanese, finds its fullest expressions in the postcards which are sent out as New Year's greetings. Many Japanese spend the last weeks of the old year, after the cards are on sale in the post offices, in composing *tanka*, or other greetings, which are then written out with a *fude*-pen – a combination of a fountain pen and a writing brush, which can be used as a surrogate for the traditional *fude*. These are then sent to any number of friends and relatives. The composition of *tanka* for the New Year is a long-standing tradition in the imperial family, and at least since the Meiji era a selection of the poems have been read out at the New Year Poetry Party at the imperial court. In the era of the Chrysanthemum Curtain, a small number of members of the public, chosen for the high quality of their work, are invited to be present on this occasion. Such an invitation is, needless to say, regarded as an exceptional honour. The poetry-reading, in the late Showa era, was, except for the emperor's birthday, his only regular contact with his people.

The *jimintō* government which established the *jōyō kanji* in 1982 never linked this particular reform to the imperial court, but it is worth recalling (from Chapter 4) that the great Meiji, in his day, when compared with the German Kaiser Wilhelm I, was seen to excel in his gifts as a poet. Not long after the introduction of the *jōyō kanji* the minister at the head of the *mombushō*, Mitsuyo Setoyama, attributed the increasing lack of discipline in Japanese schools to the work of SCAP officials operating more than thirty years earlier. It is hardly surprising, then, that his successor, Masayuki Fujio, went a step further and urged the reintroduction of the moral code of the Imperial Rescript on Education. In Japanese politics the *mombushō* requires much closer watching than parallel departments of education in Western countries.

None of these policy trends assigns any specific role to the emperor. If anything, the opposite is the case. What is most in the interests of the *jimintō* oligarchy is that the taboo surrounding the emperor should be maintained. In the course of the 1980s the increasing age of the emperor helped keep the Chrysanthemum Curtain tightly drawn. The last foreign visit, to the United States, had taken place in 1975, and this was the last occasion when the emperor and his wife were really in the public eye for any extended period of time. One of the last informal photographs of the emperor in public shows him signing the visitors' book at Disneyland, with Mickey Mouse standing in the background. In 1986 Nakasone, then Prime Minister, took the initiative in commemorating the completion by the Showa Emperor of an unprecedented reign of sixty years, but this provided practically no scope for photo-journalism (as I have already noted in Chapter 1). The ten million commemorative gold coins issued by the Bank of Japan carried no likeness of the emperor (in accordance with strict Shinto principles relating to possible defilement).

The emperor's formal duties were for the most part carried out behind the scenes, although he did, significantly, make a yearly visit to Ise, the home of the sun-goddess. For the rest he continued to perform the private Shinto ceremonies in the three shrines within the Imperial Precinct. Their most important purpose was to honour the imperial ancestors, but prayers were also said for the preservation of the country and the fertility of its soil. The status of these rituals, as much as that of their performer, was equivocal. A government spokesman, in a written answer to a question asked by Peter Crome, declared that ' . . . the emperor, in the private sphere, shares the traditional beliefs of the imperial family, as expressed in State Shinto, and performs the ceremonial rites of the court. The emperor has no fixed rank as a leader, whether of State or sect Shinto. Japanese mythology describes the emperor as a descendant of the sun-goddess, Amaterasu. According to traditional belief, the imperial family regards Amaterasu Omikami as its founding ancestress. Since this tradition is not historical it requires no official judgement. Within the court the emperor carries out the ceremonial rites as a private individual, and not as leader of Shinto nor as a Shinto priest. Before the war, when the ceremonial rites of the court were officially sanctioned by the State, the emperor performed these rites as the highest in rank within State Shinto.'

Looking back on the twilight years of the Showa Emperor, his identity remains a conundrum: it is better not even to try to solve it.

However, three years before the end came, a Tokyo journalist, Naoki Inose, published a book, *Mikado no Shōzō* (or Portraits of the Mikado), which put forward not one solution, but any number of alternative solutions. It is open to any group of people to project their own conception of the emperor, which is no more than what the young officers of the *ni-ni-roku jiken* did in 1936, or Mishima and his followers in the *tate no kai* in 1970. The emperor himself can also play this game, and the Showa Emperor did his best to appear as a sort of Japanese equivalent of his British contemporary, King George VI (1895–1952). No attempted projection ever becomes definitive: every image, as soon as it comes into focus, dissolves. The succession of *jimintō* governments which have been in power since 1956 have never succeeded in finding a convincing role for the emperor, which is why they have preferred to keep him on ice, ensuring, thereby, that their opponents do no better.

Robert Guillain, in his book *La Guerre au Japon*, comes as close to the truth as anyone when he describes the emperor as 'the man who has no right to be man, first because he is kept at a distance behind a wall insurmountable by ordinary people, and then because he is himself in some way Japan, its living history, its aspirations, its beliefs. He is an ensemble of institutions; he is a crown; and his image is inseparable from the background upon which it is projected – a multitude of seventy-five million people.' The concept of reflection is particularly apt in an imperial culture one of whose most important symbols is a mirror. Following in the footsteps of Alice (whose dreams have been translated into Japanese), and passing through the looking-glass, the emperor becomes the Red King, and everyone becomes an actor in his dream. Tweedledee put it in a nutshell:

'He's dreaming now,' said Tweedledee: 'and what do you think he is dreaming about?'

Alice said, 'Nobody can guess that.'

'Why, about you!' Tweedledee exclaimed, clapping his hands triumphantly. 'And if he left off dreaming about you, where do you suppose you'd be?'

'Where I am now, of course,' said Alice.

'Not you!' Tweedledee retorted contemptuously. 'You'd be no-where. Why, you're only a sort of thing in his dream!'

'If that there King was to wake,' added Tweedledum, 'you'd go out – bang! – just like a candle!'

The 'unbroken line of succession' means that the dream has lasted since time immemorial. The emperor himself cannot be asked what he thinks, because then it would be necessary to wake him up. No wonder the Japanese prefer not to talk about him. This is why the unscripted drama of Japanese life remains open to any number of alternative and conflicting interpretations.

The Showa Legacy

In a 'conversation with the philosopher, N', which forms an appendix to Inose's book, *Mikado no Shōzō*, the court is referred to as *mienai seido*, the 'invisible institution'. This is also the point I reached in Chapter 11. When, however, in September 1988 the Showa Emperor succumbed to an illness from which he had no hope of recovery, the invisible insitution became only too visible, just as it had seventy-six years earlier when the Meiji Emperor fell ill in the summer of 1912.

The transformation was accomplished first of all by the use of photography, supplemented in 1989 by every possible type of media coverage, including live TV broadcasts of the crowds waiting outside the Imperial Precinct. This lies at the heart of the cultural paradox of the imperial institution. The death of the emperor released a torrent of photographic documentation: where in 1987 it was difficult to find any popular publication detailing the life of the emperor (so that I had to visit about ten bookshops before I found one with Inose's book), in 1989, when I went to Japan for the funeral, every possible retail outlet carried an enormous display of such material, produced for every possible intellectual level, and coming from every possible source; even the Communist Party, the Kyōsantō, had its own contribution, entitled simply *Tennō Mondai*, 'The Emperor Problem'. What is more, every publication was dated according to the Heisei era, whose name was not known until the accession of the new emperor, Akihito. Before I left Japan on 25 February, the day after the funeral, an eighteen-volume encyclopaedia of the Showa era was already on sale. True the publishers must have been hard at work at least from the day that the Showa Emperor first fell ill, five months beforehand, but even so, their productivity was simply staggering.

The flood of lavishly illustrated publications about the Showa Emperor, and his era, was but a part of the media coverage. The television crews had been waiting for months outside the Imperial Precinct, but so long as the emperor lived the only information supplied by the court consisted of numerical factors relating to his physical state: he became a person described in terms of body temperature, pulse rate, blood pressure, and respiration. Some details were also given of the medical treatment, and at one stage the doctors seem to have been uncertain whether the transfusion of ordinary blood was acceptable for their august patient. Once the emperor died, two whole days of uninterrupted broadcasting covered every aspect of his life and times. From that time on, until the day of the funeral, any number of programmes were devoted to the same theme, with the funeral itself being covered from every possible angle.

How then did the Japanese public react to all this: were people really that interested and concerned? With a population in Japan of well over a hundred million, no complete answer to this question is possible. The media were busy with it the whole time. Both TV and the newspapers reported, for instance, that the shops hiring video-cassettes had never done such good business as in the two days after the death, when the public were denied their normal TV diet of sumo-wrestling, blood-curdling period dramas and coy English lessons. On the eve of the funeral, six weeks later, the Ueno station in Tokyo, where the main-line trains depart for the north, was crowded with skiers (and foreign TV crews denied all facilities to cover the funeral itself) leaving for a windfall three-day weekend. The newspapers confirmed that the ski-resorts (which the government had tactfully exempted from any sort of mourning) were booked solid. There was never any doubt that any number of Japanese had more than had their fill of mourning. More generally, in the weeks after the Showa Emperor's death there was little, on the surface of life, to show that the country was involved, somehow, in a protracted series of *rites de passage*, involving the very centre of its being, and taking place for the first time in more than sixty years. Perhaps more surprising is the fact that even such places as the Inner Shrine at Ise or the Meiji Shrine in Tokyo, so closely associated with the imperial institution, gave no sign that anything extraordinary was taking place.

For ordinary people the lifting of the taboo had released a pent-up, and almost obsessive, interest in the emperor. Some sat out the whole two-day TV coverage following the death, others recorded the whole transmission on video. Many a family compiled a thick scrap-book filled with newspaper cuttings about the emperor. Everyone was ready to talk about the Showa Emperor, and discuss in detail such matters as the relationship between the imperial institution and Shinto.

This brought in another paradox. A death must be followed by a funeral, but what is to be done in a country such as Japan, where the only possible funeral for an emperor, with any sort of religious validity, is apparently unconstitutional? It was clear to all that the funeral of an emperor was a special case. (An ordinary Japanese would find it difficult to believe that an English sovereign was buried with the normal rites of the Church of England.) All this is but part of the legacy from the period of State Shinto established in the Meiji era (1868–1912), and terminated by the Showa Emperor's disclaimer in 1946, and the new constitution in 1947. So successful was State Shinto that few today would accept the possibility that the emperor might have a Buddhist funeral, which is the standard practice with more than 90 per cent of the Japanese population. The fact that the Meiji Emperor's predecessor, Komei, had a Buddhist funeral when he died in 1866 is not generally known, although in a TV-panel broadcast on the day of the Showa Emperor's funeral, Inose was asked why a Buddhist funeral could not be held. To this question he could give only an equivocal answer.

Given that the funeral brought the whole question of the relationship between Shinto and the emperor into focus, the question arises, is there any sort of minimal position held by the great majority of Japanese, and if so, what is it? The following answer is probably near to being correct. The unbroken line of succession to the Chrysanthemum Throne, established before the dawn of recorded history, does mean, for the Japanese, that the emperor's continued well-being is somehow tied, supernaturally, to that of the nation as a whole. This is essentially the position summed up in the official answer to Peter Crome's question, which I have quoted in Chapter 11. In the urban civilization of modern Japan many go no further than this.

Nevertheless, this belief, in the context of Shinto, accepts that the prosperity of Japan's traditional agricultural economy, based upon the cultivation of rice, depends, at every season of the year, upon the favour of the appropriate *kami*. The calendrical rites traditionally carried out by the emperor, or *tennō* – however low-keyed – are still seen by many as essential for gaining such favour, even if this requires that the *tennō* (notwithstanding his disclaimer on New Year's Day, 1946) is himself a living *kami* (although not necessarily the only one at any given time). The point is that it is the office, rather than its holder, which is effective: the succession is apostolic in the sense of that to the Holy See, whose theocratic powers, whatever they are, depend upon much the same factors. In both cases there is a definite mythical starting point located somewhere between heaven and earth: the link between the two, in both cases, is maintained by those that successively represent that starting point. In the Japanese case, it is as if the succession of Popes were conflated with all the numerous, and sometimes nearly forgotten, local saints, often the patron of some distinctive human activity, so that the distinction between the two categories became blurred. In comparison to the saints of the Church, many *kami* are curiously disembodied – spirits enshrined in such natural features as trees, rocks and waterfalls – but even then every one of the old Japanese cities sends its delegation of a fixed number of *kami* to the Yoshida shrine in Kyoto, to represent it at the feast of *setsubun* which, on 2 February every year, marks the end of winter. True the imperial ancestors still retain their identity, but it is one conferred upon them after their death. It must not be thought that Shinto, in whatever form, has any doctrine of resurrection, even for the *tennō*: Shinto is a religion of this world, not of the next, for which the Japanese must look to Buddhism. Part of the whole paradox is that Shinto is the religion of the living, whereas it is Buddhism which is the religion of the dead. It is not for nothing that in the history of Japan the emperors have been among Buddhism's most important patrons.

The funeral itself, on 24 February, treated the thin crowds on the streets of Tokyo to a spectacle which provoked a palpable sense of disappointment. A steady, heavy drizzle, at a temperature just above freezing point, suggested that the weather *kami* were not pleased by the way things were organized. Shortly after 9.30 a.m. the constant cawing of crows and the incessant drone of police helicopters were interrupted by a twenty-one-gun salute followed by the sad strains of the 'Kanashimi no Kiwami', 'The Height of Sorrow', composed by a forgotten German composer for the funeral of the Showa Emperor's great-grandmother. It did not take long for the cortège to appear, nor for it to pass by: a motorcade, with police outriders, in which the last vehicle, incongruously, was a white bus from Kokusai Tours, provided a supremely depressing spectacle in a country rightly renowned for the splendour and magnificence of its ceremonial. The funeral of the Emperor Taisho, held along the same route on a cold winter's night almost exactly sixty-two years before, with a bier drawn by seven sacred bulls, followed by a long procession, on foot, of men clad in traditional costume, the whole lit by blazing logs in tall iron braziers, provided a model which the present government, no doubt supported by the *kunaichō*, the Imperial Household Office, chose not to follow. It seemed almost as if the message to the crowds, both on the streets and in front of TV sets across the land, was simply, 'See what you get if you ask for a secular funeral.' In fact it was more the fear of terrorism which had decided the form taken by the funeral procession: the government also took refuge in the fact (noted in a book on the Taisho funeral which appeared in December 1988) that the 1909 Imperial Household Mourning Ordinance, which had governed the 1926 funeral, had been repealed by the 1947 constitution.

This legal point was dealt with by making the Shinto funeral a private ceremony paid for by the Imperial Household. The final destination of the cortège was a park, the Shinjuku Gyoen, which had been closed to the public since the emperor's death. There a temporary shrine, the *sōjōden*, was constructed by skilled craftsmen, out of unseasoned wood, on a traditional model. The Shinto funeral ceremony, the *sōjōden no gi*, began as soon as the cortège arrived, and had all the splendour which the crowds on the streets of Tokyo had been denied. Fortunately the TV cameras provided a unique opportunity for observing it.

The ceremony, as is normal with Shinto rites, was long on action and short on words. Before it could begin, the imperial coffin was carried into the *sōjōden* in a palanquin weighing one and a half tons, carried by fifty-one members of the Imperial Guard dressed in the style of the Heian period of some 1,000 years ago. This, and the accompanying music, was the most moving part of the whole ceremony. The ceremony carried out by Shinto priests in the *sōjōden* itself consisted mainly of ritual offerings, including two and a half cups of rice, twenty quail, a wild duck, seven carrots, three lotus roots, sweet bean paste, sake, nine apples, assorted fresh-water fish and bales of silk – a collection so heterogeneous, at least to Western eyes, as to defy any sort of 'theological' analysis. The distinguished guests, freezing in the tents provided for them, were able to watch this on closed-circuit television, enjoying a view no better than that provided for the millions of ordinary Japanese who watched TV in the comfort of their homes.

The *sōjōden no gi* was followed by the 'great mourning ceremony', or *taisō no rei*, which is what representatives from some 160 different countries had come to participate in. This purely secular event, which had cost the Japanese government some $74 million to stage, according to *Time* 'at times . . . seemed more a convention of world leaders than the occasion to mourn the death of an aged and controversial Emperor'. It started with a very short and moving speech by the new emperor, who was followed by Takeshita, the Prime Minister, and three other prominent figures. These four speeches, equally short and appropriate to the occasion, were read aloud, in the form of letters, each ending with the date and the writer's name, and written in beautiful calligraphy on Chinese folding scrolls. Even after his death, the Showa Emperor, both in the public and in the numerous private rituals, was treated as someone who could be communicated with, a property he would retain, as an imperial ancestor, into the indefinite future.

The eulogies took up little time, and were followed by the representatives of the foreign states being called up one by one to pay their respects to the deceased emperor, simply by bowing to the coffin, a procedure which lasted for about an hour, and completed the *taisō no rei*. The official funeral, in this form, was little different from that of many a secular funeral in the Western world. One is tempted to ask whether it has to be that a funeral, once denied any 'theological' content, must be based upon a standard international model of this kind. In Japan (and elsewhere), TV viewers also had the chance to compare the demeanour of an unprecedented assembly of world leaders. The palpable misery of President Bush (who had just heard that the United States Senate had rejected John Tower, his nominee for Secretary of Defence) could be compared with the composure of President Mitterand, the relaxed attitude of the King and Queen of Spain, or the perplexity of many Third World leaders. The Japanese dignitaries, led by the new emperor, far surpassed any of their guests in bearing the strain of a very long day: their performance was, in the true meaning of the word, exemplary.

At the end of the *taisō no rei*, the palanquin, once more containing the coffin, was carried back to the hearse, and the funeral cortège proceeded, over a distance of some 28 kilometres, to the outer suburb of Hachioji, where the Showa Emperor would be finally laid to rest in the *sanryō*, or funeral mound, specially constructed for him next to that of his father, Taisho. The rites conducted there on the day of the funeral, which lasted some five hours, were attended only by members of the Imperial Household and were not televised. Although the rites still to be performed will not be completed until 1990, the Showa Emperor has at least reached his last and only permanent resting place. It is significant that the *rites de transition*, such as have so far been performed, were all carried out in temporary structures. Hardly a month after the funeral, the Shinjuku Gyoen, once more open to the public, showed no traces of the *sōjōden*, nor of the ceremonies witnessed there by millions of people over the whole world. *Sic transit gloria mundi*.

It is difficult, so soon after the event, to pronounce any definitive judgement about the funeral of the Showa Emperor. The Japanese government on the one hand, and the Imperial Household on the other, had to conflate a number of different traditions of uncertain validity into a form subject to unprecedented political constraints, both national and international. Much of the problem is defined by conflicts about time. The undoubted antiquity of the imperial line provides no real argument for reinstating the State Shinto rites, ruled out by the 1947 constitution, particularly when the historians can prove that their mythopoeic basis is hardly a hundred years old. As of now, the funeral of the Emperor Taisho, in 1927, is the only complete instance of this tradition, at least if one accepts the position that the *sōjōden no gi*, as performed in 1989, was a private court ceremony in which the State was not involved.

The funeral which took place on 24 February in fact comprised a number of rites, of which only the *taisō no rei*, a strictly secular event, was public. The remaining rites, which were all Shinto, culminated in the *sōjōden no gi* which, although not directly visible to the thousands of guests invited to the *taisō no rei*, could be seen by them – and by countless millions of others, both in Japan and overseas – on television. For this of course there was no historical precedent. The rites preceding the *sōjōden no gi*, performed in the *kōreiden*, the shrine of the imperial ancestors in the Imperial Precinct, and those following it, performed at the *ryōsho*, the place of final burial in Hachioji outside Tokyo, were strictly private.

The rites taking place on the day of the *taisō no rei* were only part of a long series, comprising in all nearly thirty different ceremonies, not due for completion until the end of the year. At the same time, the first rite of accession for the new emperor, the *sensō* (which I describe in Chapter 6), has also taken place. The interesting questions now concern not the funeral, whose status in Shinto is very uncertain, but the rites of accession yet to be performed.

At the moment both the Japanese government and the court are enjoying something of a breathing space. The two main rites described in Chapter 6, the *sokuirei* and the *daijōsai*, will not take place earlier than the end of 1990, if they take place at all. This is the real issue. The government has already announced that the *sokuirei* will take place, but with details to be announced later. As to the *daijōsai*, Prime Minister Takeshita, shortly before the Recruit Cosmos scandal forced him to resign his office, conceded, in answer to a parliamentary question, that this ceremony was ruled out by the 1947 constitution. On the other hand a committee was to be appointed to study the question further.

The whole discussion is taking place against the background of what may be judged to be the most serious government scandal of the twentieth century. In the first two months of 1989 the names of Recruit Cosmos and its egregious founder, Hiromasa Ezoe, dominated the media as much as those of the Showa Emperor and his son, who became the Emperor Akihito on 7 January. Ezoe, with a view to gaining official support for furthering his own interests, and those of the Recruit group of companies, provided the opportunity for almost every prominent member of the *jimintō* government to subscribe for unlisted shares in the Recruit Cosmos company. The result was that when, following expectation, the shares were listed on the Tokyo Stock Exchange, they increased enormously in value, so that those favoured by Ezoe could reap a handsome profit, often of the order of millions of yen.

Ezoe's operation provides an interesting sidelight on both the working of the Japanese bureaucracy and the operation of the labour market. The hard core of Ezoe's business consisted of publishing directories listing jobs available for young people, at various levels of competence and attainment, looking for employment. Given the Japanese custom of remaining true to one employer for the whole of one's working career, the importance of the services provided by the Recruit companies could hardly be over-estimated. At the same time the goodwill of the bureaucracy was essential for the success of the operation. Not only did the Recruit publications rely on the support of the *mombushō* (Ministry of Education), which in Japan is critical for a business of this kind, but Ezoe's involvement in the construction industry made him look for good contacts in the local bureaucracy throughout the country. All this fitted in with an electoral system which involves all politicians in very considerable expenditure: *jimintō* members of the Diet are notorious for the size and scope of the hand-outs in their constituencies.

In the end the Recruit Cosmos scandal not only led to the fall of Takeshita as Prime Minister, but made it difficult to find an untainted successor from within the *jimintō*. Now none of this directly concerns the court: involving members of the imperial family in matters of this kind is quite out of the question. The first question asked by almost everyone in the early months of 1989 was whether the government could hide its own problems behind the popular interest in the succession to the Chrysanthemum Throne. In this the government plainly failed. But then the question arises as to whether the attention paid by the media to the Recruit Cosmos affair does not provide the government with the opportunity to proceed, unnoticed, with plans for carrying out all the rites of succession which I describe in Chapter 6, notwithstanding the constitutional objections. It is true, the Takeshita government has fallen, but the *jimintō* so far remains in power.

Two factors will influence the course of events. The first is public opinion, which according to every survey is content to see the 1947 consitution enforced. It is suprising but true that the *jimintō*, for all the attention it pays to voter relations at grassroots level (which explains the constant need for funds from sources such as Recruit Cosmos), has little regard for public opinion. If the voters can be fixed in the right number of constituencies, then the *jimintō* remains in power, and that is all that Japanese politics is about.

The second factor, of course, is the emperor himself: is he ready to take part in a traditional *sokuirei*, followed by the *daijōsai*? The path of least resistance would be simply to act on the advice of his government, but this will not be easy if, according to the same constitution as established the emperor's position, that advice is illegal. It is here that the funeral rituals may have established a precedent which will solve the problem. Just as the *sōjōden no gi* was a private ceremony paid for out of the funds of the Imperial Household, so also could the same be said of the *daijōsai*. There is no lack of historical precedent for this: in the period when the emperor was confined to the *kindairi* in Kyoto, the *daijōsai* was a private matter of the court. On the other hand it did always take place, and if it had not, the consequences for the unbroken line of succession would have been extremely grave. If the government left it up to the emperor as to whether and how the traditional rites of accession would be carried out, his position would not be at all easy. There is not only the constitutional question, but also the Showa Emperor's disclaimer of 1 January 1946. The *daijōsai* is almost meaningless unless the emperor accepts the status of *arahito-gami*, or 'divine present emperor'. No previous emperor has ever been confronted with this issue at the time of his accession.

The uncertain factor is the advice, if any, given by the Showa Emperor to his son. It could well be that the new emperor, Akihito, will see his father's disclaimer of 1946 as decisive, and out of filial piety and respect to the throne, become the first emperor in Japanese history to forgo the *daijōsai*. No government could question this display of the virtue of *chūkō* (which I discuss in Chapter 2). Any appeal made by the present emperor to the memory of his father would have to be granted, and in this sense the Showa Emperor is, for any Japanese government in the present Heisei era, a hostage to fortune who cannot be disregarded. Until the question of the *daijōsai* is decided, the initiative rests with the new emperor.

The Emperor Akihito could, however, decide in favour of the *daijōsai* on either one of two grounds. First, he could simply maintain that the Showa Emperor, in the last years of his life, had withdrawn from the extreme position taken in the 1946 disclaimer, if only because the circumstances in which it was made were so exceptional. This may well have been a matter of discussion between father and son. Second, the present emperor could equally well maintain that as a constitutional monarch his first duty was to act on the advice of his ministers: the difficulty here is Takeshita's admission (while he was still Prime Minister) that the *daijōsai* was not permissible under the 1947 constitution. If the government, following the advice of the committee yet to be appointed, changes its mind on this, it will certainly be asked some very searching questions.

The consequences for the political climate of modern Japan could be particularly significant if the *daijōsai* were carried out, for this would be a further, and even decisive, step in effacing the era of the MacArthur shogunate, and all that was then achieved, from the historical record presented to the Japanese public. The *jimintō* has long been concerned to use the continuity of the imperial line, as represented in the present century by the Showa Emperor, as the basis for establishing the continuity of government. The catharsis carried out in the years of SCAP is the great obstacle in the way of achieving this position. If this is worked out of the system, the result is an orderly transition from Taisho Democracy to a Showa democracy, of which the *jimintō*, since 1955, have been the self-appointed guardians. If the ship of state survives the storms of Recruit Cosmos (which is what everyone expects), then with the *jimintō* still at the helm, it will enter the period of Heisei democracy, and the second half of the twentieth century will be established as the golden age of Japanese history.

What about the role of the emperor in this golden age? The government would be well served if the new emperor, and his successors, were to see the *kōkyo*, the Imperial Precinct in Tokyo, as a sort of latter-day *kindairi*, where the court can live in style, and play the role of leading patrons of Japanese culture. Ceremonial functions, such as opening parliament and receiving ambassadors, would still be carried out, and State visits abroad could still provide the opportunity for maintaining a favourable public image. At home, visits to Ise would certainly be favoured, but for the rest the public would have to be content with the New Year's poetry reading and the celebration of the emperor's birthday. The emperor would maintain his country homes for vacations, and once official duties were done, chamber music, tennis, marine biology, and above all life with his family would take up his time. The routine of private Shinto rites, performed in the shrines within the Imperial Precinct, established by the Showa Emperor after the disclaimer of 1946, could be continued. Certainly the new emperor was punctilious in carrying out the succession of mortuary rites for his father. But if there is no *daijōsai*, the status of the visits to Ise and the Shinto rites would be extremely uncertain, for the *daijōsai* is at the very heart of Shinto. Would the Japanese public accept this? True enough, an opinion poll conducted by the newspaper, *Asahi Shimbun*, whose results were published on 7 April 1986, had shown that 84 per cent of the people supported the present constitutional status of the emperor, but then the *daijōsai* was hardly a live issue. Other surveys show that of this 84 per cent a very great number will be at least nominal believers in Shinto: more than half of all *ie* still contain a *kamidana*, on which the central position is taken up by a tablet from Ise on which the name of the sun-goddess is written. As the reign of the Showa Emperor moved into its seventh decade, the number of those who had any memory of the last *daijōsai* became progressively smaller, and so the essential relationship between the *daijōsai* and the sun-goddess was lost on the greater part of the Japanese population. Now that the Showa Emperor has died, they are certain to be reminded of its importance, whichever way the decision goes.

The Emperor Akihito, more than any of his predecessors, must trust to his own judgement, and here he has the advantage of his age and experience. No one can provide him with the support which the young Showa Emperor received from the Prince Saionji. The legacy bequeathed by the Showa Emperor is extremely problematic. It was inevitable that the consequences, for the imperial line, of the 1946 disclaimer and the 1947 constitution would only become acute after the Showa Emperor's death. Even the continuation of the imperial line is uncertain, for neither of the new emperor's two sons is yet married (although the court must certainly be able to solve this problem). All that is certain is that there is a new emperor: the definition of his office has yet to be worked out.

If there is one lesson that the Emperor Akihito must have learnt from his father, it is that decisions cannot always be left to others. The Showa Emperor will be remembered for the decisions he took on his own initiative: the surrender in August 1945, the visit to MacArthur a month later, and the disclaimer of his divine status on New Year's Day, 1946, all turned the course of Japanese history. For a man who always shunned the limelight none of these decisions could have been easy. The judgement of history will favour the Showa Emperor because, at every critical moment, he took the right path. True, he failed to curb Japanese militarism, and from this failure followed the most disastrous war in Japanese history. This, however, is saying no more than that he failed to achieve the impossible. The ultimate crisis of the summer of 1945 was without precedent in world history. Its resolution was left to a man who, in the end, would interpret a role on the world stage for a period lasting nearly seventy years – the greater part of the twentieth century. In a government tradition in which responsibility is divided and the position of every leading figure, from the Prime Minister downwards, always precarious, the Japanese emperor is a constant, enduring focus of respect. Only a metaphor can do justice to his role. As the eye of the hurricane, he moves with the storm, but is not part of it. The storm may abate, but it never blows out, and in the years up to 1945 it engulfed the whole world.

Afterword to the paperback edition

I WROTE this book in the early summer of 1989 after having spent the month of February in Japan, where, as an anthropologist, I was able to take note of the succession of rites following the death of the Showa Emperor on 7 January of the same year. As far as the general public, and particularly the world outside Japan was concerned, these culminated in a public ceremony on 24 February, the *taisō no rei*, which I describe in Chapter 12. After having witnessed this ceremony (for the most part on television) I returned to Europe the following day, and after a month spent in collecting source material, I started writing. The manuscript was delivered in July, the proofs corrected in August, and the book published at the beginning of November. At this date the private mortuary rites for the Showa Emperor were not yet complete, and *a fortiori* no decision had been published about the installation rites for the new emperor, Akihito.

The actual one-year period of mourning prescribed for the death of an emperor, which is known as *ryōan*, expired in January 1990. A month earlier the Japanese government had let it be known that the installation rites for the new emperor would follow the traditional forms which I described in Chapter 6. The emperor himself made the formal announcement to his divine ancestress, the sun-goddess, Amaterasu Omikami, on 23 January, setting the date of the civil ceremony of the *sokui no rei* for 12 November, and that of the religious ceremony of the *daijōsai* for the night of 22–23 November.

The policy adopted by the government and the court for the installation of the new emperor is clearly based on the same principles as that adopted in relation to the funeral of his father. Just as the funeral ceremony of the *taisō no rei* was presented as a public, secular occasion, fit to be attended by court and government representatives from abroad, so also would the *sokui no rei* be presented as the public rite by which the new emperor would assume his constitutional position as symbolic head of state. In this case the *sokui no rei* would once more be fulfilling its historical function, as established by the T'ang dynasty in China some 1,500 years ago. On this basis the present emperor assumed the temporalities of his office on the 12 November 1990.

The *taisō no rei* and the *sokui no rei* are ceremonies carried out within the space of a single day. At least in the case of the former, there was hardly any distinctive Japanese note, beyond the few special details noted in Chapter 12. A historical purist could almost say the same for the *sokui no rei*. The purport of this ceremony would have been clear enough to the foreign dignitaries invited to it even without the explanatory notes supplied to them by the Imperial Household Agency. The pageantry, also of Chinese origin, was that described in Chapter 6, and although colourful, its meaning was transparent enough. Nothing that the foreign guests were allowed to witness should have caused them any misgivings about the status of the new emperor. This is precisely the message which the Japanese government wished to convey.

What then is the significance of the fact that in the year 1990 the *daijōsai* was also performed as part of the installation ceremonies? In this case, just as the *sōjōden no gi* was but the climax to a series of Shinto funeral rites carried out in the course of the year of the *ryōan*, so also was the *daijōsai* no more than the culmination of a long series of preparatory rites, the first of which had taken place some ten months beforehand. The critical question is whether the *daijōsai* made, at least by implication, any sort of theological statement open to question in the light either of the Showa Emperor's disclaimer of divine status on New Year's Day 1946 or of the provisions of the 1947 constitution separating state and religion. Although this point is considered in Chapter 12, the possibility of the new emperor not proceeding to celebrate the *daijōsai* is left open and the reasons given which would justify such a decision. We know that he decided otherwise. Although no-one can tell precisely what factors influenced this decision, we do know that it was framed in a particular context, that of the emperor's private religious life, already established by the funeral rites centred on the *sōjōden no gi*. The message is quite simply that it was the emperor's personal decision, on a matter relating to his own private life, in which the government would, or could not interfere. We are concerned therefore with a new religious dimension, which can best be called 'Court Shinto'.

What then are the implications of this position, and to what extent are they credible? In the first place it is plain that every care has been taken to avoid any suggestion that *Court Shinto* commits the state or the Japanese public to any position not allowed by the 1947 Constitution. This itself is not entirely credible in the light of the renewed cult of the national Yasukuni shrine in Tokyo, which I described in Chapter 11, but it could be argued that the emperor himself is only marginally involved in this. In any case Yasukuni never had anything to do with the rites to be performed on the succession of an emperor.

In a briefing given at the Foreign Press Club in Tokyo on the 22 June 1990 by Nubuo Ishihara, Deputy Chief Cabinet Secretary, the official position was stated as follows:

> The Constitution provides that succession is hereditary, so that the government considers itself authorized to organize a *daijōsai* at state expense, for otherwise succession, as provided for in the constitution, would not be possible.

It was also stated that, following the advice of fifteen experts, in all walks of life, this involved no conflict with Articles 20 and 89 of the constitution, dealing with religion (which I discuss on pages 157–58).

This historical rationale is clear enough. The principle is that a Japanese emperor performed the rites of the *daijōsai* some time in the course of his reign, on the basis of a precedent which had ruled throughout the whole course of Japanese history. This still leaves unanswered the question what, at the present stage in Japanese history, does the precedent mean, when the rite which it establishes does not belong to the public domain?

From almost any official Japanese perspective, this is an unfair question, designed to force the issue to a false syllogism. The western world is used to the idea that ritual makes a statement about doctrine. Certainly the priority of doctrine over ritual is central to any Christian theology. The communion service is based upon a quite explicit historical assertion about the occasion, that is the Last Supper, when the ritual was established. The putative historical event upon which the *daijōsai* is based does not have anything like the same status. In theological terms, the old Japanese chronicles, such as the *kojiki* and the

Nihon shoki, which describe this event, are in no sense canonical. They are in no way a part of Shinto worship, even though without the events related in them Shinto would be a lesser religion than it is. Shinto, to cite a recent article in the *Japan Echo*, is 'a complex of religious rituals centred on *matsuri* – acts of worship, especially religious festivals, addressed to a deity'.

This puts in a nutshell. What then is the *daijōsai*, but the special *matsuri* which every emperor, once in his reign, addresses to the sun-goddess, Amaterasu Omikami? One look at the record relating to this extraordinarily original ceremony should convince anyone that it has nothing to do with policy in the public domain, so that, for instance, any link between the *daijōsai* and the lot of the *kamikaze* pilots which I described in Chapter 8 is no more than an accident of history. But why then, if the *daijōsai* is so innocuous, are so many, both inside and outside Japan, so troubled at its being performed as part of the installation of the new emperor?

The explanation must be largely psychological. The fact that the reign of the Showa Emperor was allowed to continue after the complete and utter defeat of Japan in 1945 was a very considerable concession by the allied powers. Although the emperor's disclaimer of any divine status on New Year's Day, 1946, was freely given on his part, it was seen as a definitive break with tradition, and it is not surprising that many, in Japan as well as abroad, still see it as such. This position was confirmed by the 1947 constitution. In the remaining years of his reign the Showa Emperor gave no sign of having changed his position. The most that could be said is that his tacit consent to the Shinto cult of the Yasukuni shrine implied in some way that he was ready to affirm the old tradition.

If then, the celebration of the *daijōsai* by the present emperor in 1990 does not restore the previous position, what is its significance? Once again one must look at *Court Shinto*, which is really something quite new in the religious history of Japan. It would be easy to accept that it adds up to nothing more than a restoration of the religious position of the emperor as it was in the days of the Tokugawa Shoguns (1600–1868), which I described in Chapter 3. True, in this long and relatively recent historical period, the court was hidden away in the *kindairi* in Kyoto, where it was mainly engaged in 'the production of ritual'. At the same time the real government of the country was carried on from Edo, which in 1868 became the capital city of Tokyo.

I have already suggested, in Chapter 12, that the court may be entering a new *kindairi* period, although its present day engagement in Shinto ritual must be at a far lower level than that of the old days in Kyoto. There is, however, one significant difference. In Kyoto the emperors always remained Buddhists, and even the very last of this line, the Meiji Emperor's father, Kōmei, had a Buddhist funeral. For the court this was still the period of *shinbutsu-shūgō*, the conflation of Buddhism and Shinto which is still the religion of the Japanese man in the street.

There has been no sign of restoring Buddhism as a court religion (even though this was how it was introduced into Japan in the first place, not far short of 1,500 years ago). True, any member of the imperial family, other than the emperor himself, would have a Buddhist funeral, as one saw with the death of Prince Takamatsu, a younger brother of the Showa Emperor, in February 1987. But the emperor, religiously speaking, is on his own. Some time in this course of his reign he performs a rite, the *daijōsai*, of which he himself is the only possible object. On the face of it, the only interpretation of this rite in the context of the present emperor is that it belongs to a private religion, of which he is the only representative. This, once again, makes any explanation of the elaborate construction of the two buildings used for the rite in 1990 extremely problematical.

There is no need to discuss the logical difficulties inherent in the idea of a private religion, which are in some ways parallel to those which arise in relation to the possibility, examined by Wittgenstein, of a private language. The question is simply whether the essentially private rite of the *daijōsai* is intended to have any public or state consequences. Considering the controversy which it has given rise to in the first two years of the reign of the present emperor, there are certainly many who believe that this was precisely what was intended. No one can doubt that if the Japanese government had not wanted the *daijōsai* to be performed, the emperor would have accepted its decision.

It must be then that the historical fact of the *daijōsai* in the year 1990 does amount to a political statement, and the Japanese government can hardly contend otherwise. This is precisely the reason for the psychological problems which have now arisen. Let it first be noted that, if the opinion polls are right, government policy on this question is in no way a response to any sort of majority will. Some three-quarters of the Japanese population had no wish to change the position under the allied government in the late 1940s; indeed a number of prominent figures made all too clear their opposition to the renewal of the *daijōsai*.

The opposite position is equally difficult to prove: government policy cannot be just a concession to vocal right wing opinion, expressed through the numerous patriotic paramilitary organizations which maintain a conspicuously high profile in present-day Japan. Ultra-right wing opinion may be a factor in government policy, but it is hardly a decisive one, and relatively few Japanese believe otherwise.

The key is to be found in a search for legitimacy by the Liberal Democratic Party (*jimintō*), which has been continuously in power since its original formation in the mid-1950s. A succession of scandals has dented the image of the party, to the point that it was defeated in the Upper House elections in July 1989, following the fall of two Prime Ministers involved in the Recruit Cosmos affair described in Chapter 12. Yet the party remains in power. This may be the result of there being no credible alternatives, but even so, the party, much more than any other, has succeeded as establishing itself as in some way the authentic voice of Japan. Needless to say, unprecedented economic success has played a major part in this process.

Tradition, more than any other factor, is the basis of authenticity, particularly in Japan. None the less, the whole history of modern Japan, starting with the Meiji restoration in 1868, has rested on invented tradition, in which the religious component has always been critical. Once again, Japan has a government concerned to re-invent tradition, as a sort of charter for its own policies. The whole history of the Imperial Rescript on Education (which I described in Chapters 4 and 9) shows how important this can be for those who govern Japan. The fact that this has now led to the emergence of a *Court Shinto*, recognized by the government as the emperor's private religion, may be paradoxical, but all religion, particularly other people's, contains an element of paradox. (Even St Paul recognized that the doctrine he preached was to 'the Greeks a foolishness, and to the Jews a stumbling-block'.)

Within Japan the government's position is nearly impregnable. To those opposing its stand on the *daijōsai* it can simply point out that they are free, under the 1947 constitution, to reject it. Certainly the press has been free enough in its comment and criticism. None the less, the government has scored a victory. Its version of tradition has been decisively affirmed. The *daijōsai* of 1990 will be a part of history which cannot be rewritten. This explains the frustration felt by many both inside and outside Japan.

A final word should also be said about possible foreign reactions. The allied occupation of Japan ended nearly forty years ago. It is no longer realistic to deny Japan the right to regulate the succession of its emperors in its own way, although the course now being taken in relation to the *daijōsai* may only be possible because the Showa Emperor survived the 1947 constitution by more than forty years. What is more, whatever the correct historical judgement on the Showa Emperor, with his death at the beginning of 1989 the issue has been settled once and for all. The traumas suffered by the powers involved in the Pacific War may not yet be healed, but the Japanese have effectively closed the case against them, whatever its merits might have been. The new emperor, who was eleven years old at the end of the Pacific War, has nothing to answer for. Nor is there anything to be gained by laying the restoration of the *daijōsai* at his door. A chapter of Japanese history has been closed, and it is beyond anyone's power to open it again.

Further Reading

EVER since Japan became known to the West, some 400 years ago, countless books and articles have been written about the country, its people and institutions. For modern Japan, Edwin Reischauer's *The Japanese Today* (Harvard University Press) is a readable, popular introduction, brought up to date in 1988. Roland Barthes' *L'Empire des Signes* (Skira) is much to be recommended as a short, imaginative interpretation of Japan, which is particularly good for its insights about the emperor. For Japanese history, Richard Storry's *A History of Modern Japan* (Penguin) is an excellent, short introduction, while for Japanese contact with the West, Sir George Sansom's *The Western World and Japan* (Cresset Press) is the best-known study. For the imperial institution itself, Jerrold M. Packard's *Sons of Heaven* (Queen Anne Press) is a readable popular study, with few pretensions to scholarship. For a summary of events in the Showa era *Fifty Years of Light and Dark: the Hirohito Era*, written by the staff of the *Mainichi Daily News*, is for its length remarkably complete, but somewhat disorganized. Leonard Mosley's *Hirohito: Emperor of Japan* (Weidenfeld and Nicolson) is complete for all but the last twenty years of the reign. The two books about the Showa Emperor to appear after his death, Edward Behr's *Hirohito: the Man behind the Myth* (Hamish Hamilton) and Peter Crome's *Der Tenno* (Verlag Kiepenheuer & Witsch) are both concerned to establish the Showa Emperor as being at least partly responsible for the wars in which Japan was involved from 1931 to 1945, and for the crimes then committed by the Japanese military. If a choice has to be made between these two tendentious works, Peter Crome's *Der Tenno* is to be preferred for its more

[227]

imaginative interpretation of events. Much the most interesting book about the Showa Emperor, Naoki Inose's *Mikado no Shōzō* (Images of the Emperor) (Tokyo, Shogakkan), has, unfortunately, only appeared in Japanese. For general background to Japan (including the court and the nobility) B. H. Chamberlain's *Japanese Things* (Charles E. Tuttle), which first appeared at the beginning of the century, is a mine of information. At much greater length, the recent Kodansha Encyclopedia of Japan is also to be recommended.

In addition to the general studies, a number of specific works are relevant to the separate chapters of the book. The calendrical material in Chapter 1 is largely to be found under the entries 'Calendar', 'Dates and Time' and 'Periodization' in the Kodansha Encyclopedia. The development of written Japanese is fully described and illustrated in Yaeko Sato Habein's *The History of the Japanese Written Language* (Tokyo University Press). Yuji Aida's *A Prisoner of the British*, which I cite in the text, is published by Cresset Press. Much of the remaining material in Chapter 1 is derived from Japanese newspaper articles appearing in the seven-week period between the death of the Showa Emperor and his funeral, at the beginning of 1989.

For Chapter 2, Robert J. Smith's *Ancestor Worship in Contemporary Japan* (Stanford University Press) is indispensable. For the structure of the *ie*, see Chie Nakane's *Kinship and Economic Organization in Rural Japan* (Athlone Press) or John Embree's *Suye Mura: a Japanese Village* (University of Chicago Press). For the religious background Neil McMullin's *Buddhism and the State in Sixteenth Century Japan* (Princeton University Press) and Robert Bellah's *Tokugawa Religion: the Cultural Roots of Modern Japan* (Collier Macmillan) are both first class. For the development of Confucianism see Masao Maruyama's *Studies in the Intellectual History of Tokugawa Japan* (University of Tokyo Press).

The description of the court in Kyoto in Chapter 3 is largely based on Herschel Webb's *The Japanese Imperial Institution in the Tokugawa Era* (Columbia University Press). For the reader interested in seeing how different Japan can be from any Western Country this fascinating book is much to be recommended. For a glimpse of the last days of the Kyoto court A. B. Mitford's account, recently republished as *Mitford's Japan* (Athlone Press), is as readable as the better known works of his granddaughters, Nancy and Jessica. For this chapter also R. A. B. Ponsonby-Fane's *The Fortunes of the Emperor* and *The Imperial*

House of Japan (both University Publications of America) are standard works. For the intellectual background see Ronald Dore's *Education in Tokugawa Japan* (Athlone Press). For those interested in the Yakuza, Alec Dubro and David Kaplan's *Yakuza* is a modern popular account.

The Meiji era, examined in Chapter 4, has been the subject of a great number of studies. In relation to the emperor Carol Gluck's *Japan's Modern Myths* (Princeton University Press) is greatly to be recommended. K. B. Pyle's *The New Generation in Meiji Japan* (Stanford University Press) is good for its description of the new governing classes, where G. W. Beckmann's *The Making of the Meiji Constitution* (Greenwood Press) is important for the political reforms.

As for Chapter 5, the early years in the life of the Showa Emperor are well described in Leonard Mosley's biography. For the political background and for the consequences of General Nogi's suicide Carol Gluck's *Japan's Modern Myths* is once again invaluable.

For the accession ceremonies described in Chapter 6, two books published by Tokyo's Sophia University are indispensable: these are Robert Ellwood's *The Feast of Kingship* and D. C. Holtom's *The Japanese Enthronement Ceremonies*. Takakuni Hirano's *Daijōsai no Kōzō* (The Structure of the Daijōsai) (Tokyo, Perikankai) is the standard Japanese text.

For Japan before the Pacific War, described in Chapter 7, Hyoe Murakami's *Japan: the Years of Trial 1919–52* (Kodansha International) and Louis Allen's *Japan: the Years of Triumph* (American Heritage Press) are good short studies. For the *ni-ni-roku jiken* and its background, Ben-Ami Shillony's *Revolt in Japan: the Young Officers and the February 26, 1936 Incident* (Princeton University Press) is indispensable. Two books by Yoshitake Oka, *Konoe Fumimaro: a Political Biography* and *Five Political Leaders of Modern Japan* (both Tokyo University Press) portray the leading political figures of this period. For Japan, as seen by an outsider during this period, the American ambassador, Joseph C. Grew's *Ten Years in Japan* (Simon and Schuster) is the classic text.

For Chapter 8, Robert Guillain's *La Guerre au Japon* (Paris, Stock) is absolutely first class. In English, Ben-Ami Shillony's *Politics and Culture in Wartime Japan* (Oxford University Press) is a good short study. For the Chinese side Barbara Tuchman's *Sand against the Wind* (Futura Publications) could hardly be bettered. Akira Iriye's *The*

Origins of the Second World War in Asia and the Pacific (Longmans) is good for the general historical background. The hopeless prospects for Japan in the Pacific War are analysed in both Barbara Tuchman's *The March of Folly* (Collins) and Paul Kennedy's *The Rise and Fall of the Great Powers* (Vintage Books).

The study which best captures the work of SCAP, described in Chapter 9, is Toshio Nishi's *Unconditional Democracy: Education and Politics in Occupied Japan* (Stanford, Calif., Hoover Institution Press). This should be read in conjunction with Elizabeth Gray Vining's *Windows for the Crown Prince* (Charles E. Tuttle), which describes how the imperial family adjusted to the post-war situation.

As for Chapter 10, the political background to the International Military Tribunal is well described in Meirion and Susie Harries' *Sheathing the Sword* (Heinemann). A historical judgement on the trial is to be found in Richard H. Minear, *Victors' Justice: the Tokyo War Crimes Trial* (Princeton University Press). For the scope which the crime of conspiracy allows the prosecution it is worth while to look at Jessica Mitford's *The Trial of Doctor Spock* (Vintage Books). The Dutch experience of the Japanese occupation is well described in L. G. M. Jaquet, *Aflossing van de Wacht* (Relieving the Guard) (Rotterdam, A. D. Donker). For the allied use, for the purposes of wartime propaganda, of racial prejudice against the Japanese, see J. W. Dower's *War Without Mercy* (Pantheon). For the historical background to the Nuremberg trials see Alan Bullock's *Hitler: a Study in Tyranny* (Penguin).

For Japanese politics in the period of the Chrysanthemum Curtain, described in Chapter 11, Karel van Wolferen's monumental *The Enigma of Japanese Power* (Knopf) is significant for its almost complete disregard of any role played by the Showa Emperor. Kishimoto Koichi's *Politics in Modern Japan* (Japan Echo) is useful for its detailed chronology of major political events from the beginning of the Meiji era to the present day. The cultural background is to be found in the two books cited in the text, Peter Dale's *The Myth of Japanese Uniqueness* (Routledge) and Roy Miller's *Japan's Modern Myth* (New York, Weatherhill). For extremism in this period see Yukio Mishima's *On Hagakure: the Samurai Ethic and Modern Japan* (Penguin).

Chapter 12 is largely based on reports in both the Japanese and foreign press, but Nobumasa Tanaka's *Taishō Tennō no Taisō* (The Taisho Emperor's Funeral) (Tokyo, Daisan Shokan) provides essential historical background. This, much more briefly, is also to be found in Adrian Mayer's *The Funeral of the Emperor of Japan* (*Anthropology Today*, June 1989).

Finally, the *Japan Echo* for spring 1989 contains a discussion by Shunpei Ueyama, Takeshi Umehara and Tōru Yano, entitled 'The Imperial Institution in Japanese History', followed by an article by Takeshi Muramatsu, 'The Emperor as Priest-King'.

Glossary

Amakudari lit. 'descending from heaven': refers to top bureaucrats who join outside organizations, and then make use of their government contacts.

Ama no hagoromo lit. 'heavenly feather robe', the garment which the new *tennō* wears during the *daijōsai*.

Arabia sūji Arabic (as opposed to Chinese) numerals.

Arahitogami the term which recognizes the *tennō* as a *kami*.

Arigatō 'thank you', lit. 'it is difficult'.

Ashigari the *samurai* who served as common foot soldiers.

Bakufu the government of the Shoguns.

Banzai lit. 'ten thousand years', a cry wishing success.

Banzai no hata the *banzai* banner used in the *sokui rei*.

Bentōbako Japanese lunch-box.

Bon the Buddhist annual ancestor festival.

Bonzai miniature tree.

Burakumin the current word for the untouchable class.

Bushidō the *samurai* code of chivalry.

Butsudan the household Buddhist altar.

Chinkonsai the ceremony taking place the night before the *daijōsai*.

Chonin tradesmen, traditionally a lower order than the farmers.

Chūkō filial piety combined with respect for the emperor.

Daijōgu the precinct where the *daijōsai* takes place.

Daijōsai the first fruits festival celebrated to inaugurate a new emperor.

Daikan the official entrusted by the *daimyō* with the administration of his fief.

Daimyō lit. 'great name': the highest rank in the feudal order of the Shoguns.

Daitōa Kyōeiken lit. 'Great East Asia co-prosperity sphere', the term coined by the Japanese for the part of Asia occupied in the course of the Pacific War.

Dandanbatake the step-terraces characteristic of Japanese wet-rice cultivation.

Densai the purification rite for the buildings used in the *daijōsai*.

Dōgu lit. 'tool', a word sometimes used to refer to the emperor.

Ekikyō Japanese for the *I Ching* or *Book of Changes*.

Fudai a *daimyō* who is an hereditary vassal of the Shogun.

Fude the brush traditionally used to write Japanese.

Gai 'outside', the *on*-reading corresponding to *soto*.

Gaijin 'outsider', so foreigner.

Genrō the elder statesmen, constituted by those who held high office in the Meiji oligarchy, of which the Prince Saionji was the last survivor.

Giyōden the hall where the imperial family put on their ceremonial robes for the *sokui rei*.

Go a traditional board game.

Gokoku lit. 'defending the country', a term referring to Shinto shrines dedicated to this purpose.

Gokōmon a special prayer to the *kami* made by the emperor towards the end of the *daijōsai*.

Goryō an imperial tomb.

Gosaimon the message sent by the emperor to the deities of the Yasukuni shrine.

Go-sekke the five top-ranking families in the *kuge*.

Gosho the old imperial palace in Kyoto.

Gun county.

Gyoen the enclosure in Kyoto containing the homes of the *kuge*.

Gyoji the imperial seal.

Hagakure nyūmon Mishima's introductions to the classic *samurai* text, *hagakure*.

Haiku a traditional seventeen-syllable, three-line poem.

Haizen a maiden serving the emperor during the *daijōsai*.

Han the fief of a *daimyō*.

Harakiri traditional *samurai* suicide, better referred to as *seppuku*.

Hasshinden lit. 'hall of the eight gods', one of the buildings next to the *saiden*, where the rice for the *daijōsai* is grown.

Heika 'Majesty' as a title.

Heisei the era name chosen by the present emperor, Akihito, which will become also the name by which he will be known after his death.

Himorogi a traditional Shinto shrine used in the course of the emperor's accession ceremonies.

Hinkyū the temporary mortuary in the Imperial Precinct for the emperor's body in the period preceding the *taisō no rei*.

Hinoki the wood of the Japanese cypress, used in the construction of the temporary buildings used for the funeral and accession ceremonies.

Hiōgi a fan of traditional design carried by the empress.

Hiragana the most commonly used of the two *kana* syllabaries, sometimes referred to as *onna no te*, lit. 'women's hand'.

Hito man or person.

Honji suijaku the process by which Buddhist principles are incorporated in Shinto.

Hōon the obligation to make some return for blessings, *on*, received from a deity.

Hotoke a departed spirit, acknowledged as a Buddha.

Ie the traditional Japanese household.

Ikebana Japanese flower arranging.

Ikigami lit. 'living *kami*', of which the emperor, as *arahitogami*, is the prime exemplar.

Inanominoya lit. 'rice fruit house', where the rice harvested from the *saiden* is worshipped as a *kami*.

Inatsuki uta the song sung at the traditional rice-pounding, or *inatsuki*, preparatory to the *daijōsai*.

Ishin term commonly used for the Meiji restoration.

Jichinsai the ritual used to guard against earthquakes.

Jimintō the Liberal Democratic Party, in power since its formation in 1955.

Jogen abbot of a Buddhist monastery.

Jōi expulsion of foreigners.

Jōyō kanji the new (since 1982) form of *kanji* for everyday use.

Jūdō judo.

Junshi the *samurai* custom of following one's lord unto death.

Kagami mirror, in this book generally the *yata* mirror, one of the *sanshū no shinki*.

Kagura the sacred dance performed at the end of the *sokui rei*.

Kaikoku the policy of opening the country to foreigners, as opposed to *sakōku*.

Kairyūden the building in which the emperor makes the ritual preparations for the *daijōsai*.

Kami generally translated as 'god', but can be almost any sort of supernatural being.

Kamidana the shelf for domestic Shinto offerings.

Kamikaze lit. 'divine wind', used for the suicide air attacks on allied warships at the end of the Pacific War.

Kana the syllabaries developed by the Japanese in the eighth century to represent their language phonetically.

Kanashimi no kiwami lit. 'The height of sorrow', the music composed for the funeral of the *kōgō* of the Emperor Kōmei at the end of the nineteenth century.

Kanbun the version of Chinese adopted in medieval Japan.

Kanji the Chinese characters used to write Japanese.

Kanji seijen hantai 'opposition to the limitation of *kanji*', a policy adopted by some members of the *jimintō* during the 1970s.

Kanreki lit. 'returning to the calendar', refers to the sixty-first year of life, in which the *kanshi* calendar begins to repeat itself.

Kanshi the cyclic system of numeration, based on the ten *kan* and the twelve *shi*, which repeats itself in cycles of sixty.

Kashikodokoro the portable shrine, generally kept in the Imperial Precinct, containing the copy of the *yata* mirror, of which the original never leaves the *naigū* at Ise.

Katakana the less commonly used of the two *kana* syllabaries.

Kempeitai the name given to the secret police before 1945.

Kenji the sword and the jewel of the imperial insignia.

Kenjinogodoza a rite focused on the *kenji*.

Kenjitō Shōkei no Gi the ceremony by which the *kenji* are transmitted to a new emperor.

Kenkoku kinenbi the public holiday commemorating, on 11 February in every year, the accession of the first emperor, Jimmu.

Kezuriki a *hinoki* wand used by a Shinto priest to cast out evil.

Kichijitsu the first day after *setsubun*, the feast celebrating the end of winter.

Kikoku shijo lit. 'child returning to its own country', refers to Japanese children who return home after living abroad.

Kindairi the enclosure within the Gyoen where the members of the imperial family lived in Kyoto in the Edo era.

Kōbu gattai the policy of combining the functions of the emperor and the Shogun.

Kōgō the consort of the *tennō*, though not generally the mother of the *kōnaishi*.

Kōhai lit. 'junior' in opposition to *senpai*, 'senior'.

Kojiki the oldest Japanese epic text, from the beginning of the eighth century.

Koku a unit of measure of rice, approximately 180 litres.

Kokugo Shingikai the National Language Commission, which advised on the reform of the *tōyō kanji*.

Kokuji the state seal.

Kokuryūkai the Black Dragon Company, an ultra-nationalist secret society.

Kokutai lit. 'essence of the nation', the basis of Japanese patriotism established in the Meiji era, and maintained officially until 1945.

Kōkyo the Imperial Precinct in Tokyo.

Konrō the two covered corridors reserved for guests attending the *sokui rei*.

Kōreiden the ancestor shrine in the *kōkyo*.

Kōso the imperial ancestors.

Kōtaishi the Crown Prince, see also *tōgū*.

Ku a ward or district.

Kuge the families traditionally attached to the imperial court in Kyoto.

Kun the autochthonous Japanese reading of a *kanji*.

Kunaichō the Imperial Household Agency, the form taken by the *kunaishō* after it was downgraded in 1947.

Kunaishō the Imperial Household Ministry, as established in the Meiji era, with its own minister in the cabinet.

Kuzu a song sung by the court musicians at the beginning of the *daijōsai*.

Kwazoku the name given to the old *kuge* and *daimyō* families after the reforms of the Meiji era.

Kyōsantō Communist Party.

Kyūkana tsukai futtatsu lit. 'restoration of old *kana* usage', a policy advocated within the *kokugo shingikai* in the 1970s.

Machi town or city.

Man'yōgana the phonetic use of *kanji* occurring in the *man'yōshū*.

Man'yōshū the earliest Japanese anthology of poems.

Matsuri festival.

Meishi visiting card.

Michōdai the empress's throne in the *sokui rei*.

Mienai seido lit. 'invisible institution', a phrase used to describe the Chrysanthemum Throne.

Mikado a traditional word for the emperor, to which *tennō* is now preferred, largely for ideological reasons.

Miki the sacred black and white sake presented to the emperor during the *daijōsai*.

Minseitō with the *seiyūkai*, one of the major parties in the pre-war Diet.

Misasagi an imperial tomb, generally in Kyoto: see also *goryō*.

Misogi the body-cleansing rite which the emperor undergoes just before the *daijōsai*.

Mitamanowo the sacred rope representing the life of the emperor in the *daijōsai*.

Miyu no fune lit. 'hot bath boat', in which the emperor, wearing the *ama no hagaromo*, purifies himself before the *daijōsai*.

Mochi rice-cake.

Mogari the state of the deceased emperor during the period of lying in state in the *hinkyū*.

Mombushō Ministry of Education.

Mondai problem, sometimes trouble.

Monsai the rite of purification and consecration of the brush-wood fence surrounding the *daijōgū*, and carried out on the day preceding the *daijōsai*.

Mura village.

Nai 'within' or 'inside', the *on*-reading equivalent to *uchi*.

Naigū the inner shrine of Ise.

Nanten the 'southern' court in which the *sokui rei* takes place.

Nengō the name of an era.

Nihonjinron roughly 'how to be Japanese', as the Japanese themselves see it.

Niinami matsuri the first fruits ceremony corresponding to the *daijōsai* in a normal year.

Ni ni roku jiken the incident of 26 February 1936.

Norito a Shinto prayer.

Nukiho the September rite of plucking the heads of rice to be used in the *daijōsai*.

Okayu the offering of boiled rice and millet consumed by the emperor in the *daijōsai*.

On a blessing received from the *kami*.

On lit. 'sound', but refers to the Chinese reading of *kanji*.

Onaobinokami a *kami* recognized as correcting all wrongs, and worshipped in the course of the *chinkonsai*.

Onaorai the table reserved for the emperor's own food in the *daijōsai*.

Onusa a wand used by a Shinto priest in the purification ritual preceding the *daijōsai*.

Ōseifukkō restoration of monarchy.

Otanushi the owner of the *saiden* on which the rice for the *daijōsai* is grown.

Reishi a kite, a sacred bird in the imperial mythology.

Reizen ancestral spirit.

Renketsu no jō 'falling in love with the imperial family'.

Rensō the imperial funeral ritual.

Risshō Kōseikai a modern Buddhist sect.

Ritsu-ryō the traditional law of the court from the Heian era.

Rōmaji Latin characters.

Ryōkiden the shrine in the *kōkyo* where the *chinkonsai* takes place in a normal year.

Ryōsho the final burial place of an emperor.

Saiden the fields where the rice is grown for the *daijōsai*.

Saiko the sacred storehouse in Kyoto for the rice to be used in the *daijōsai*.

Saisei itchi the 'unity of rites and governance' established at the beginning of the Meiji era.

Saishi 'rites' as opposed to 'doctrine' (*shūkyō*).

Sakaki a sacred tree in Shinto hung with strips of hemp and white paper.

Sakatsuko young virgins who traditionally gathered the first heads of rice used in the *daijōsai*.

Sakoku 'closing the country', as opposed to *kaikoku*.

Sakura a cherry tree.

Sakurakai a secret society of young army officers active in the 1930s.

Samurai the traditional military order in Japanese feudalism, subservient to the *daimyō*.

Sankyō itchi the union of the three faiths, Buddhism, Shinto and Confucianism.

Sanryō an emperor's funeral mound.

Sansai the three calamities of fire, flood and storm.

Sanshū no shinki the mirror, sword and jewel of the imperial insignia.

Seiga the second rank of the *kuge*, below the *go-sekke*.

Seiyūkai one of the two major parties in the pre-war Diet.

Senpai 'senior' as opposed to 'junior' (*kōhai*).

Sensō the opening rite of accession of a new emperor.

Senzo ancestor.

Seppuku traditional *samurai* ritual suicide: see also *harakiri*.

Setsubun the festival celebrating the end of winter.

Shaku the wand carried by a Shinto priest.

Shichi-go-san lit. 'seven-five-three', a Shinto feast for children of these years.

Shinkaden the temporary Shinto shrine specially constructed for the celebration of the first 2,600 years of the imperial line in 1940.

Shinkansen the ultra-rapid express, sometimes known as the 'bullet train'.

Shinkō shūkyō the so-called 'new religions'.

Shinbutsu shūgō conflation of Shinto and Buddhism.

Shinden the shrine to the *kami* in the Imperial Precinct.

Shintō lit. 'way of the gods', the traditional religion of Japan.

Shinza the throne in the *yuki* (*suki*)-*den* in the *daijōsai*.

Shishinden the temporary hall in which, as part of the *sokui rei*, the accession of the emperor is announced to the people of Japan.

Shosei commoners admitted, on the basis of merit, to the special schools for *samurai*.

Shōshidai the representative of the Shogun at the Kyoto court.

Shōwa the era, and posthumous name, of the Emperor Hirohito.

Shūkyō religion.

Shunkōden the shrine in Kyoto which is the proper resting place of the *kashikodokoro*.

Shūshin traditional Japanese morality.

Sōjōden the temporary building used for the Shinto funeral of an emperor.

Sokui rei the accession ceremony proper, preceding the *daijōsai*.

Sonnō lit. 'revere the emperor', combined with *jōi*, the name given to the policy of closing Japan to the outside world.

Soto lit. 'outside', the *kun*-reading corresponding to the *on*-reading, *gai*. See also *uchi*.

Suiden the field used for wet-rice cultivation.

Suijaku see *honji*.

Sukiden one of the two identical structures used for the *daijōsai*.

Sumi-e the traditional art of painting in black ink.

Ta a rice-field: see also *suiden*.

Tachibana an orange tree.

Taireshi kōtōkan the twenty high-ranking officials who look after the guests at the *sokui rei*.

Taisei Yokusankai the Imperial Rule Assistance Association, formed by Konoye in 1940, after the parties in the Diet had been disbanded.

Taisō no rei the funeral of an emperor, used in the case of the Showa Emperor for the public ceremony, as opposed to the private Shinto ceremony in the *sōjōden*.

Takamikura the throne of the emperor in the *sokui rei*.

Tanka traditional poem of five lines, and thirty-one syllables.

Tatami the mats used as floor covering in the Japanese home.

Tate no kai lit. 'company of the sword', the patriotic society led by Yukio Mishima.

Tennō the term for the emperor officially used since 1936. See also *mikado*.

Tennō chūshinsetsu the doctrine of the *tennō* as a supernatural ruler.

Tenno kikansetsu the doctrine of the *tennō* as a constitutional monarch.

Tenryō the regions of Japan in direct fief to the Shogun.

Terakoya temple school.

Tōgū the Crown Prince: see also *kōtaishi*.

Tōgū gogakumonsho a special institution set up for the education of the Crown Prince.

Tokonoma the alcove in a Japanese home where the *butsudan* is placed.

Tōseiha a faction of army officers in the 1930s.

Torii the symbolic gate found before Shinto shrines.

Tōyō kanji the *kanji* adopted for everyday use in 1946: see also *jōyō kanji*.

Tozama the *daimyō* who were not vassals of the Shogun.

Tsuigō hōkoku no gi the rite announcing the deceased emperor's new name to his departed spirit.

Tsunami tidal wave.

Uchi 'inside', corresponding to the *on*-reading *nai*: see also *soto*.

Ujidera clan temple.

Ukefune platform for a priestess's ritual dance in the course of the *daijōsai*.

Uyoku lit. 'right wing', referring to the patriotic right in Japanese politics.

Wabun autochthonous Japanese, as opposed to *kanbun*.

Yakudoshi unlucky years in the life of an individual, against which Shinto provides ritual defences.

Yakuza the general word for organized crime in Japan.

Yata the name for the sacred crow represented on one of the banners displayed in the *sokui rei*.

Yata kagami the sacred mirror of the imperial insignia.

Yōhaishiki ceremonies from afar, carried out throughout Japan as part of the ritual following the death of the Meiji Emperor.

Yukiden one of the two identical structures used for the *daijōsai*.

Yūmei mujitsu lit. 'having name, no substance', one of the ways of describing the emperor's role.

Zaibatsu a giant industrial combine.

Zekke a household that has died out.

Index

OXFORD

MORE OXFORD PAPERBACKS

Details of a selection of other Oxford Paperbacks follow. A complete list of Oxford Paperbacks, including The World's Classics, Twentieth-Century Classics, OPUS, Past Masters, Oxford Authors, Oxford Shakespeare, and Oxford Paperback Reference, is available in the UK from the General Publicity Department, Oxford University Press (RS), Walton Street, Oxford, OX2 6DP.

In the USA, complete lists are available from the Paperbacks Marketing Manager, Oxford University Press, 200 Madison Avenue, New York, NY 10016.

Oxford Paperbacks are available from all good bookshops. In case of difficulty, customers in the UK can order direct from Oxford University Press Bookshop, 116 High Street, Oxford, Freepost, OX1 4BR, enclosing full payment. Please add 10 per cent of the published price for postage and packing.

HISTORY IN OXFORD PAPERBACKS

Oxford Paperbacks' superb history list offers books on a wide range of topics from ancient to modern times, whether general period studies or assessments of particular events, movements, or personalities.

THE STRUGGLE FOR
THE MASTERY OF EUROPE 1848–1918

A. J. P. Taylor

The fall of Metternich in the revolutions of 1848 heralded an era of unprecedented nationalism in Europe, culminating in the collapse of the Hapsburg, Romanov, and Hohenzollern dynasties at the end of the First World War. In the intervening seventy years the boundaries of Europe changed dramatically from those established at Vienna in 1815. Cavour championed the cause of *Risorgimento* in Italy; Bismarck's three wars brought about the unification of Germany; Serbia and Bulgaria gained their independence courtesy of the decline of Turkey— 'the sick man of Europe'; while the great powers scrambled for places in the sun in Africa. However, with America's entry into the war and President Wilson's adherence to idealistic internationalist principles, Europe ceased to be the centre of the world, although its problems, still primarily revolving around nationalist aspirations, were to smash the Treaty of Versailles and plunge the world into war once more.

A. J. P. Taylor has drawn the material for his account of this turbulent period from the many volumes of diplomatic documents which have been published in the five major European languages. By using vivid language and forceful characterization, he has produced a book that is as much a work of literature as a contribution to scientific history.

'One of the glories of twentieth-century writing.' *Observer*

Also in Oxford Paperbacks:

Portrait of an Age: Victorian England   G. M. Young
Germany 1866–1945   Gorden A. Craig
The Russian Revolution 1917–1932   Sheila Fitzpatrick
France 1848–1945   Theodore Zeldin

OPUS

General Editors: Christopher Butler,
Robert Evans, Alan Ryan

OPUS is a series of accessible introductions to a wide range of studies in the sciences and humanities.

METROPOLIS

Emrys Jones

Past civilizations have always expressed themselves in great cities, immense in size, wealth, and in their contribution to human progress. We are still enthralled by ancient cities like Babylon, Rome, and Constantinople. Today, giant cities abound, but some are pre-eminent. As always, they represent the greatest achievements of different cultures. But increasingly, they have also been drawn into a world economic system as communications have improved.

Metropolis explores the idea of a class of supercities in the past and in the present, and in the western and developing worlds. It analyses the characteristics they share as well as those that make them unique; the effect of technology on their form and function; and the problems that come with size—congestion, poverty and inequality, squalor—that are sobering contrasts to the inherent glamour and attraction of great cities throughout time.

Also available in OPUS:

The Medieval Expansion of Europe   J. R. S. Phillips
Metaphysics: The Logical Approach   José A. Bernadete
The Voice of the Past 2/e   Paul Thompson
Thinking About Peace and War   Martin Ceadel

WOMEN'S STUDIES FROM
OXFORD PAPERBACKS

Ranging from the *A–Z of Women's Health* to *Wayward Women: A Guide to Women Travellers*, Oxford Paperbacks cover a wide variety of social, medical, historical, and literary topics of particular interest to women.

DESTINED TO BE WIVES
The Sisters of Beatrice Webb

Barbara Caine

Drawing on their letters and diaries, Barbara Caine's fascinating account of the lives of Beatrice Webb and her sisters, the Potters, presents a vivid picture of the extraordinary conflicts and tragedies taking place behind the respectable façade which has traditionally characterized Victorian and Edwardian family life.

The tensions and pressures of family life, particularly for women; the suicide of one sister; the death of another, probably as a result of taking cocaine after a family breakdown; the shock felt by the older sisters at the promiscuity of their younger sister after the death of her husband are all vividly recounted. In all the crises they faced, the sisters formed the main network of support for each other, recognizing that the 'sisterhood' provided the only security in a society which made women subordinate to men, socially, legally, and economically.

Other women's studies titles:

A–Z of Women's Health   Derek Llewellyn-Jones
'Victorian Sex Goddess': Lady Colin Campbell and the Sensational Divorce Case of 1886   G. H. Fleming
Wayward Women: A Guide to Women Travellers
Jane Robinson
Catherine the Great: Life and Legend   John T. Alexander

POLITICS IN OXFORD PAPERBACKS

Oxford Paperbacks offers incisive and provocative studies of the political ideologies and institutions that have shaped the modern world since 1945.

GOD SAVE ULSTER!
The Religion and Politics of Paisleyism

Steve Bruce

Ian Paisley in the only modern Western leader to have founded his own Church and political party, and his enduring popularity and success mirror the complicated issues which continue to plague Northern Ireland. This book is the first serious analysis of his religious and political careers and a unique insight into Unionist politics and religion in Northern Ireland today.

Since it was founded in 1951, the Free Presbyterian Church of Ulster has grown steadily; it now comprises some 14,000 members in fifty congregations in Ulster and ten branches over-seas. The Democratic Unionist Party, formed in 1971, now speaks for about half of the Unionist voters in Northern Ireland, and the personal standing of the man who leads both these movements was confirmed in 1979 when Ian R. K. Paisley received more votes than any other member of the European Parliament. While not neglecting Paisley's 'charismatic' quali-ties, Steve Bruce argues that the key to his success has been his ability to embody and represent traditional evangelical Protestantism and traditional Ulster Unionism.

'original and profound . . . I cannot praise this book too highly.'
Bernard Crick, *New Society*

Also in Oxford Paperbacks:

Freedom Under Thatcher   Keith Ewing and Conor Gearty
Strong Leadership   Graham Little
The Thatcher Effect   Dennis Kavanagh and Anthony Seldon

LAW FROM OXFORD PAPERBACKS

Oxford Paperbacks's law list ranges from introductions to the English legal system to reference books and in-depth studies of contemporary legal issues.

INTRODUCTION TO ENGLISH LAW
Tenth Edition

William Geldart
Edited by D. C. M. Yardley

'Geldart' has over the years established itself as a standard account of English law, expounding the body of modern law as set in its historical context. Regularly updated since its first publication, it remains indispensable to student and layman alike as a concise, reliable guide.

Since publication of the ninth edition in 1984 there have been important court decisions and a great deal of relevant new legislation. D. C. M. Yardley, Chairman of the Commission for Local Administration in England, has taken account of all these developments and the result has been a considerable rewriting of several parts of the book. These include the sections dealing with the contractual liability of minors, the abolition of the concept of illegitimacy, the liability of a trade union in tort for inducing a person to break his/her contract of employment, the new public order offences, and the intent necessary for a conviction of murder.

Other law titles:

Freedom Under Thatcher: Civil Liberties in Modern Britain
Keith Ewing and Conor Gearty
Doing the Business   Dick Hobbs
Judges   David Pannick
Law and Modern Society   P. S. Atiyah

OXFORD LETTERS & MEMOIRS

This popular series offers fascinating personal records of the lives of famous men and women from all walks of life.

JOURNEY CONTINUED

Alan Paton

'an extraordinary last testament, told in simple and pungent style . . . for anyone new to the period and to Paton, it will be a revelation' *Independent*

This concluding volume of autobiography (the sequel to *Towards the Mountain*) begins in 1948, the year in which Paton's bestselling novel, *Cry, the Beloved Country*, was published, and the Nationalist Party of South Africa came to power. Both events were to have a profound effect on Paton's life, and they represent two major themes in this book, literature and politics.

With characteristic resonance and trenchancy, Paton describes his career as a writer of books, which were received with extreme hostility by his fellow South Africans, and also covers his political life, notably the founding—and later Chairmanship—of the Liberal Party of South Africa, the multi-racial centre party opposed to apartheid.

'required reading for anyone who wants to understand, compassionately, the full tragedy of South Africa' *Daily Express*

Also in Oxford Letters & Memoirs:

LITERARY BIOGRAPHY AND CRITICISM IN OXFORD PAPERBACKS

Oxford Paperbacks's impressive list of literary biography and criticism includes works ranging from specialist studies of the prominent figures of the world literature to D. J. Enright on television soap opera.

BRITISH WRITERS OF THE THIRTIES

Valentine Cunningham

'He has steeped himself in the period . . . *British Writers of the Thirties* is by far the best history of its kind published in recent years . . . and it will become required reading for those who wish to look back at a society and a culture in which writers, for all their faults, were taken seriously.' Peter Ackroyd, *The Times*

'a serious and often brilliant book, provoking one to argument, forcing one back to known texts and forward to unread ones . . . it is simply so packed with information that it will speak as much to readers with an interest in social history as to the students of literature for whom it was first intended.' Claire Tomalin, *Independent*

'this should henceforth be the standard treatment . . . a minor classic of literary history' Frank Kermode, *Guardian*

'brilliant survey and analysis . . . Mr Cunningham's narrative is cleverly constructed, wonderfully detailed, and he deploys his findings to great effect.' Charles Causley, *Times Educational Supplement*

Also in Oxford Paperbacks:

Fields of Vision D. J. Enright
Modern English Literature W. W. Robson
The Oxford Illustrated History of English Literature edited by Pat Rogers
The Pursuit of Happiness Peter Quennell